Philippine–American Military History, 1902–1942:
An Annotated Bibliography

YOUNG MEN HEED YOUR COUNTRY'S CALL!

REGISTER FOR MILITARY INSTRUCTION APRIL 1-7, 1936.

ONLY THOSE WHO SHALL ATTAIN THE AGE OF 20 YEARS DURING THE CALENDAR YEAR 1936 ARE REQUIRED TO REGISTER.

# Philippine–American Military History, 1902–1942

## An Annotated Bibliography

*by* RICHARD B. MEIXSEL

Richard B. Meixsel

To Bruce Moore
with all best
wishes

New Orleans 2015

McFarland & Company, Inc., Publishers

*Jefferson, North Carolina, and London*

Frontispiece: A military registration poster from 1936 printed in Manila newspapers of the time.

Library of Congress Cataloguing-in-Publication Data

Meixsel, Richard B., 1955–
    Philippine–American military history, 1902–1942 : an annotated bibliography / by Richard B. Meixsel.
        p.    cm.
    Includes index.

    ISBN-13: 978-0-7864-1403-1
    ISBN-10: 0-7864-1403-0
    (softcover : 50# alkaline paper) ∞

    1. Philippines—History, Military—20th century—Bibliography.
    2. United States—History, Military—20th century—Bibliography.
    3. United States—Armed Forces—Philippines—Bibliography.
    4. World War, 1939–1945—Philippines—Bibliography.    I. Title.
    Z3298.A5 M45    2003
    [DS671]
    016.355'0330599—dc21                                                2002011896

British Library cataloguing data are available

Manufactured in the United States of America

*Cover photograph:* Soldiers of the Philippine Scouts at Regan Barracks, Albay Province, circa 1907 *(Courtesy Samuel Rockenbach, Virginia Military Institute Archives)*

*McFarland & Company, Inc., Publishers*
  *Box 611, Jefferson, North Carolina 28640*
    *www.mcfarlandpub.com*

To Helen Mendoza, Mike Billig, Gay Iglesias,
Rico Jose, Lew Gleeck, and Scott Harrison—
friends and colleagues who've made the study of
Philippine history professionally and personally rewarding.

# Acknowledgments

This bibliography had its unwitting origins in the mid-1980s, when I began researching the history of the US Army in the Philippines in the early twentieth century [see entry 145]. Completion of a study of the pre-war Philippine Army [entry 81], of a history of my boyhood home, Clark Air Base, Pampanga ("Clark Field and the Army Air Corps in the Philippines, 1919-1942," forthcoming from New Day Publishers of Quezon City), and the commencement of research for a biography of Brigadier General Vicente P. Lim led to the acquisition of many more titles. In gathering the information that resulted in this bibliography, I spent many hours at the Library of Congress, the US Army Military History Institute, and other libraries, but I also benefited immensely from the hard work of Susan Huffman, Debra Ryman, and Anna Lee Newman of the interlibrary loan staff at James Madison University. Their "above and beyond the call of duty" perseverance turned up many difficult-to-find titles.

In the Philippines, I examined the holdings of the Philippine National Library, the Ayala Museum Library (now the Filipinas Heritage Library), the Lopez Memorial Library, the Jose P. Laurel Library, the library of the Veterans Federation of the Philippines (hard-to-find but rich in veterans' memoirs), the library at the Philippine Army Museum, the AFP Command and General Staff College library, the American Historical Collection (now located within the Ateneo de Manila University library), the Jorge B. Vargas Library (on the campus of the University of the Philippines, Diliman), and the main libraries of the University of the Philippines, Diliman, the University of Santo Tomas, De La Salle University, and the Ateneo de Manila University in Quezon City. I am grateful to the many librarians at those institutions who, more often than not, indulgently suffered my many impositions. Finally, my sincere thanks go to Professor Ricardo T. Jose of the University of the Philippines, who allowed me to peruse his own extensive collection of Philippine military history books and then read the completed manuscript.

# Table of Contents

# Introduction

For much of the forty-year American occupation of the Philippine Islands, military obligations rested lightly upon the Philippine people. The annual levy for conscripts (albeit relatively small given the size of the population involved) that scooped up the poor and those without influence and sent others fleeing into the countryside five hundred miles to the west across the South China Sea in French Indochina, for example, was unknown to Filipinos. Nor did a large occupying army underpin a "garrison state" and have first call on state revenues, as some historians have argued was the case in British India where the largest army in the dependent East was to be found. Indeed, in contrast, the United States government paid all military and naval expenses in the Philippines, a sum estimated to have amounted to about 700 million dollars from 1902 to 1940. Also, most American colonial officials opposed as unworkable and unnecessarily burdensome the conscription-based military system adopted by the Philippine government when it became semi-independent in the 1930s.

There was military activity in the Philippines during the period of American rule. Both the army and navy enlisted Filipino auxiliaries for local service, Filipino cadets attended the military academy at West Point and the naval academy at Annapolis, the Philippine and United States governments sponsored a national guard division during World War I, and the army supported several officer-cadet programs at Philippine colleges and universities. Most of these activities and organizations involved relatively few people or were, like the national guard, short-lived. Given the small size and intimacy of pre–World War II Philippine society, however, the activities or interests of an influential few could have great impact. Only a handful of Filipinos graduated from West Point before World War II, for example, but they were the only Filipinos with extensive professional military training and thus assumed leadership roles in the indigenous Philippine military forces that began to take shape in the mid–1930s. The national guard was active for only three months before disbanding in 1919, but it was the only modern example of a Philippine national army and thus provided a model for future development.

For most of this period, however, military developments in the Philippines primarily centered around the actions of the United States Army and Navy. The army was the dominant military service in the Philippines during the American occupation, but the navy was the first to arrive. Commodore George Dewey's defeat of the Spanish fleet off Cavite, in Manila Bay, on the morning of 1 May 1898 ushered in a year-long period in which Dewey was the most important American official in the islands. There is no need to read between the lines of Dewey's autobiography [entry 259] to discern that he thought the army generals who took over negotiations with the Spanish and Filipino commanders were out of their depth. "It was a time for statesmanship if we were to avoid a conflict," Dewey declared, but the army generals proceeded to establish American authority in the Philippines "by force against the very wishes of the people whom we sought to benefit."[1] Dewey washed his, and the navy's, hands of the entire affair.

With Dewey's departure in May 1899, the navy would play little further role in Philippine affairs, although that was neither inevitable nor immediately apparent. Initial plans that a significant naval force might remain in Far Eastern waters came to nothing, but for several years the navy and army supported placing a major navy base in the Philippines, a project that generated considerable contemporary rancor and a number of scholarly books and articles later. (William Braisted [entries 240–241] provides the most comprehensive account of the "bases controversy.") The navy believed that Subic (spelled contemporaneously as Subig) Bay was the appropriate location for a base; the army preferred Manila Bay. The inability to agree combined with the growing perception that, militarily, the Philippines had become, in President Theodore Roosevelt's famous phrase, America's "heel of Achilles," ensured that no significant navy base was ever built.[2] To the army, it was probably less important that a base be built in Manila Bay than that one *not* be built at distant and isolated Subic Bay. A major installation at Subic would invariably have focused money and authority on the navy and made it the dominant military service in the Philippines, just as it was on Guam and, arguably, Hawaii. Had that happened, the course of Philippine history might have been significantly altered.

As it was, the Asiatic "Fleet"—a courtesy title that gave unwarranted stature to the small collection of third-class cruisers, destroyers, and gunboats that showed the American flag in Asian waters—spent much of the year in China. A few commissioned officers (perhaps sixty or so at any one time, including doctors, dentists, and marines) found themselves assigned to the Cavite naval station in Manila Bay, with its marine barracks and adjacent Cañacao naval hospital, or to the smaller Olongapo naval station and marine barracks, at Subic Bay.[3]

Although the Philippines may have had little impact on the navy, the navy could have significant influence on Filipinos and their communities. Many Filipinos chose the navy as a means of social mobility, financial security, or merely as a way of getting to the United States. One of the delegates to the Philippine constitutional convention in 1934–35, for example, was a retired navy petty officer. Paulino Santos, the Philippine Army's first chief of staff, had hoped to join the navy in 1908, but a cholera epidemic put a stop to local enlistments that year. Service in the navy was limited to the role of messman, but that did not dissuade applicants. A recruiting campaign during World War I drew so much interest that a Manila newspaper advised its enlistment-inclined readers "to hasten to Manila or to the Naval Station at Cavite and appear at the recruiting station at once if they desire to see service in the United States Navy."[4]

Service came at a cost, however. Fifty-six Filipinos died on duty with the navy during the war and another Filipino sailor went down with the *Reuben James* in October 1941.[5] The navy also maintained an "insular force" of some one thousand Filipinos for duty on navy ships and installations in the Philippines. Naval officer Kemp Tolley mentions the organization [entry 461], but nothing more is known about it. Aside from passing mention in a few biographies of navy and marine officers [entries 247–261] and Gerald Anderson's brief history of Subic Bay naval base [entry 294], navy and marine activities in the Philippines prior to 1941 await exploration.

The United States Army's far more prominent involvement in the Philippines can be divided into four periods: first, from 1898 to 1902, during which the army defeated Spanish and Filipino forces to take possession of the Philippines; second, from 1902 to 1917, during which the army remained undecided about its role in the islands even as a large portion of the army was on duty there; third, from World War I to 1940, during which the army garrison was increasingly Filipinized and correspondingly marginalized; and fourth, the Philippine Campaign of 1941–1942. The first period of the army's involvement in the Philippines is beyond the scope of this bibliography, but the following few paragraphs introduce the period and survey the literature.

The military campaign waged by the United States to win Filipino acquiescence to American rule lasted from February 1899 until President Roosevelt declared the war to be over on 4 July 1902, although fighting for which soldiers continued to be awarded the army's Philippine Campaign Medal [entry 681] flared off and on until 1917, mostly on the large southern island of Mindanao.[6] Despite repeated requests from the

Philippine government that it redesignate the war, the US government continues to label the war the "Philippine Insurrection." The title has long fallen out of use by historians. Nonetheless, there is no widely agreed upon replacement. Philippine War, Philippine-American War, and Filipino-American War are commonly used today. The varied names suggest the lack of consensus about the significance and nature of the war among historians.

Institutionally, the army learned nothing from the Philippine-American War, a disinterest mirrored for years by military historians. Historian John Gates has pointed out that the army's own military history textbook, published in 1973, devoted more space to Zachary Taylor's Monterrey Campaign during the Mexican War than to the entire war in the Philippines.[7] For decades, the only military history of the war to be published was then-Captain William Thaddeus Sexton's *Soldiers in the Sun* (Harrisburg, PA: Military Service Publishing Co., 1939). The reviewer for the *New York Times*, William Rivers, himself a veteran of the Philippine-American War and former chief of the Philippine Constabulary, thought the book a "capital adventure story—in addition to being good history." Sexton, a 1924 graduate of West Point who had interviewed veterans of the war when stationed in the Philippines, ended his account of the war in mid-1901, when paramount authority in the islands passed from the army to a civilian commission headed by William Howard Taft. Sexton had no patience for stories of the army's use of "so-called tortures" and was scathing in his denunciation of the army's political enemies at home.[8]

Those were precisely aspects of the war on which historians focused when growing American military involvement in Asia in the 1960s generated renewed interest in America's first Asian war. Journalist Leon Wolff emphasized anti-imperialist rhetoric from the turn-of-the-century, American racism, and the consequent ruthlessness of the army's war-waging methods in *Little Brown Brother: How the United States Purchased and Pacified the Philippine Islands at the Century's Turn* (Garden City, NY: Doubleday & Co., 1961), a book subsequently reprinted (most recently in 1991) in Britain, the Philippines, and Singapore. Other American authors (not military historians) picked up the same themes, which made John Gates' *Schoolbooks and Krags: The United States Army in the Philippines* (Westport, CT: Greenwood Press, 1973) something of a revisionist work. (The "Krag" in the title was the name of the US Army's rifle of the day.) Gates did not deny that some soldiers had acted improperly or that military force had not been an important component of the American victory, but he argued that stories of army atrocities and the numbers of Filipino casualties had been grossly inflated for political purposes. According to Gates, the army had actively demonstrated the positive aspects of American rule through a policy of beneficial civil affairs works, a policy continued with great success by the islands' civilian administrators after the war. Stuart Creighton Miller responded with *"Benevolent Assimilation": The American Conquest of the Philippines, 1899–1903* (New Haven and London: Yale University Press, 1982) in which he dismissed Gates' argument as "the latest attempt to whitewash the army's conduct." For Miller, drawing mostly and uncritically on contemporary newspaper accounts of the war (sources Sexton, Gates, and others held suspect), the conduct of the war—from the politicians in Washington to the commanders in Manila to the private soldiers in the field—symbolized America's enduring racism, contempt for foreign cultures, and dismissal of other peoples' legitimate nationalist aspirations. The emergence of two clearly distinct schools of thought, what might be called the "army fought honorably despite provocation" view of the war articulated by Gates, strongly supported by historian Brian Linn in *The U.S. Army and Counterinsurgency in the Philippine War, 1899–1902* (Chapel Hill, NC: University of North Carolina Press, 1989), and Miller's "atrocity-filled precursor to Vietnam and My Lai" view of the Philippine-American War, generated mutually dismissive book reviews and vituperative exchanges of correspondence in academic journals in the 1980s and early 1990s.[9]

In the Philippines, "military history"—however defined—hardly exists in academia. Filipino historians have shown little interest in the military heritage of Spanish and American colonialism or in how the Philippine-American War was fought, either by the Philippine or American armies (that American soldiers, sailors, and marines brutalized the Filipinos is mostly taken for granted and thus not a matter for controversy), although the survey military histories of the Philippines that have begun to appear in recent years (usually written by non-academics) [entries 26-30] devote some attention to the topics. Rather, their interest has focused on the class dynamics of the war. The late Teodoro A. Agoncillo's influential *Malolos: The Crisis of the Republic* (Quezon City: University of the Philippines, 1960) played freedom-loving masses off a corrupt, collaborating elite, who sold out to the Americans. Glenn Anthony May's *Battle for Batangas: A Philippine Province at War* (New Haven and London: Yale University Press, 1993; reprinted in the Philippines by New Day, 1993) was an attack on Agoncillo's thesis, as well as an outstanding work of military history that showed how American soldiers fought the war and how Filipinos fought back. May sought to demonstrate, at least in Batangas Province, how elites led the war effort, sometimes only begrudgingly followed by peasants and townsmen.[10] In *The War Against the Americans: Resistance and Collaboration in Cebu, 1899–1906* (Quezon City: Ateneo de Manila University Press, 1999), Resil B. Mojares countered that May merely reversed Agoncillo's equation, "ascribing to an ill-defined 'elite' the primary impetus for the resistance" rather than to an equally ill-defined "masses."

From a traditional military history perspective, Brian Linn's recent *The Philippine War, 1899–1902* (Lawrence, KS: University Press of Kansas, 2000) is authoritative. Drawing on a vast array of official documents and officers' personal papers (but ignoring virtually anything written by an enlisted man) Linn has written a detailed and nuanced history of American military and naval operations during both the conventional and guerrilla phases of the war. Linn made good use of the invaluable Philippine Insurgent Records to assay Filipino military strengths and weaknesses, as well.[11] Linn's interest is military operations, however, and he gives short shrift to other aspects of the war. Three times as many American soldiers died as a result of disease as were killed in combat, yet Linn does little more than acknowledge that disease was a problem.[12] He also says nothing about what motivated Americans to enlist to fight in what can be called the United States' last "all-volunteer war."[13] On that fascinating topic, interested readers might begin with Richard E. Welch's *Response to Imperialism: The United States and the Philippine-American War, 1899–1902* (Chapel Hill, NC: University of North Carolina Press, 1979) and Kristin L. Hoganson's *Fighting for American Manhood: How Gender Politics Provoked the Spanish-American and Philippine-American Wars* (New Haven and London: Yale University Press, 1998), books that examine domestic attitudes toward the Philippine adventure.

Older histories of the war provide substantial information. Karl Irving Faust's heavily illustrated *Campaigning in the Philippines* (San Francisco, CA: The Hicks-Judd Company, 1899) is a remarkably even-handed depiction of military operations during the initial conventional stage of the war, before the stresses of guerrilla war made the US Army and its civilian chroniclers less sympathetic to Filipino aspirations. Faust's is probably the best of the many "quickie histories" of the war produced for the American public at the time and is available in a modern reprint edition.[14] Francis D. Millet's richly detailed *The Expedition to the Philippines* (New York and London: Harper & Brothers, 1899) describes the fighting against Spanish forces in 1898. Millet's book is little-known today, but it was used as the "military history of the Philippines" textbook in Philippine Army training camps in the 1930s.

The second period of the army's involvement in the Philippines lasted until World War I. From 1902 to 1917 the War Department kept a substantial part (close to 20 percent, annually) of the army in the Philippines. During this period, the demands of insular duty forced the army to devise and implement a foreign service policy both integrative within the wider organizational framework of the army while still fulfilling the more distinct and specialized function of an overseas garrison. Solutions did not come easy as army and civilian officials clashed over the numbers of military forces needed in the islands and their purpose. Were they there to prevent insurrection, or to defend against foreign (that is, other foreigners') aggression?

The obligations of Philippine service also required a reappraisal of many aspects of traditional army life and administration. New enlistment, promotion, pay, and retirement regulations, for example, had to accommodate, or were even dictated by, the requirements of foreign service. The problems of distance, climate, and unfamiliarity with local conditions posed tremendous hurdles for both individual soldiers and their families, as well as the army's various staff departments, to overcome. It was a colorful, exciting and aggravating time in the army's history. Aside from Brian Linn's recent kaleidoscopic survey of the pre–World War II army garrisons in the Philippines and Hawaii [entry 144] and one older unpublished master's thesis [entry 145], it is a period that has attracted almost no interest from historians.

Biographies provide the closest look at the army's occupation of the archipelago, during both this period and the one that followed. Before World War II, duty in the Philippine Islands was one of the most common shared experiences of military service. As Colonel R. Ernest Dupuy wrote in his history of the United States Army, "It would be hard to find an Army family some member of which has not at some time been stationed there."[15] In fact, many officers spent significant portions of their army careers in the Philippines. Douglas MacArthur [entries 91–104] was stationed in the Philippines three times prior to becoming Commonwealth military advisor in 1935, and his experience was not out of the ordinary. George Marshall [entries 174, 175, 186, 187, 207] was sent to the islands twice before World War I and turned down an offer to return a third time after the war. John J. "Black Jack" Pershing [entries 211, 213] arrived in the Philippines in 1899 and was there off and on almost continuously until 1913. Henry "Hap" Arnold [entries 171, 179, 183] grew familiar with Luzon's terrain as an infantryman long before he gained fame as head of the army air forces in World War II. Lyman Lemnitzer [entry 173], army chief of staff in 1959–60 and chairman of the Joint Chiefs of Staff in 1960–62, lived for five years on Corregidor in the 1920s and 1930s. Lewis Brereton [entries 442, 452] spent a tour of duty on the same island in 1916–1917 before returning a quarter of a century later to begin his short and controversial tenure as MacArthur's air commander in late 1941. Medal of honor winner Charles Kilbourne (no biography) traveled across the Pacific for five tours of duty in the archipelago over the course of his army career. Given the prevalence of Philippine service before World War II, biographies of army officers almost invariably have something (albeit sometimes very little) to say about military life in the Philippines.[16]

Soldiers made up a large component of the American population in the Philippines, and the power and prestige of the garrison's commanding generals was such that they could enhance or impede the civil government's authority. The last military governor of the Philippines (General Arthur MacArthur, the father of Douglas MacArthur) had only reluctantly given up power to the first civil governor, William Howard Taft, and many Americans living in the islands continued to hope that the generals would resume authority. When Major General J. Franklin Bell returned to the Philippines in 1911, for example, he made a point of publicly dousing such expectations. (The Republican-appointed governor-general made a point of publicly thanking him for doing so.)[17] A few years later a Democratic-appointed governor-general, Francis B. Harrison [entry 138] wrote that he was "constantly preoccupied with the effort to keep these relations [with the US Army] upon a uniform level of cordiality and cooperation." Harrison was back in the Philippines in 1935 and expressed his amazement that a departing army commanding general, Major General Frank Parker (no biography), appeared to believe "that he [Parker] and the governor-general [Frank Murphy] had governed this country for the past two and a half years!"[18]

When he was commanding general of the army in the Philippines, Major General Leonard Wood argued that only officers possessing "the maximum of activity and energy" should be placed at the helm of the Philippine garrison, which Wood saw as one of the most important assignments in the army.[19] Wood's biographers [entries 188, 196] have entirely overlooked Wood's perception that the Philippines, far from Congressional and public oversight, provided the perfect arena for trying out unpopular army reform policies of the Progressive era. Wood was one of the earliest of the roughly three dozen officers who commanded the garrison (known as the Division of the Philippines or Philippines Division to 1913 and then as the Philippine Department) between the end of the Philippine-American War in July 1902 and the establishment of Douglas MacArthur's US Army Forces Far East (USAFFE) command in July 1941.[20] Unfortunately, only the most prominent—and their prominence had little or nothing to do with the command of the Philippine Department—

have been subjected to book-length biographies. These officers are Wood, commanding general from 1906 to 1908, Tasker Bliss, 1908–1909 [entry 206], Pershing, 1910–11, and MacArthur, 1928–30.

The Philippine command of the last Department commander, George Grunert, 1940–41, has been the subject of a scholarly article [entry 429]. The controversial J. Franklin Bell, who emerged from the Philippine-American War as one of the army's most famous soldiers and who would command the Philippine garrison longer than any other officer, from January 1911 to April 1914, has no published biography nor any study that examines his peacetime years in the islands.[21] The once equally well known Hunter Liggett, the Philippine Department commander in 1916–17, is, in the words of military historian Allan R. Millett, worthy of "at least a memoir and several biographies" but, aside from the general's own writings on World War I [entry 198], has neither. General Liggett was a strong supporter of the World War I–era Philippine National Guard [entries 71–75], and the sad history of that potentially important organization might have been much different had he remained in the islands.

The army withdrew most of the American garrison from the islands in World War I. That many officers who gained prominence with the American Expeditionary Forces had spent a considerable portion of the prewar years assigned to the army or constabulary in the Philippines is a commonplace observation, but exactly how, or if, the skills and experience acquired during their Philippine years translated into success in France awaits serious evaluation.

The army hoped to rebuild the garrison after the war, but financial, manpower, and treaty constraints prevented it from doing so. The army now entered its third period of occupation. Unable to return significant numbers of troops to the archipelago, the army made the "Philippine Scouts" the mainstay of the garrison. Recruited largely from among the non–Tagalog peoples of Luzon and the Visayas, Filipino soldiers had been serving with the army since 1899. The Army Reorganization Act of February 1901 had regularized their status and authorized the army to recruit as many as 12,000 Filipino soldiers. At first serving in widely dispersed companies under the command of American enlisted men who held local, renewable, four-year commissions, during World War I the Scouts had been brought together in provisional regiments. These Filipino-manned and (mostly) American-officered units of cavalry, infantry, engineers, field artillery, and coast artillery had been made permanent after the war. Long-serving, well-trained, and intensely loyal, the soldiers of the Philippine Scouts would prove to be the greatest stumbling block to Japanese ambitions in 1941–42.

Colonial armies have attracted considerable interest in recent years—witness such works as Myron Echenberg's *Colonial Conscripts: The Tirailleurs Sénégalais in French West Africa, 1857–1960* (Portsmouth, NH: Heinemann, 1991), Timothy H. Parsons' *African Rank and File: Social Implications of Colonial Military Service in the King's African Rifles, 1902–1964* (Portsmouth, NH: Heinemann, 1999), and the innumerable books on the British Indian army—but no such fascination with America's "colonial army" has emerged, either on the part of American or Filipino historians. The standard scholarly history remains James Woolard's quarter-century old unpublished doctoral dissertation [entry 169] that focuses mostly on the origins of the Scouts during the Philippine-American War. Of the Philippine Scout organizations, one, the 57th Infantry, has been the subject of a traditional regimental history, written by an officer who served with the regiment during World War II [entry 498].[22]

For American soldiers, the nature of Philippine service changed significantly after World War I. The garrison was smaller and no longer assigned to remote regions of the country. By contrast to trends in the United States, servants remained plentiful and affordable in the Philippines; nor did the Volstead (Prohibition) Act apply in the islands. With Douglas MacArthur the notable exception, after the war the army's senior billet in the Philippines became mostly a pleasant twilight tour for senior generals approaching retirement. It was during this period, the two decades between World Wars I and II, that a Philippine assignment acquired its reputation as "a two-year vacation with pay in a tropical playground."[23]

For all the army's disinterest in the Philippines, the 1930s was an important period in Philippine military history. The US Congress's passage of the Tydings-McDuffie Act in 1934 established a Philippine Commonwealth government in 1935 in preparation for independence, projected to come in 1946. (Philippine independence from the United States did arrive as scheduled on 4 July 1946; World War II neither delayed nor contributed to the timing of Philippine independence.) With autonomy in domestic affairs, the Philippine government was free to develop an indigenous military capacity. In 1934, Commonwealth President-to-be Manuel Luis Quezon invited US Army chief of staff General Douglas MacArthur to prepare a plan for a military system for the Philippines and then to lead a military mission to the islands to implement it.

MacArthur drew partly on the availability of the Philippine Scouts and Philippine Constabulary (PC) to establish a new military force in the islands. The Scouts provided a few officers and enlisted men, mostly in advisory capacities, but the Philippine Constabulary essentially became the

Philippine Army in January 1936. Founded in July 1901 as the national law enforcement and security arm of the Philippine government, the constabulary had originally been officered by Americans and Europeans and had, at first, performed much the same tasks as the army's Philippine Scouts. Over the years, it had become more of a law enforcement agency, but both officers and men prided themselves on the PC's military heritage and preferred the title "soldier" to that of constable or policeman. The impact of police forces on colonial societies and emerging nations has attracted scholarly investigation in recent years, but, again, such interest has not extended to the Philippines.[24] The few existing histories of the now-defunct organization [entries 31–42] tend uncritically to chronicle its successes and gloss over its failures.

Biographies of senior PC officers have yet to be published. With few exceptions, Philippine biographies remain restricted to paeans to prominent political leaders. "Filipino biographers write," one historian has noted, "as if death were a cleansing sacrament that somehow exempts their subjects from critical examination."[25] Military biography has not achieved even that level of accomplishment. The Philippine Constabulary officer corps rapidly Filipinized and as early as 1917 received its first Filipino chief, Brigadier General Rafael Crame, but neither Crame nor any of his American or Filipino successors have biographies.[26] Of the US Army officers who commanded the constabulary from its founding in 1901 until 1917, when the passage of legislation in the United States limited the army's ability to assign officers to the PC, only the first, Henry T. Allen, has a published biography [entry 47]. The first Philippine Army chief of staff, Major General Paulino Santos, began his career in the PC, and his speeches have been published (in books difficult to obtain [entries 45–46]). His family also had printed a very brief sketch of the general [entry 44], who retired from the army in 1939 and died in 1945.

The constabulary gave its officers and traditions to the Philippine Army, but MacArthur was unwilling to be constrained by the limitations of existing military organizations. He told an American journalist that the Philippines "had the opportunity to start from scratch and cut through traditions and out-of-date methods that gum up a lot of armies."[27] The military system he devised for the defense of the soon-to-be-independent country was vastly different from anything the Philippines (or the United States) had previously experienced. It held profound social and political implications, all entirely overlooked by historians of both Philippine and military history. Historically, inhabitants of the Philippines had confronted little obligation to perform military service. The new military system, however, would introduce annually some forty-thousand conscripts drawn from every region of the archipelago to a modern army based on the Western concept of the citizen-soldier. The military system was disruptive of traditional patterns of community and personal relations and held the potential to reshape political ties between the capital city of Manila and provincial centers of authority. The successful implementation of conscription laws required far more competent and intrusive local and national bureaucracies. The nationalizing influence of the military system could strengthen the central government's control of provincial governments, but the system could also enhance the power of provincial leaders capable of mobilizing (or at least coercing) public support for the new citizen-army.

Curiously, despite the military system's obvious and wide-ranging implications, nothing is said about it in the otherwise impressively researched body of provincial history monographs that has come to dominate the study of Philippine history in recent years.[28] Most historians have relied on the papers of Quezon, MacArthur, and a handful of other officials to portray the Commonwealth army only as it responded to the concerns of Manila and Washington-based authorities. Their examinations of the military system reflect civilian and military elites' perception of Philippine defense needs (or the elites' career aspirations) and say virtually nothing about the military system itself. The history of the Philippine Commonwealth army has become little more than a footnote to the careers of such luminaries as Quezon or MacArthur.[29]

Contemporaries had greater ambitions for the Commonwealth-era army than current histories and biographies suggest. From the perspective of the US Army officers who devised the scheme of defense for the Philippines, the Commonwealth army offered a rare opportunity to articulate and act upon an ideal military system. The plan for a Philippine military system (written by American officers at the United States' Army War College) served to illuminate attitudes toward a host of issues that, as a result of budgetary constraints or ideological hostility, rarely passed beyond the rhetorical in the United States. To Filipino soldiers and civilians participating in building the new army, its social utility was at least equal to its purely military potential. The Philippine Commonwealth army was to be a vehicle for nation-building, education, and modernization. The publication in recent years of book-length histories of the Philippine Army has begun to remove the army from MacArthur's long shadow, but much remains to be done. Still almost entirely missing from virtually all military histories are the conscripts themselves. For them, participation in the military system offered both challenges and opportunities. Some resisted the heavy hand of government authority; others saw social and economic advancement in military service.

The obscurity of the conscripts underlines the most significant weakness in the much written about fourth period of American military occupation of the Philippines, and that is the role of the Philippine Army in the Philippine Campaign of 1941–42. Douglas MacArthur, Bataan, Corregidor—these names continue to resonate with a wide readership, as the success of such recent books as Elizabeth Norman's *We Band of Angels* [entry 471] and Hampton Sides' *Ghost Soldiers: The Forgotten Epic Story of World War II's Most Dramatic Mission* [entry 651] make evident. By their very popularity, however, these books reinforce the greatest myth of Bataan and Corregidor: that the Philippine Campaign was largely fought by Americans, while Filipinos played a supportive, subordinate role in the desperate struggle against Japan.

In fact, nearly 90 percent of the soldiers found in MacArthur's US Army Forces Far East command in early December 1941 were Filipinos. Close to 12,000 were in the Philippine Scouts; the rest—about 100,000— were in the Philippine Army.[30] Historians of the Philippine Campaign have had little to say about the Philippine Army. Drawing almost invariably on reminiscences of the war by American participants, military historians view the army through the eyes of its American commanders and instructors, most of whom had arrived in the Philippines only weeks before the outbreak of war and knew little of the men they led. In these accounts (some of which were written by officers, see entry 437 for example, specifically to excuse their own poor performance and thus focused entirely on the army's shortcomings), the ill-fated Philippine Army appears suddenly in late 1941, its poorly trained recruits drawn inexorably into the maelstrom of Bataan. In one of the earliest and still most comprehensive history of the Philippine Campaign [entry 334], army historian Louis Morton set the tone for treatment of the Philippine Army. Briefly describing MacArthur's appointment as military adviser and summarizing the Philippine military system, Morton then moved to the mobilization of the Philippine Amy in late 1941. Morton chose one of the army's ten reserve divisions as typical of all: The 31st Division, he wrote, suffered from shortages of personal and organizational equipment, outmoded weapons, inadequate training of officers and enlisted personnel, and nonexistent logistical support.[31] John Whitman, author of the most extensive history of the Bataan campaign [entry 356] to appear in the half-century since the publication of Morton's classic, offered much the same description of the Philippine Army, also using the 31st Division as a representative example.

Neither Morton nor Whitman are wrong—the Philippine Army did have those problems—but the commonplace depiction of an undifferentiated "Filipino" army is both inadequate and misleading. The Philippines in the 1930s was a country of disparate cultural communities, all of which the Commonwealth military system hoped to encompass. Veterans themselves draw clear distinctions between the fighting capacities of men conscripted from different regions of the archipelago. The example of the Philippine Army of 1941–42 provides an opportunity to elucidate the relationship between culture and combat performance. Were the Philippine Army's failings those common to all quickly raised, poorly trained and poorly armed military forces, or do the army's difficulties highlight the dilemma of attempting to introduce Western military organization to the non-Western world? Ironically, the Philippine Army division that arguably performed most ably on Bataan, the 41st Division, obtained its soldiers from a region of the country that the US Army avoided when it recruited for the Philippine Scouts, since army officers considered those Filipinos politically unreliable.

After several false starts, attempts to provide Filipino-centered histories of the campaign resulted by the end of the 1970s or early 1980s in the publication of official histories of the army [entry 49], army air corps [entries 60–61], and navy [entries 65–67], and brief histories of the ten Philippine Army reserve divisions [entries 484–497]. In addition to being hard to find, the division histories tend to say little about the common soldier in the Philippine Campaign.[32]

When Leon Wolff wrote *Little Brown Brother*, he complained of being handicapped by the almost complete lack of biographies and autobiographies of the generals who had directed the American war effort.[33] Much the same can be said of the Philippine Campaign. Thirty-nine soldiers and sailors of general officer grade (twenty-seven US Army; eight Philippine Army; four US Navy) served in the Philippines during the campaign of 1941–42. Only six of them—Admiral Thomas C. Hart [entry 458], General Douglas MacArthur, Lieutenant General Jonathan Wainwright [entries 436, 440], Major General Brereton, Brigadier General Bradford Chynoweth (commanding general of the 61st Philippine Army Division) [entry 420], and Brigadier General William Brougher (commanding general of the 11th Philippine Army Division) [entry 560]—had their memoirs or diaries published or found biographers. Aside from the wartime MacArthur hagiographies, Wainwright was first off the mark. The publication in 1946 of his version of what happened in the Philippines in 1941–42, Louis Morton opined, ensured that most other officers would be reluctant to tell their own stories.[34]

The Philippine Army contributed several division commanders (six of its eight generals) to the Philippine-American forces that confronted

Japan in December 1941. Three—Vicente Lim, Fidel Segundo, and Mateo Capinpin—had begun their military careers with the US Army's Philippine Scouts; three others—Guillermo B. Francisco, Luther Stevens, and Guy Fort—had served in the Philippine Constabulary. The Philippine Army's senior officers have generated no book-length biographies, although Brigadier General Lim's informative but heavily edited letters written from 1938 to 1942 [entry 57] have been published by the Lim family. The US Army's official historians made a deliberate decision to say nothing about the role of Filipino generals in the Philippine Campaign.[35]

The paucity of books by or about senior officers is countered, at least on the American side, by the innumerable personal accounts of participation in the Philippine Campaign written by enlisted men and some junior officers. These are mostly in the form of prisoner-of-war memoirs. Few of the thousands of American reinforcements rushed to the islands in 1941 died in battle, but few were able to evade capture by the Japanese, either. An effort was made to evacuate some air corps pilots and other personnel, but the 19th Bombardment Group, to cite just one example, managed to get only 380 (mostly officers) of 1,510 surviving personnel out of the Philippines before the surrender.[36] The ability of other soldiers to escape was inversely related to their perceived usefulness to the beleaguered garrison's continued resistance: older officers, of demonstrated incompetence or in poorer health and unlikely to withstand the rigors of imprisonment, were more likely to find passage aboard a departing submarine or aircraft. Perhaps 25,000 Americans were captured in the Philippines; of these, close to 15,000 survived to be liberated, a few by advancing American or Russian troops, most by Japan's surrender in August 1945 [see entry 532 for figures]. Conditions in the prison camps were extremely harsh and continuation of the war would undoubtedly have led to the death of many POWs, but many prisoners who died were killed in 1944 and 1945 when US Navy submarines and aircraft sunk the unmarked "Hell Ships" transporting POWs from the Philippines to Japan. For Filipino POWs conditions were even worse. Those who survived were released from the prison camp by the end of 1942, but many did not survive. About twice as many Filipino POWs died at Camp O'Donnell in 1942 alone, as did American POWs over the course of the entire war [see entry 342].

Those who did survive have been prolific writers. POW memoirs began appearing even before the war's end, and their publication has accelerated in recent years. Gavin Daws [entry 529] writes that "there is no comprehensive up-to-date list of published works on POWs" and such a list is impossible to compile given that many POW memoirs are privately published. He estimated their total number "in the hundreds." While most former POWs focus on their prison camp experiences, many also recall enlistment and training (if any) in the United States, the voyage to the Philippines, activities prior to the outbreak of war, and fighting on Bataan, Corregidor, or the southern islands. Americans whose books are listed in this bibliography served with virtually every American and Philippine Scout unit assigned to the Philippines in 1941; many of those units have no other published "histories" than what these veterans have written. Several of the authors served with the Philippine Army, as well.

These prisoner-of-war memoirs are an immensely valuable and underused source of information about both the American military presence in the Philippines and the 1941–42 Campaign. In this bibliography, books that cover mostly the authors' years in prison are listed under the prisoner of war heading; those that cover mostly the fighting prior to surrender are listed as campaign memoirs. In either case, it is worth remembering that old men's memories can be unreliable sources of historical knowledge. Veterans' activist and former POW Richard Gordon [entry 584] sounds a cautionary note. Some former prisoners, he writes, have become "professional prisoners of war," peddling stories of horrific experiences and supposed heroics that should be taken with a grain of salt.

The bibliographic entries that follow address military-related affairs in the Philippine Islands from the years 1902 to 1942. The entries are largely restricted to books or bound book-length manuscripts that can be found in libraries (as opposed to those that can be found only in manuscript collections). Articles have been included when they address topics about which few if any books have been written. The titles frequently overlap in subject matter. For example, general histories of Philippine military forces include within them histories of the Philippine Constabulary, the Philippine Army, and the Off Shore Patrol. An officer's biography might describe a peacetime assignment to the Philippines in the 1920s or 1930s and the officer's participation in the Philippine Campaign of 1941–42. A Filipino officer possibly served in both the Philippine Constabulary and Philippine Army. The bibliography's organization is, therefore, somewhat arbitrary. Subject headings denote the major focus of any given title, but many bibliographical entries might easily have been included under several subject headings. The reader is invited to consult them all.

# Notes

1. *Autobiography of George Dewey, Admiral of the Navy* (New York: Charles Scribner's Sons, 1913), p. 285.

2. From a letter Roosevelt sent to William Howard Taft in August 1907, reprinted

in Elting E. Morison, ed., *The Letters of Theodore Roosevelt*, vol. 5 (Cambridge, MA: Harvard University Press, 1953), pp. 761-62.

3. *Navy Directory* (1 March 1920), pp. 238-39.

4. *Manila Times* (25 June 1918).

5. The figure is from George A. Malcolm, *The Commonwealth of the Philippines* (New York and London: D. Appleton-Century Co., 1936), p. 272.

6. The authors of entry 681 give 1913 as the terminal year for the award of the army's Philippine Campaign Medal, but the late Albert F. Gleim, a leading authority on American military medals, tentatively identified an engagement on Mindanao in July 1917 involving Philippine Constabulary and Scout troops as marking the last award of the medal. See Thomas J. Nier and Allen R. Menke, comps., *The Gleim Medal Letters, 1971–1997*, 2nd ed. (San Ramon, CA: Orders and Medals Society of America, 2001), p. 27.

7. John M. Gates, "The Pacification of the Philippines, 1898-1902," in Joe C. Dixon, ed., *The American Military and the Far East* (USAF Academy, 1980), p. 82. The textbook, prepared for the use of ROTC cadets, is Maurice Matloff, gen. ed. *American Military History*, rev. ed. (Washington, DC: Office of the Chief of Military History, 1973).

8. The review is in the *New York Times*, part 6 (5 May 1940). Sexton's book has been reprinted several times, sometimes under the title *Soldiers in the Philippines.*

9. Kenton J. Clymer, "Not so Benevolent Assimilation: The Philippine-American War," *Reviews in American History* 11, no. 4 (December 1983): 547-52, surveys the differing approaches to writing about the Philippine-American War.

10. May lays out his criticism (which mirrors criticism made of Agoncillo's book when it was published in 1960) most completely in Glenn Anthony May, *A Past Recovered* (Quezon City: New Day, 1987), chap. 5.

11. This vast collection of captured Filipino documents was translated, edited, and prepared for publication by army officer John Taylor early in the century. William Howard Taft decided that much of what Taylor had to say was best left unsaid and suppressed its publication, but Taylor's compilation can be seen in the US national archives. The collection was published and distributed (it was not at first for sale) in the Philippines as John R. M. Taylor, with a new introduction by Renato Constantino, *The Philippine Insurrection Against the United States: A Compilation of Documents with Notes and Introduction*, 5 vols. (Pasay City: Eugenio Lopez Foundation, 1971).

12. Curiously, Linn does not provide comprehensive casualty figures for American forces. These are from Allan R. Millett and Peter Maslowski, *For the Common Defense: A Military History of the United States of America*, rev. ed. (New York: The Free Press, 1994), p. 653: 126,468 served; 1,004 battle deaths; 3,161 other deaths; 2,911 wounded. For how the army confronted the significant health problems posed by operations in the Philippines, see entries 123, 136, 139, and 153.

13. On the American side, the Philippine-American War was fought almost entirely by men who enlisted in the army—either in regular or so-called "volunteer" regiments—specifically to fight in the war. The military forces in World Wars I and II, Korea, and Vietnam included many draftees. The Gulf War was fought by "volunteers" who, of course, had joined the military services during peacetime.

14. Faust's book was intended to be sold as a souvenir to soldiers of the state volunteer (national guard) regiments who served in the islands and was published with the appropriate regimental history and unit roster appended. Arno Press' 1970 reprint is the most accessible edition; it concludes with a history of the 10th Pennsylvania Infantry. The most widely available version of the original 1899 printing contains the history of the 1st California Regiment.

15. R. Ernest Dupuy, *The Compact History of the United States Army*, rev. ed. (New York: Hawthorn Books, Inc., 1961), p. 209.

16. Not every officer served in the islands. Omar Bradley performed his obligatory "foreign service" in Hawaii. George Patton successfully schemed to avoid Philippine duty, and the War Department rescinded Mark Clark's orders to the islands and never reissued them. But these were exceptions to the general rule.

17. *The [Manila] Cablenews-American* (27 January 1911).

18. Michael P. Onorato, ed., *Origins of the Philippine Republic: Extracts from the Diaries and Records of Francis Burton Harrison* (Ithaca, NY, 1974), p. 25.

19. Letter, Wood to Theodore Roosevelt, 30 January 1908, Leonard Wood Papers, Library of Congress.

20. The "A" in USAFFE stands for "Army," not "Armed," no matter how often the latter is written.

21. Edgar Frank Raines, Jr., has written "The Early Career of Major General James Franklin Bell, USA, 1856-1903," (MA thesis, Southern Illinois University, 1968), and "Major General J. Franklin Bell and Military Reform: The Chief of Staff Years, 1906-1910," 2 vols. (PhD dissertation, University of Wisconsin, 1976).

22. There have been other efforts to write histories of the Scouts. Eugene Ganley was an army officer who collected documents and interviewed Philippine Scout officers for nearly twenty years, starting in 1959, for a projected two-volume history, but he died before completing his work. Fortunately, his family donated his papers to USAMHI, where they have remained in fourteen archival boxes, virtually untouched, for more than two decades. Similarly, the late John Vinson, a former cavalryman and District of Columbia police officer, taped and transcribed dozens of interviews with officers, enlisted men, and dependent wives for a never-completed history of the 26th Cavalry Regiment (PS). The Vinson Collection remains in the possession of his family.

23. This characterization is from Duane Schultz, *Hero of Bataan: The Story of General Jonathan M. Wainwright* (New York: St. Martin's Press, 1981), p. 43.

24. See, for example, the articles in David M. Anderson and David Killingray, eds., *Policing and Decolonization: Politics, Nationalism, and the Police, 1917-1965* (Manchester and New York: Manchester University Press, 1992).

25. Alfred W. McCoy, "'An Anarchy of Families': The Historiography of State and Family in the Philippines," in A. W. McCoy, ed., *An Anarchy of Families* (Quezon City: Ateneo de Manila University Press, 1994), p. 4. Teodoro Agoncillo, the Philippines' preeminent twentieth century historian, wrote [entry 297] that he "eschew[ed] character portrayal" because "in the Philippines, an unflattering characterization will surely end either in court or in physical combat [and he] was prepared for neither."

26. Clarence H. Bowers, the last American chief of constabulary, is reported to have authored an autobiography that has been lost. The family of the last chief of constabulary prior to that organization's subsumption within the Philippine Army in 1936, Basilio Valdes (sometimes spelled Valdez), has reportedly commissioned a biography of the general.

27. *Collier's* (5 September 1936).

28. Representative works are John Larkin, *The Pampangans: Colonial Society in a Philippine Province* (1972; reprint, Quezon City: New Day, 1993), Rosario M. Cortes, *Pangasinan, 1901-1986: A Political, Socioeconomic, and Cultural History* (Quezon City: New Day, 1990), and Violeta B. Lopez-Gonzaga, *The Negrense* (Bacolod City: University of St. La Salle, 1991). Alfred McCoy's "Ylo-ilo: Factional Conflict in a Colonial Economy, Iloilo Province, Philippines, 1937-1955" (PhD dissertation, Yale University, 1977) offers the most incisive look at provincial-level politics under the Com-

monwealth regime, but it remains unpublished. "Popular" histories are more likely to discuss the military system and its local impact, albeit briefly. See, for example, journalist and publisher Modesto P. Sa-Onoy's *A History of Negros Occidental* (Bacolod City: Today Publishers, 1992).

29. Every MacArthur biography falls into this category, none more so than the most recent, Geoffrey Perret's thick *Old Soldiers Never Die* [entry 100] in which the author traces the rise and fall of the Commonwealth army over the course of five chapters without mentioning a single Filipino soldier. Even more scholarly biographies of the general that putatively center on his Philippine service, such as Carol Petillo's *Douglas MacArthur* [entry 101], offer only a cursory description of the military system and prefer instead to concentrate on MacArthur's stormy relationship with Quezon and his US Army superiors in Washington. Studies of Philippine-American relations in the 1930s take essentially the same approach. The military system is discussed briefly only as background to explain MacArthur's decision to accept an appointment as Commonwealth military adviser. See, for example, Theodore Friend, *Between Two Empires* [entry 78], H. W. Brands, *Bound to Empire: The United States and the Philippines* (New York and Oxford: Oxford University Press, 1992), and Frank Golay, *Face of Empire: United States-Philippine Relations, 1898-1946* (Madison, WI: Center for Southeast Asian Studies, 1998).

30. Morton [entry 334] lists a US Army garrison of 31,095 on 30 November 1941, of whom just under 12,000 were Philippine Scouts. Americans numbered just over 19,000. (The higher estimate of American POWs given later in the introduction includes sailors and marines not initially part of USAFFE.) Morton estimated the Philippine Army at "over 100,000 men" within a week of the war's start. Using Morton's figures, Filipinos comprised 85 percent of USAFFE in early December. The Veterans Administration numbered the "Commonwealth Army (USAFFE)" at 149,300 and calculated that 13,800 Filipinos had served in the Philippine Scouts. Using those figures, Filipinos made up 89.5 percent of USAFFE.

31. The army's then-chief historian, Kent Roberts Greenfield, was an in-house reviewer of the pre-publication manuscript of *The Fall of the Philippines* [entry 334]. He wrote that Morton's scant coverage of the Philippine Army and comments about its problems left him "wondering what General MacArthur had been doing since 1935." That, Greenfield opined, was probably Morton's intention. His critique, dated 14 December 1951, is found in Records of the Office of the Chief of Military History, Record Group 319, US National Archives.

32. Apparently the effort to publish division histories began not long after the war was over. The history of the 1st Regular Division [entry 496], published in 1953, was supposed to be "the first part of a series of 'after action reports' of the Philippine Army divisions that had participated in the Philippine Defense Campaign of 1941-1942," but until the 1970s only the 2nd Regular Division history [entry 495] was published. Manuscript histories prepared in the 1950s of some Philippine Army divisions can be found in archival collections.

33. At the time, Wolff thought only Frederick Funston's *Memories of Two Wars* (New York: Charles Scribner's Sons, 1911) was in print. He overlooked William Carter's *The Life of Lieutenant General Chaffee* (Chicago: University of Chicago Press, 1917). Since then, Rudolph Rau has self-published a "commemorative biography" of Major General Henry Lawton, the senior American officer killed in the war, *Lawton, Forgotten Warrior* (1998). Kenneth Ray Young's *The General's General: The Life and Times of Arthur MacArthur* (Boulder, CO: Westview, 1994) filled a long-felt void. Funston's adventures before he became a general officer have been the subject of two books by Thomas Crouch, including one *A Leader of Volunteers: Frederick Funston and the 20th*

*Kansas in the Philippines, 1898-1899* (Lawrence, KS: Coronado Press, 1984), that describes his rise to fame in the Philippine-American War.

34. Brereton's controversial diary [entry 442] also appeared in 1946, several months after Wainwright's book.

35. See letter, George Groce to Maj. Gen. K. L. Berry, 23 January 1950, box 2, Morton Collection, USAMHI.

36. Figures are taken from Maj. J. H. M. Smith, response to "request for historical information concerning 19th Bombardment Group (H)," dated 2 November 1943, a copy of which is published with entry 444.

# Bibliographies and Other Reference Works

1   Ancell, R. Manning, with Christine M. Miller. *The Biographical Dictionary of World War II General and Flag Officers: The U.S. Armed Forces.* Westport, CT: Greenwood Press, 1996. Pp. xii, 706. Coverage of Philippine generals is spotty in this book. One of the American-born Philippine Army generals, Guy Fort, is included, but not the other, Luther Stevens. Vicente Lim is included (although his entry has several errors of fact) but not Fidel Segundo or Mateo Capinpin. More usefully, some of the entries give details of an officer's Philippine assignments prior to his promotion to general officer, such as the one for Frederick Manley, who as a colonel worked in the office of the High Commissioner in 1935-36, for which he was awarded the Philippine Constabulary's Distinguished Service Star.

1A   *Bataan and Corregidor: World War II Commemorative Bibliography, No. 3.* Washington, DC: Washington Navy Yard, Navy Department Library, 1992. [Pp. 8.] Bound typescript. Includes a list of articles appearing in popular and official military journals (e.g., *Leatherneck, Marine Corps Gazette, Life, Newsweek*).

2   Beede, Benjamin R. *Intervention and Counterinsurgency: An Annotated Bibliography of the Small Wars of the United States, 1898–1984.* New York: Garland Publishers, 1985. Pp. xxxviii, 321. Numerous entries in a chapter titled "Philippine Campaigns, 1902-1936," with emphasis on "The Moro Wars." Does not cover the Philippine-American War.

3   Beede, Benjamin R., ed. *The War of 1898 and U.S. Interventions, 1898–1934: An Encyclopedia.* New York: Garland Publishers, 1994. Pp. xxvi, 751. Forty-eight entries contributed by American and Filipino authors describe persons, themes, places, and events of "the Philippine War, 1899–1902." There are a further twenty-four entries under "Moro Campaigns, 1902–1913." Sample entries include "Atrocities in the Philippine War," "The Philippine Scouts," "Moro Cotta."

4   Bell, Walter. *The Philippines in World War II, 1941–1945: A Chronology and Select Annotated Bibliography of Books and Articles in English.* Westport, CT: Greenwood Press, 1999. Pp. viii, 276. Pages 4–117 of this book consist of a chronology of events from January 1941 to September 1945. The bibliography lists many

standard titles but is far from comprehensive, and there are some curious omissions and inclusions: "Filipino Unit Histories," for example, lists only one title (*The Philippine Scouts* [entry 166]); "Historical surveys" of Philippine-American relations includes journalist Stanley Karnow's derivative *In Our Image: America's Empire in the Philippines* (New York: Random House, 1989) but not historian Theodore Friend's authoritative *Between Two Empires* [entry 78]; and a short list of the Philippines in World War II-related websites includes the "Battling Bastards of Bataan" veterans' group website (http://home.pacbell.net/fbaldie/Battling_Bastards_of_Bataan.html), but not the more extensive (and more useful to researchers) ADBC website (http://harrisonheritage.com/adbc/). The annotations are useful, and the book does list some little-known articles.

**5**  Brown, Russell K. *Fallen in Battle: American General Officer Combat Fatalities From 1775.* Westport, CT: Greenwood Press, 1988. Pp. xxvi, 243. Page-long biographies of Philippine Scout and Army officers Vicente Lim [see entry 57] and Fidel Segundo find a place in this book, as does one for Guy Fort [see entry 322], the Philippine Army general who commanded the 81st Division, PA, on Mindanao. All of the US Army generals who served in the Philippine Campaign of 1941-42 survived the war; one-half of the Philippine Army generals survived. The Japanese executed Lim, Segundo, and Fort.

**6**  Coletta, Paolo E. *An Annotated Bibliography of U.S. Marine Corps History.* Lanham, MD: University Press of America, 1986. Pp. xiii, 417. Most of the Philippine-related entries here deal with the Spanish-American War and World War II.

**7**  Coletta, Paolo E. *A Selected and Annotated Bibliography of American Naval History.* Lanham, MD: University Press of America, 1988. Pp. xi, 523. (Revised edition of the author's earlier navy-history bibliographies.) Includes entries relating to Commodore George Dewey in the Philippines and to the operations of the Asiatic Fleet in 1941-42.

**8**  Controvich, James T. *United States Army Unit Histories: A Reference and Bibliography.* Manhattan, KS: Department of History, Kansas State University, 1983. Pp. viii, 591. Bound typescript. 6,672 entries include a half-dozen dealing with the Philippine Scouts, Constabulary, and Philippine National Guard. A "1987 Supplement" added 1,055 entries, few of which relate to the Philippines. Two further supplements, B (1992) and C (1996) have also appeared, each with additional Philippine-related entries. Controvich incorporated the listings found in Dornbusch [entry 10] and Pappas [entry 20]. Like those, his book is most useful for identifying unit histories of regular US Army regiments which served in the Philippines before World War I.

**9**  Cornejo, Miguel R., editor and comp. *Cornejo's Commonwealth Directory of the Philippines, 1939 Encyclopedic Edition.* Manila: Privately Published, 1939. Pp. xciii, A1-A176, 2626. This is a major source for any Commonwealth-era research which, thanks to Cornejo's interest in Things Military, includes Philippine and

US Army personnel directories, a directory of naval officers, biographical sketches of senior officers, and reprinted newspaper articles dealing with Philippine defense issues in the 1930s. A postwar reprinting divided the encyclopedia into two volumes, but the contents remained the same. Earlier versions of Cornejo's directories (the first appeared in 1918) are less useful and are, at any rate, very rare.

**10**    Dornbusch, Charles E. *Histories, Personal Narratives—United States Army: A Checklist*. Cornwallville, NY: Hope Farm Press, 1967. Pp. 402. 2,743 entries compiled by America's leading expert on the topic. Entries for the 26th Cavalry, 14th Engineers, and 24th Field Artillery Philippine Scout Regiments—all articles found in US armed forces journals—are included. Dornbusch also prepared a bibliography of air force unit histories which has been published and reprinted several times under various titles, but it includes no Philippine-related entries.

**11**    Fletcher, Marvin. *The Peacetime Army, 1900–1941: A Research Guide*. Westport, CT: Greenwood Press, 1988. Pp. xxi, 177. Many entries under "Philippines" and, despite the book's title, "Philippine-American War." Fletcher excluded first-person books and sources published before 1945 and did not search journals published in the Philippines.

**12**    Floyd, Dale E. *Military Fortifications: A Selective Bibliography*. Westport, CT: Greenwood Press, 1992. Pp. xxii, 361. Twenty-six entries for the Philippines, emphasizing, but not limited to, the US period and World War II.

**13**    *A Guidebook to the Military, Police & Veterans Museums*. 3rd ed. Manila: National Commission for Culture and the Arts, 1998. Pp. 32. Includes photographs, descriptions, locations, and contact information (some now out of date) for the Armed Forces of the Philippines, Philippine Army, Navy, Air Force, National Police, Manila Police Department, and Veterans Federation of the Philippines museums and libraries. All are located in Metro Manila. Also lists other military-related museums found on Luzon and Panay.

**14**    Higham, Robin, ed. *A Guide to the Sources of United States Military History*. Hamden, CT: Archon Books, 1975. Pp. xiii, 559. Many titles dealing with US military forces in the Philippines can be found in this invaluable volume and its supplements (four to date [1998], all co-edited with Donald J. Mrozek), but their organization makes it difficult to identify Philippine-related titles. The Philippine-American War and early period of occupation, for example, are subsumed within a chapter titled "Civil Military Relations, Operations, and the Army, 1865-1917."

**15**    Higham, Robin, ed. *Official Histories: Essays and Bibliographies from Around the World*. Manhattan, KS: Kansas State University Library, 1970. Pp. xi, 644. A one-page essay titled "The Historical Branch of the AFP" gives a history of the organization and lists its chiefs and publications. The essay also includes the titles of AFP service journals that contain history articles. Higham edited a second edition of this work (*Official Military Historical Offices and Sources*, 2 vols. [Westport, CT: Greenwood Press, 2000]), but it included nothing about the Philippines.

**16**   Kelly, Thomas E., III. *The U.S. Army and the Spanish-American War Era, 1895–1910, Part I, Special Bibliographic Series, Number 9.* Carlisle Barracks, PA: US Army Military History Institute, 1974. Pp. ix, 151. Bound typescript. In 1968, USAMHI began the Spanish-American War Veterans and Widows Survey, and the questionnaires and other documents collected as a result are listed in this publication. Although most respondents were veterans of the fighting in Cuba, the Philippines, China, and Puerto Rico from 1898 to 1902, some served with post-war occupation forces. Two enlisted Filipino veterans of the Philippine Scouts responded to the survey, as did several American veterans of the Scouts and PC and others with post-1902 service in the islands.

**17**   Meixsel, Richard B. "Research Adventures in Philippine Military History." In *Bulletin of the American Historical Collection*, vol. 28, no. 1 (January-March 2000): 37–46. Identifies archives and libraries in the Philippines that hold military-related documents and books.

**18**   Netzorg, Morton J. *The Philippines in World War II and to Independence, December 8, 1941–July 4, 1946: An Annotated Bibliography.* Ithaca: Cornell University Press, 1977. Pp. xii, 232. Bound typescript. This "coverage of books, of selections from books, of theses and dissertations, of published government documents, and of journal articles" includes thousands of entries alphabetized by author, in English and other European and Filipino languages. It is a monumental work, surpassed only by Netzorg's posthumously published revised edition [next entry].

**19**   Netzorg, Morton J. *The Philippines in World War II and to Independence (December 8, 1941–July 4, 1946): An Annotated Bibliography.* Second Revised & Greatly Enlarged Edition. Detroit: The Cellar Book Shop Press, 1995. 2 vols. Pp. xviii, 1587 (continuous pagination). This vast expansion of Netzorg's earlier work [previous entry] is handicapped only by the lack of a more narrowly focused subject index (all entries are by author) and an original pricetag of US$150. These two volumes should be the starting point for any serious research into the history of World War II in the Philippines.

**20**   Pappas, George S., with Elizabeth Snoke and Alexandra Campbell. *United States Army Unit Histories, Special Bibliographic Series, Number 4.* Carlisle Barracks, PA: United States Army Military History Institute, 1978. 2 vols. Pp. xviii, 431 (continuous pagination). Bound typescript. This is a listing of "books, pamphlets, and mimeographed studies" concerning regular US Army, National Guard and Reserve unit histories found in the Institute's collection. For the Guard and other volunteer organizations, histories published before 1914 are not listed. There are no entries for any Philippine Scout regiment nor for any Philippine Army (USAFFE) unit.

**21**    Paszek, Lawrence J. *United States Air Force Histories: A Guide to Documentary Sources.* Washington, DC: Office of Air Force History, 1973. Pp. v, 245. Reprinted by Arno Press, NY, 1980. Guide to air force-related document and manuscript sources in United States archives and libraries. A few entries deal with air force activities in the prewar Philippines.

**22**    Rasor, Eugene L. *General Douglas MacArthur, 1880–1964: Historiography and Annotated Bibliography.* Westport, CT: Greenwood Press, 1994. Pp. xxii, 217. Considerable Philippine-related material is found here, but the compiler's knowledge of the Philippines is modest. Well-known journalist and diplomat Carlos P. Romulo [entries 387, 403, 404, and 407] is described as "president of Philippines" and James Woolard's dissertation on the formative years (1899–1922) of the Philippine Scouts [entry 169] as a history of "the Philippine Army prepared and trained under command of MacArthur during the late 1930s."

**23**    Rasor, Eugene L. *The Southwest Pacific Campaign, 1941–45: Historiography and Annotated Bibliography.* Westport, CT: Greenwood Press, 1996. Pp. xvi, 279. Brief topical introductory chapters (guerrilla movement, prisoners of war, weapons and technology, and so on) discuss the state of the literature and suggest avenues for further research. 1,535 briefly annotated entries (including movie titles) complete the book. Philippine-related entries suggest the compiler does not know the material well: Walter Edmonds [entry 366] is dismissed as a novelist; Carlos Quirino's 1935 campaign biography of Manuel Quezon is included for some unexplained reason but not Quirino's *Filipinos at War* [entry 30] nor his well-known 1971 Quezon biography (which actually encompasses events of World War II) [entry 119]; several of Uldarico Baclagon's books are listed, but nothing by Primitivo Catalan nor by most other Filipino authors of military history (Ricardo Jose, Alfonso Aluit, etc.). Rasor still thinks [see previous entry] that Carlos Romulo was a "famous wartime leader of the Philippines." Of value is the compiler's discussion of periodicals that specialize in World War II topics, of archives and libraries strong in World War II material, and of veterans' associations (although there are no contact addresses).

**24**    Rebadavia, Consolacion B. *Checklist of Philippine Government Documents, 1917-1949.* Edited by Natividad P. Verzosa and Pacifico M. Austria. Quezon City: University of the Philippines Library, 1960. Pp. xv, 817. Lists existing official publications (regulations, rosters, manuals, and annual reports) of the pre-World War II Philippine Army and Constabulary.

**25**    Saito, Shiro. *Philippine-American Relations: A Guide to Manuscript Sources in the United States.* Westport, CT: Greenwood Press, 1982. Pp. xx, 256. Detailed guide to manuscript collections, many of which deal with the US Army in the prewar Philippines.

# Philippine Armed Forces

GENERAL HISTORIES

**26**   Baclagon, Uldarico S. *Military History of the Philippines*. Manila: Saint Mary's Publ., 1975. Pp. x, 411. In this book, described by the author as an up-dated edition of *Philippine Campaigns* [next entry], Colonel Baclagon begins with Pigafetta's account of the battle of Mactan in 1521 and concludes with a chapter titled "National Security and the New Society." Along the way he discusses the Philippine military participation in the Korean and Vietnam Wars. Ferdinand Marcos's exploits—real or imagined—receive a chapter of their own. About one-half of the book deals with World War II. A pictorial essay (pp. 363-99) and rolls of honor for World War II and the Korean War conclude the book. For an informed account of Baclagon's background as a military historian and role as Ferdinand Marcos's "palace historian," see entry 51.

**27**   Baclagon, Uldarico S. *Philippine Campaigns*. Manila: Graphic House, 1952. Pp. xvii, 388. A traditional military history of (mostly) World War II, focusing on the disposition of units and the decisions of senior officers. McCoy [entry 51] evaluates *Philippine Campaigns* "as a landmark work. In its documentation, analysis, and objectivity it surpassed the writing of established Filipino historians."

**28**   *Ministry of National Defense: A Brief History*. Camp Aguinaldo, Quezon City: Ministry of National Defense, Public Information Service, [c1979]. Pp. 224. Meant to commemorate the 40th anniversary (1939-79) of the National Defense Department, the book is actually a military history of the Philippines and better written than most. It says curiously little about the National Defense Department, however. Text ends on page 100; remainder of book consists of appendices (including MacArthur's 1936 *Report on National Defense*).

**29**   Pobre, Cesar P. *History of the Armed Forces of the Filipino People*. Quezon City: New Day, 2000. Pp. xi, 731. (According to the author's "acknowledgements," Ricardo Jose "did much of the research for the book [and] also prepared the draft.) Covers Philippine military history from the precolonial period to the AFP modernization act of 1995. Alongside Jose's work [entry 50], this book includes perhaps the best published history of the founding and development of the Commonwealth-era army and an excellent account of the Philippine National Guard, as well.

**30**   Quirino, Carlos. *Filipinos at War*. Quezon City: Vera-Reyes, 1981. Pp. 284. This is a profusely illustrated coffee-table book military history of the Philippines, from Mactan to Bessang Pass, in the author's always readable style. For his coverage of World War II, the author draws partly on his own experiences as an officer with the 2nd Division (PA) on Bataan.

---

# Philippine Constabulary

### GENERAL HISTORIES

**31**    Baja, Emanuel A. *Philippine Police System and Its Problems*. Manila: Pobre's Press, 1933. Pp. 604. That a serving officer could author a book so critical of the constabulary's leadership and still rise in the organization should be a cause for wonder. After a brief account of the Spanish-era police, Baja (commissioned 1913) examines the challenges faced by the PC and municipal police forces in the islands and finds the PC lacking in many particulars.

**32**    Baja, Emanuel A. *Philippine Police System and Its Problems, Book II: Police of the Commonwealth*. Manila, Philippine Education Co., 1939. Pp. xii, 222. This book continues the themes developed in the author's 1933 book [previous entry].

**33**    Coates, George Y. "The Philippine Constabulary, 1901-1917." PhD dissertation, Ohio State University, 1968. Pp. v, 410. This detailed history of the PC's early years concentrates on action in the field. It remains the standard scholarly history of the organization, although the author made no use of the voluminous BIA constabulary files in the US National Archives.

**34**    Cojuanco, Margarita R., *et al. Konstable: The Story of the Philippine Constabulary*. Manila: AboCan Enterprises, 1991. Pp. 249. This multi-authored book is engagingly written and nicely illustrated but contributes little new information about the PC.

**35**    Elarth, Harold H. *The Story of the Philippine Constabulary*. Los Angeles, CA: Philippine Constabulary Officers Association, 1949. Pp. 185. A Roll of Honor (list of officers killed, died, and wounded on duty) is followed by a narrative history of the organization. A lengthy biographical section concluding the book must be used with caution. The author was a former PC officer (served 1904-17) who had access to official PC registers, but he apparently compiled much of the biographical section by word of mouth. Some details are wrong, unpleasant information is excluded (the word "resigned" hides a multitude of sins, here), and the list includes only a few of the most senior Filipino officers. A reduced-format photocopy reproduction of this book was offered for sale in 1998. The copy reproduced belonged to Joseph V. Thebaud (served 1912-16) and includes biographical notations made by him to 1962 and photographs of PC medals not found in the original book.

**36**    Headquarters, US Army Service Forces. *Civil Affairs Handbook, The Philippines, Section 14: Public Safety.* Army Service Forces Manual, M-365-14, dated 5 February 1945. Pp. 65. Bound typescript. This history of the Philippine Constabulary and other law-enforcement agencies in the Philippines during the Spanish, American, and Japanese regimes includes a "List of Provincial Sheriffs as of 1941" and a list of "Philippine Constabulary Officers, 1939-1940."

**37**    Hurley, Vic. *Jungle Patrol: The Story of the Philippine Constabulary.* New York: E.P. Dutton and Co., 1938. Pp. 397. Reprinted by Cacho Hermanos, Manila, 1985, as Book 4 of the Filipiniana Reprint Series, with an introduction by Renato Constantino. This adventure-story writer's account of the PC emphasizes the heroism and self-sacrifice of the organization's American officers. It remains the PC's most accessible history, but the tales told in it should be verified using contemporary evidence. Hurley's version of Cary Crockett's heroics at San Ramon, Samar, in early 1905, for example, differs, in almost every particular, from the version given by Englishman Stanley Hyatt in *The Diary of a Soldier of Fortune* (London, 1911). Hyatt and his brother (Hurley mentions neither in his book) were traveling with Crockett at the time as journalists for Manila newspapers. Hyatt's book includes photographs of the PC fort at San Ramon. This book has been placed on the internet at www.bakbakan.com.

**38**    Jenista, Frank Lawrence. *The White Apos: American Governors on the Cordillera Central.* Quezon City: New Day, 1987. Pp. xii, 321. This engrossing account of the personal lives and official activities of American officers of the Philippine Constabulary charged with ruling the inhabitants of the Mountain Province of northern Luzon is based on archival sources and dozens of interviews conducted in the early 1970s.

**39**    Martir, Valeriano A. "The Philippine Constabulary, 1901–1951: An Historical Survey." MA thesis, University of Manila, 1955. Pp. iii, 146. A difficult-to-find work but one which includes some details not found in more common sources.

**40**    Miller, Richard L. "The Philippine Constabulary, 1901–1941." University of the Philippines, 1970. Pp. xvi, 144. The stated purpose of this Bachelor of Science degree research project is to illustrate the effectiveness of the Philippines' national police system and to show how the PC evolved into a para-military organization. It consists mostly of lengthy extracts from annual reports of the Philippine Commission, the Governors-General, and (from 1935) the President of the Philippines. A one-page history of the AFP finance section is appended. The author writes that one problem in obtaining documents about the AFP (of which the PC was a part) history is that the AFP's historical section was deactivated in 1959; when reactivated in 1965, many records were found to have been misplaced.

**41**  *Philippine Constabulary, 58th Anniversary.* [Camp Crame: Headquarters, Philippine Constabulary,] 8 August 1959. Pp. 202. On the anniversary of its founding (July-August 1901), the PC usually issued a souvenir publication. Anywhere from a dozen to more than 200 pages in length, the bulk of the publication was devoted to contemporary events, but it included a brief history of the PC and photographs of its chiefs. The first such publication seems to have been a special 30th-anniversary issue of the PC monthly journal *Khaki and Red* (July 1931) that included a photograph of every serving officer in the PC. This 1958 issue, which has a photo essay showing the evolution of the PC uniform, is included here as a sample of the type.

**42**  San Gabriel, Reynaldo P., *et al. The Constabulary Story.* Camp Crame: Headquarters Philippine Constabulary, Public Information Office, 1978. Pp. 384. (Subsequent editions exist; the third appeared in 1982.) Drawing on Elarth [entry 35] and PC anniversary publications [previous entry] for coverage of the PC's prewar years, the authors offer a vivid but uncritical account of the accomplishments of the organization from its inception in 1901. According to the authors, a fire at PC headquarters at Camp Crame, Quezon City, in 1958 destroyed whatever records then existed dealing with the PC's history.

## BIOGRAPHIES AND MEMOIRS

**43**  Crowder, James L., Jr. *Osage General: Major General Clarence L. Tinker.* Tinker AFB, OK: Office of History, Oklahoma City Air Logistics Center, 1987. Pp. 394. Unable to obtain a commission in the army after graduating from a military college in Missouri, Tinker joined the PC and served in the Visayas and Mountain Province, from December 1908 to June 1912 (with a month out to try his hand at selling sewing machines in Manila in early 1912). Later an army air force general, Tinker disappeared in a flight over the Pacific early in World War II. One chapter describes Tinker's experiences in the Philippines.

**44**  *Major General Paulino Santos, AFP, Retd., First Chief of Staff of the Philippine Army; Former Director, Bureau of Prisons; Manager, National Land Settlement Administration (NLSA)—His Biography.* N.p. n.d. General Santos's involvement in the founding of the Philippine Army is all but forgotten today, but he had a meteoric rise in the PC (enlisted service 1909-12; commissioned 1914; retired 1930) and was MacArthur's choice to be brought out of retirement to become the new army's first chief of staff in 1936. This twelve-page illustrated biographical tribute was published by the general's family.

**45**  Ramirez, Jong Balagtas. "Major Gen. Paulino Santos, Sr." In *Who Is Who: Databank, Gen. Santos City, Vol. II, '93,* edited by J. B. Ramirez. Privately Published, 1992. This illustrated eighty-page biography of the general draws heavily on Santos's public speeches. See next entry.

**46**  Santos, Paulino. *Speeches (formal, informal and extemporaneous) delivered* *by Major General Paulino Santos, Chief of Staff, Philippine Army (May 1936–July 1938), including some of those delivered prior to his appointment as Chief of Staff.* Quezon City: Publications Division, Philippine Army, Adjutant General Service, August 1938. Pp. 263. This is presumably the source for Santos's speeches cited in Ramirez [previous entry]. The only known library copy is reportedly held by Sophia University in Tokyo.

**47**  Twichell, Heath, Jr. *Allen: The Biography of an Army Officer, 1859–1930.* New Brunswick, NJ: Rutgers University Press, 1974. Pp. xiii, 358. This scholarly biography of the first Chief of Constabulary, Captain Henry T. Allen, US Army (USMA 1882), provides one of the better accounts of the PC's formative years. Allen commanded the PC from 1901 to 1907.

**48**  White, John R. *Bullets and Bolos: Fifteen Years in the Philippine Islands.* New York and London: The Century Co., 1928. Pp. 343. (This book has also been seen in a modern paperback edition, with no publishing details provided.) A number of PC officers wrote book-length memoirs, but White seems to be the only one who got his published. An army enlisted man during the Philippine-American War, White joined the constabulary in 1901 and served on Negros, Mindanao, as warden of the Iwahig Penal Colony, and as head of the constabulary school at Baguio. White, who retired as a colonel in 1914, describes the isolated life of a PC officer, his position in the local community, and the PC's relationship with the Scouts and regular army.

Research note: The University of Oregon library's special collections holds the papers of fourteen Americans who served in the Philippine Constabulary, including those of Harold Elarth [entry 35] and John White [48]. The official personnel files of prewar PC officers no longer exit, but information about many PC officers (mostly Americans) can be found in the BIA's "personal name file," and BIA files include nine separate boxes of material related to individual PC officers, filed alphabetically. BIA files are located in Record Group 350 at the US National Archives at College Park, MD. Manuel L. Quezon's papers at the Philippine National Library, Manila, include lengthy extracts from the personnel file of PC officer George Bowers (no relation to PC officer Clarence Bowers [entry 675]).

---

# Philippine Army

## GENERAL HISTORIES

**49**  Army Historical Division, Philippine Army, *History of the Philippine Army*

*(1897–1945)*. Ft. Bonifacio: Army Historical Division, 1981. Pp. xvii, 300. The first of a planned two volumes, this history of the Philippine military experience concentrates on the revolutionary period and World War II. Appendices include "Aguinaldo's Manifesto of October 31, 1896," and the "Constitution of Biak-na-Bato." Prepared for the internal educational needs of the army, this book saw only limited distribution and is difficult to find. The second volume has been written but not published.

**50**    Jose, Ricardo Trota. *The Philippine Army, 1935–1942.* Quezon City: Ateneo de Manila University Press, 1992. Pp. x, 268. This is the published version of the author's University of the Philippines masters thesis. A professor at the University of the Philippines whose expertise is Philippine military history and the Japanese occupation period, Jose has been described as a "walking encyclopedia" of information about the Philippine military, and he displays only some of that knowledge in this well-written book, which explores the problems surrounding the implementation of MacArthur's Commonwealth-era military system in great detail.

**51**    McCoy, Alfred W. *Closer Than Brothers: Manhood at the Philippine Military Academy.* New Haven and London: Yale University Press, 1999. Pp. xx, 425. (Philippine edition published by Anvil Publishing, Manila.) The author studied the experiences of the graduates of the PMA classes of 1940 and 1971 to explore "the military's changing role in Philippine political life"—changes largely for the worse. A portion of this book dealing with the 1940 PMA class appeared earlier as "'Same Banana': Hazing and Honor at the Philippine Military Academy," in *The Journal of Asian Studies* 54, no. 3 (August 1995): 689–726, reprinted in *The Military and Society*, Vol. 2, *The Training and Socializing of Military Personnel* (Hamden, CT: Garland Publishing, 1999), edited by Peter Karsten.

**52**    McCoy, Alfred W. "Philippine Commonwealth and the Cult of Masculinity." In *Philippine Studies* 48, no. 3 (2000): 315–46. The author argues that "in building an Army on the American model, the Commonwealth imported a foreign model of masculinity and then, through mass mobilization, drilled Filipino males to its standard."

**53**    *Philippine Army: The First 100 Years.* Headquarters Philippine Army, 1997. Pp. xi, 297. About sixty pages of this well-illustrated, coffee-table style book cover the period 1902 to 1945. Includes rare prewar training photos and pictures of unit insignia.

**54**    Philippine Research and Information Section, Advance Echelon, USAFFE. *The Philippine Army: Its Establishment, Organization, and Legal Basis.* 26 January 1945. Pp. iv, 21, plus 81 pages of appendices. Bound typescript. A brief narrative overview of the organization of the constabulary and army is followed by appendices which include Commonwealth Act no. 1 (National Defense Act), as amended to 1940, and assorted executive orders and presidential proclamations pertaining to the army.

BIOGRAPHIES AND MEMOIRS

**54A**   Carunungan, Celso Al. "The Courtmartial of Capt. Rufo C. Romero." This was a nineteen-part serial that ran in the *Kislap-Graphic* (sometimes catalogued under the title *Graphic*) weekly newspaper from 22 July to 25 November 1959. Rufo Romero was a Filipino officer of the Philippine Scouts (graduate of the West Point class of 1931 with the highest academic record ever achieved by a prewar Filipino cadet) who was court-martialed in 1940 for having stolen classified maps from his office at the 14th Engineers and sentenced to ten years in prison. Here he tells his version of what happened to a sympathetic journalist.

**55**   Galang, Ricardo C. *Hammer and Anvil.* Quezon City: Phoenix Publ., 1989. Pp. viii, 344. The author, a 1938 graduate of the Philippine Army's Reserve Officers Service School at Los Baños, offers an irreverent recollection of the Philippine Military Academy—"spawning ground for heroes and villains"—where he taught English from 1938 to 1941. Armed with a scholarship to study at Boston University, Galang sailed from Manila in November 1941. He joined the army in 1942 and returned to the Philippines as an intelligence officer in November 1943.

**56**   Navarro, Edmundo G. *Beds of Nails.* Manila: Privately Published, 1988. Pp. 334. Navarro's adventuresome life saw him graduate with the 1940 PMA class, serve in North Luzon during the Philippine Campaign, followed by imprisonment at Ft. Santiago and participation in guerrilla activities. After the war he joined the "new" Philippine Scouts, then the Veterans Administration, and finally ended up in Vietnam with the US Agency for International Development. The author's recollections of his childhood as the son of PC officer Colonel Celestino Luna Navarro are especially fascinating and include a scathing portrait of some of the American officers serving with the PC in the 1930s. Three hundred copies of this book were produced, the first 100 in typescript, a second 100 printed and bound, and the final 100 printed and bound corrected copies.

**57**   Perez, Adelaida L., ed., *To Inspire and to Lead: The Letters of Gen. Vicente Lim, 1938–1942.* Introduction by Edilberto C. de Jesus. Manila: Privately Published, 1980. Pp. 262. De Jesus's biographical sketch of Philippine Army deputy chief of staff Vicente P. Lim (USMA 1914) is followed by an edited collection of letters written by Lim to family members in the United States. Lim expected the letters to form the basis for a history of the Philippine Army and thus provided considerable detail of the inner workings of the army's central general staff. A bound collection of the unedited letters was donated by the family to the US Naval Academy library. The book version of the letters deletes some personal information and most of Lim's references to other PS officers.

**58**   Rimando, Juanito R. "Brigadier General Vicente Lim and the 41st Division in Bataan." MA thesis, University of the Philippines, 1978. Pp. xx, 492. This thick work made use of sources now difficult or impossible to obtain. One fascinating chapter sets out to explain how General Lim could legitimately (through sound business investments) have more spending money in the 1930s than his army salary seemed to justify—a sad commentary on the modern AFP?

**58A**    Unson, Ben Cailles. "General Vicente P. Lim." This was a six-part serial that appeared in *The Manila Times Magazine* on 7, 8, 9, 10, 11, and 13 April 1959. This newspaper biography of the general was based on interviews and Lim's, at that time unpublished, letters [see entry 57]. Includes several photos of Lim at West Point and on Bataan.

Research note: Near-complete series of Philippine Army general orders (but not special orders), bulletins, and training directives from 1936 to 1941 can be found at the US National Archives, Library of Congress, and USAMHI.

---

# Philippine Army Air Corps

## GENERAL HISTORIES

**59**    Jose, Marte Ernesto. *Wings of Philippine Independence*. Los Angeles, CA: Wetzel Publishing, 1940. Pp. 63. Jose, graduate of the Curtis-Wright technical institute, argued that Japan would inevitably attempt to conquer the Philippines, and therefore the Philippines should commit itself to building a strong air defense force.

**60**    Nemenzo, Eldon Luis G., with Guillermo Molina, Jr., II. *The Philippine Air Force Story*. Pasay City: Office of the Commanding General, Philippine Air Force, 1992. Pp. vii, 437. Detailed and opinionated history of military aviation—Philippine and American—in the islands from the earliest years. For the prewar period, the authors rely heavily on Santos [entry 62]. Includes many photos.

**61**    PAF Historical Committee, *Guardian of Philippine Skies, 1917–1968*. Nichols Air Base: Philippine Air Force, 1969. Pp. xi, 201. (A second edition appeared in 1970.) Nemenzo's work [previous entry] supersedes this official air force history, copies of which are difficult to obtain. The only library in the US that reported holding a copy of this book was the library of the Central Intelligence Agency, and its copy could not be found.

**62**    Santos, Enrique B. *Trails in Philippine Skies: A History of Aviation in the Philippines from 1909 to 1941*. Manila: Philippine Airlines, 1981. Pp. v, 328. An invaluable record of the prewar development of civil and military aviation in the Philippines, based mostly on newspaper accounts. Includes twenty pages of photographs.

**63**   Hasdorff, James C. "Jerry Lee: Founding Father of the Philippine Air Force." In *Aerospace Historian* 20, no. 4 (Winter/December 1973): 208-14. William "Jerry" Lee arrived in the Philippines in 1935 and volunteered to help the PC establish an air arm. Lee's recollections of that experience—based on interviews he gave to air force historians in the 1970s—do not always agree with what he wrote in his diaries in the 1930s. (The diaries are now found at the Eisenhower Library in Abilene, KS.)

**64**   Villamor, Jesus A., as told to Gerald S. Snyder. *They Never Surrendered*. Quezon City: Vera-Reyes, 1982. Pp. xvi, 335. One of the original PAAC pilots, Villamor devotes a few pages of this posthumously published memoir to prewar flight training in the Philippines (and adds his name to the list of pilots who claim to have taught Dwight Eisenhower how to fly) and the US and to the exploits that won him the Distinguished Service Cross in the 1941-42 Campaign. Most of this book documents his guerrilla activities on Negros in 1943. Villamor felt that infighting amongst MacArthur's subordinates in Australia and their distrust of Filipino leadership in the guerrilla movement undermined his ability to establish an effective intelligence network and kept many legitimate guerrillas from receiving postwar recognition.

Research note: The Philippine Air Force maintains a website with historical information at www.paf.mil.ph

---

# Philippine Navy/ Off Shore Patrol

## GENERAL HISTORIES

**65**   Edralin, Fernando L. *The Filipino Navy*. Manila: Headquarters, Philippine Navy, 1973. Pp. xviii, 152. Introductory chapters on Philippine geography and the law of the sea are followed by a brief account of General Aguinaldo's "mosquito fleet," chapters on the Off Shore Patrol, World War II, and the post-war transition from re-created OSP (1945) to Philippine Naval Patrol (1947) to Philippine Navy (1951). Confronted by a dearth of official prewar Philippine Navy documents, the author made good use of newspaper accounts, official US War Department and Navy records, and interviews with OSP veterans to recreate the history of the Commonwealth-era naval force.

**66**   Giagonia, Regino. *The Philippine Navy, 1898–1996.* 2nd ed. Manila: Headquarters Philippine Navy, 1997. Pp. lvi, 436. This history of the OSP is probably the most thorough that will ever be published. It includes chapters on the development of the OSP, the activities of the Q-boats during the war, and the participation of OSP officers and men in the guerrilla war. It also discusses personality conflicts amongst the OSP officers and clashes with the American officers of the Military Mission.

**67**   Silvero, Aquilino C., and Isidro G. Espela, *History of the Philippine Navy.* Manila: Headquarters, Philippine Navy, 1976. Pp. viii, 312. The authors' account of the OSP draws heavily on Edralin [entry 65] and also includes a roster of officers and men in the OSP in November 1941.

**68**   Tangco, Reuben V., *et al. Tides of Change: The Philippine Navy Looks Back a Hundred Years and Peers into the Next Century.* Manila: Headquarters Philippine Navy, with Infinit-I Communications Services, 1998. Pp. 183. This picture-laden coffee table-style book concentrates on the navy's postwar development but does have a unique approach to the Off Shore Patrol. Relying mostly on Camilo Osias's biography [entry 117], the authors take army general MacArthur to task for not doing more to develop a Philippine navy in the 1930s.

BIOGRAPHIES AND MEMOIRS

**69**   Huff, Sid, with Joe Alex Morris. *My Fifteen Years with General MacArthur.* New York: Paperback Library, 1964. Pp. 142. (This book reputedly first appeared in 1951, but that edition proved impossible to find.) Sidney Huff's book is the main source of anecdotes about MacArthur's home life with wife Jean and son Arthur. Before becoming the MacArthur family factotum, however, retired naval officer Huff was the Military Mission member responsible for overseeing the acquisition of motor torpedo boats for the Off Shore Patrol, and Huff recalls a few details of that assignment.

**70**   Rodriquez, Ernesto O. *Commodore Alcaraz: First Victim of President Marcos.* New York: Vantage Press, 1986. Pp. xviii, 268. Ramon Alcaraz was one of seven graduates of the 1940 PMA class to join the OSP. During the Philippine Campaign, he commanded the Q-112, aboard which General MacArthur made his single visit to Bataan. Although the bulk of the book deals with Alcaraz's later confrontation with President Ferdinand Marcos, Rodriquez also offers a rare insider's look at the activities of the OSP.

# Philippine National Guard

**71**   David, Manuel H. *Our National Guard*. Manila, [c1921]. Pp. xi, 34. The author, who had been a second lieutenant in the Guard, described this brief and very rare account of the short-lived, World War I-era, Philippine National Guard division as a "first edition" meant for young readers. Includes a list of Filipinos killed while serving with the US Army in World War I.

**72**   Hill, Alva J. "The Philippine Army During the World War." Two parts. In *The Philippine Forum* 1, no. 12 (November 1936): 53-61, and vol. 2, no. 1 (December 1936): 52-61. First person account of the trials and tribulations of the guard by an American lawyer who was there.

**73**   Jose, Ricardo T. "The Philippine National Guard in World War I." In *Philippine Studies* 36 (1988): 275-99. Overview of the PNG's organization and activities based largely on documents in the Manuel L. Quezon Papers in the Philippine National Library.

**74**   Paterno, Feliciano P., ed. *The Ninth Regiment of Infantry, Roster, First Philippine Division, USA*. [Manila, c1919] Pp. 107. Intended as a souvenir for members of the regiment, this roster includes group photographs and lists every officer and enlisted man in the regiment. Character sketches of the officers and brief essays on the significance of the National Guard experience conclude the book. Paterno commanded the machine-gun company.

**75**   Schaefer, Christina K. *The Great War: A Guide to the Service Records of All the World's Fighting Men and Volunteers*. Baltimore, MD: Genealogical Publishing Co., Inc., 1998. Pp. xiv, 189. Briefly describes Philippine National Guard records, as well as some Spanish-era conscription rolls.

Research note: The PNG is extensively documented in BIA records at the US National Archives and the Francis Burton Harrison Papers at the Library of Congress. The organization's officer and enlisted personnel records survive in the Philippine National Archives, Manila, and have been microfilmed (on 300 reels) by the family history center of the Church of Jesus Christ of Latter Day Saints. For specific reel numbers, consult www.familysearch.org.

# The Commonwealth
# Military Mission

## GENERAL HISTORIES

**76**   Baldoria, Pedro L. "A Study of the Problems Involved in the Neutralization of the Philippines." PhD dissertation, University of Southern California, 1940. Pp. vi, 295. The Tydings-McDuffie Act of 1934 called for the President of the United States to negotiate the neutralization of the Philippines. The author evaluates the success or failure of neutralization in Switzerland, Belgium, Luxembourg, Cracow (Poland) and the Aaland Islands (near Finland) and concludes that the Philippines could be successfully neutralized. One chapter evaluates the contrasting views (largely of American authors) concerning the defensibility of the islands, describes the Philippine military forces being raised under the Commonwealth, and concludes that MacArthur's new army was "a very important element towards effecting the perpetual neutrality of the Philippines." Appendices include copies of the Tydings-McDuffie Act (with amendments), the Philippine Constitution, and the National Defense Act.

**77**   Carpenter, Suzanne Gronemeyer. "Toward the Development of Philippine National Security Capability, 1920–1940: With Special Reference to the Commonwealth Period, 1935-1940." PhD dissertation, New York University, 1976. Pp. 560. Filipino views of military needs as offered in a wide array of newspapers and periodicals (those that could be found in the NY Public Library) are discussed in this dissertation. Some sources used by the author, like the library's near-complete collection of the prewar PC journal, *Khaki and Red*, are very rare. Two chapters describe the Philippine Army. Short on analysis, this often-overlooked dissertation is also marred by some unfortunate proofreading errors. However, extensive quotations from the journals and newspapers the author used make this text the next best thing to having the papers themselves.

**78**   Friend, Theodore. *Between Two Empires: The Ordeal of the Philippines, 1929–1946.* New Haven and London: Yale University Press, 1965. Pp. xviii, 312. MacArthur's belief that the US could defend the Philippines, and that later the Filipinos could defend themselves, while "orthodox military opinion despaired" of doing so, Friend writes, was a reflection of the general's "great confidence" in himself and in Filipino ability. That this nearly four decades' old study of Philippine-American relations during the Commonwealth period remains unsurpassed speaks both to the superiority of Friend's work and the subsequent paucity of serious research on the era.

**79**   Hayden, Joseph Ralston. *The Philippines: A Study in National Development.* New York: MacMillan, 1942. Pp. xxvii, 984. Hyden's chapter on national defense and the Commonwealth remains one of the more useful introductions to the problem of defending the islands and how Quezon's government went about addressing that concern.

**80**   Lopez del Castillo, Jose. *Orientaciones Diplomaticas*. Manila: Privately Published, 1939. Pp. x, 354. Collection of Spanish-language essays on Philippine military affairs and neutrality which apparently first appeared in the author's column in *La Vanguardia* newspaper.

**81**   Meixsel, Richard B. "An Army for Independence? The American Roots of the Philippine Army." PhD dissertation, Ohio State University, 1993. Pp. v, 383. Examines the development of the Philippine Scouts and Philippine Constabulary in the 1920s and 1930s and evaluates their potential for forming a Philippine army under the guidance of MacArthur's Military Mission.

**82**   Meixsel, Richard B. "Manuel L. Quezon, Douglas MacArthur, and the Significance of the Military Mission to the Philippine Commonwealth." In *Pacific Historical Review* 70, no. 2 (May 2001): 255-92. Argues that, just as some contemporaries claimed, MacArthur and Quezon hoped that building a substantial Filipino military force would justify placing an American naval base in the Philippines and thereby perpetuate mutually beneficial Philippine-American ties.

**83**   Pacis, Vicente Albano. *National Defense: A Basic Philippine Problem*. Manila: Philippine Education Co., 1937. Pp. xiv, 142. Edited and enlarged book version of a series of articles Pacis wrote for the *Philippines Herald* newspaper in 1936 in support of MacArthur's Military Mission and its plan of Philippine defense. MacArthur's 1936 *Report on National Defense* is included as an appendix.

**84**   *Primera Asamblea Nacional, Diario de sesiones de la Asamblea Nacional, periodo inaugural de sesiones, 25 de noviembre de 1935 al 21 de diciembre de 1935*. Tomo [Volume] I. Manila: Bureau of Printing, 1940. Pp. 584. This volume, apparently the only volume of prewar assembly debates that was published, includes (mostly in English but partly in Spanish) the Philippine Commonwealth assembly's debate of the national defense bill and the bill's legislative history.

**85**   *Report on National Defense in the Philippines*. Manila: Commonwealth of the Philippines, Office of the Military Adviser, 1936. Pp. 52. This is MacArthur's report touting the achievements of the first six months of the Military Mission. A copy of President Quezon's Executive Order no. 10 (Army Promotion Regulations) and a statement Quezon made on the topic of officer promotion when he signed the executive order are included. For other sources of MacArthur's *Report*, see entries 28, 83, 89, and 90.

**86**   Villamor, Blas. *Defensa Integral de Filipinia*. N.p. n.d [c1936]. Pp. 54. A Spanish-language "military geography" by a member of the 1934-35 constitutional convention's national defense committee.

**87**   Villamor, Juan. *Brevario Militar del Ciudadano Filipino*. Privately Published, 1937. Collection of six Spanish-language articles by a former officer of the Revolutionary army. They deal with 1) invasion, 2) civil war, 3) chemical warfare, 4) military duty of citizens, 5) development of natural resources, and 6) need for a national intelligence system.

**88**  Villamor, Juan. *Defensa Militar de Filipinas desde el punto de vista de los Filipinos.* Privately Published, 1930. Pp. iv, 238. Discusses the military needs of the Philippines, with a look at the experiences of the Revolution and National Guard.

**89**  Waldrop, Frank C., ed. *MacArthur on War: His Military Writings.* New York: Duell, Sloan and Pearce, 1942. Pp. 419. Another source for the Field Marshal's 1936 report on Philippine defense.

**90**  Whan, Vorin E., ed. *A Soldier Speaks: Public Papers and Speeches of General of the Army Douglas MacArthur.* With an Introduction by Carlos P. Romulo. New York: Frederick A. Praeger, 1965. Pp. xxix, 367. A chapter titled "The Philippine Years, 1936-1941" includes excerpts from MacArthur's 1936 report on Philippine defense and reprints "An address to the faculty and student body of the Command and General Staff School at Baguio, Philippine Islands, August 3, 1936." (According to the original of the latter speech, in the MacArthur Library, Norfolk, VA, the address was made before "a group of officers" at 1 Calle Victoria, Intramuros, Manila, the headquarters of MacArthur's mission.)

BIOGRAPHIES AND MEMOIRS

*General Douglas MacArthur*

**91**  Eyre, James K., Jr. *The Roosevelt–MacArthur Conflict.* Chambersburg, PA: Privately Published, 1950. Pp. 234. As a wartime advisor to Commonwealth President Sergio Osmeña, Eyre was presumably in a position to offer an insider's view of Philippine-American relations. Eyre claimed Osmeña opposed MacArthur's prewar program of military defense, and that MacArthur was left in the Philippines after being recalled to active duty in July 1941 primarily because no one in Washington, military or civilian, wanted him in the United States. "All logic," Eyre wrote, pointed to MacArthur's return to the United States for an "important assignment" had he not alienated everyone in a position to help him. In the lesser-known second edition of this book (1965), Eyre deleted some sections found in the first edition but added a lengthy and bizarre chapter titled "The Author Speaks Out," in which he discussed his relationship with Osmeña in the Philippines after the war and promised to expose (but did not) the conspiracy surrounding MacArthur's rehabilitation of Manuel Roxas.

**92**  Hunt, Frazier. *MacArthur and the War Against Japan.* New York: Charles Scribner's Sons, 1944. Pp. viii, 182. MacArthur-admirer Hunt presents a capsule history of the Philippine Army and of MacArthur's accomplishments in building the army against formidable odds.

**93**  Hunt, Frazier. *The Untold Story of Douglas MacArthur.* New York: Devin-Adair, 1954. Pp. 533. Scholars have tended to dismiss this biography because of its partisan nature, but as James points out [entry 94], as a friend of MacArthur's, Hunt had unusual access to files dealing with the general's early life and career. Hunt's acquaintance with Quezon also went back many years, and, therefore, unlike other biographers, Hunt did not uncritically accept everything MacArthur had to say about his relationship with Quezon.

**94**    James, D. Clayton. *The Years of MacArthur*, Vol. 1, *1880-1941*. Boston: Houghton Mifflin, 1970. Pp. xix, 740; Vol. 2, *1941–1945*. Boston: Houghton Mifflin, 1975. Pp. xix, 939; Vol. 3, *Triumph & Disaster, 1945–1964*. Boston: Houghton Mifflin, 1985. Pp. xvi, 848. James's much acclaimed MacArthur (USMA 1903) biography will undoubtedly remain the standard for many years to come. It forms the basis for most MacArthur biographies that have appeared since publication of James's work began in 1970. It must be said that neither Philippine history nor the history of the US Army in the Philippines are the author's areas of expertise, however. Errors range from misidentifying Charles Nathorst, a retired PC officer, as a US Army general, to misunderstanding War Plan Orange. Bibliographical essays concluding the volumes include useful appraisals of other books about MacArthur.

**94A**    Leary, William M., ed. *MacArthur and the American Century: A Reader*. Lincoln and London: University of Nebraska Press, 2001. Pp. xxi, 522. This handy compilation reprints several Philippine-related articles about MacArthur, including Carol Petillo's "Douglas MacArthur and Manuel Quezon: A Note on an Imperial Bond" and a response, "An Exchange of Opinion," by the late Paul P. Rogers with a rejoinder by Petillo. Both originally appeared in *Pacific Historical Review* in 1979 and 1983. Petillo's article revealed MacArthur's acceptance of Manuel Quezon's payment of $500,000 in 1942, which, she points out, would seem to have been a violation of army regulations. Rogers, who typed the order transferring the money to MacArthur, claimed that no attempt had been made to hide the transaction and that Petillo's explanations for the payment were "interesting excursions into mystery story writing." He did not, however, address the issue of whether army regulations allowed such payments. Also reprints Weigley's review of Manchester's biography [see entry 98], Louis Morton's review of MacArthur's autobiography [see entry 97] and entry 301. See also entries 101 and 433.

**95**    Lee, Clark, and Richard Henschel. *Douglas MacArthur*. New York: Henry Holt and Co., 1952. Pp. x, 370. All controversies are resolved in MacArthur's favor in this biography, although even the authors concede that MacArthur's insistence that the Japanese would not attack until April 1942, despite years of intelligence studies concluding that any attack on the islands would come in the months of December or January, was a reflection of the general's wishful thinking. Prewar problems in building up the Philippine Army are attributed to Quezon's waning interest and Washington's lack of support. The concluding 128-page "pictorial biography" includes many Philippine-related photographs.

**96**    Long, Gavin. *MacArthur as Military Commander*. London/Princeton: B.T.

Batsford/D. Van Nostrand Co., 1969. Pp. x, 243. This Australian-authored volume, one in a series of "military commander" studies, is based almost entirely on secondary sources but offers thoughtful evaluations of MacArthur's generalship. Of the 1941-42 Campaign, the author concludes that "MacArthur's leadership in the Philippines had fallen short of what might have been expected from a soldier of such wide experience and one held in such high esteem. In the training of the Philippine Army he and his staff had achieved far less than they might have done in the six years up to December 1941."

**97**  MacArthur, Douglas. *Reminiscences.* New York: McGraw-Hill, 1964. Pp. viii, 438. Philippine Army Field Marshal MacArthur's "treatment of his stint in the Philippines," historian Teodoro Agoncillo observed, was "rather disappointing" in these much-criticized memoirs. The memoirs are widely believed to have been ghost-written, but James [entry 94] concluded that the prewar portions of the book were probably written by MacArthur and were generally reliable. They include little about the Philippines, however: MacArthur's first three tours of Philippine duty (1903-1904, 1922-25, and 1928-30) receive about one page each; his military adviser years (up to the establishment of USAFFE) merit a further six pages.

**98**  Manchester, William. *American Caesar.* Boston and Toronto: Little, Brown and Co., 1978. Pp. xvii, 793. Best-selling biography of Douglas MacArthur, both acclaimed for its balanced treatment of the controversial general's life and dismissed for its superficiality. Some reviewers thought that this biography, in common with Perret's [entry 100], emphasized colorful anecdotes over detailed analysis. The eminent military historian Russell Weigley gave this book a long, critical, review in *Reviews in American History* 7, no. 4 (December 1979): 571-76.

**99**  Mayer, Sydney L. *MacArthur.* New York: Ballantine Books, Inc., 1971. Pp. 160. The text for "War Leader Book No. 2" in Ballentine's "Illustrated History of the Violent Century," is drawn from a handful of secondary sources, but the book is prolifically illustrated with photographs of American and Japanese military officers in the Philippines and drawings of weapons.

**100**  Perret, Geoffrey. *Old Soldiers Never Die: The Life of Douglas MacArthur.* New York: Random House, 1996. Pp. xii, 663. This gossipy biography tells the usual story but is more favorable to MacArthur than most in recent years. Perret repeats the standard MacArthur-centric account of the creation of the Philippine Army, managing to mention not a single Filipino soldier in the process. The author's research is not reliable (the Philippine-related sections of the book are filled with factual errors and sources provided in the notes do not always support the text), but Perret has some provocative things to say about the debacle at Clark Field on 8 December 1941 [see entry 362].

**101**  Petillo, Carol Morris. *Douglas MacArthur: The Philippine Years.* Bloomington: Indiana University Press, 1981. Pp. xviii, 301. This "psychological interpretation" of what drove MacArthur was (thanks to Richard Sutherland's just-opened papers) the first to reveal Quezon's payment of a half-million dollars to MacArthur in 1942, with substantial sums for subordinate officers, as well. Netzorg [entry 19] commented that it was "notable how little the book has to do with Filipinos." The doctoral dissertation on which the book is based (same title, Rutgers, 1979) includes a fuller discussion of Petillo's views on why MacArthur felt justified in accepting the money.

**102**    Schaller, Michael. *Douglas MacArthur: The Far Eastern General.* New York: Oxford University Press, 1989. Pp. xi, 320. The author is unremittingly contemptuous of his subject but contributes nothing new about MacArthur's Philippine years. Schaller's brief account of the prewar period is based almost entirely on secondary sources.

**103**    Whitney, Courtney. *MacArthur: His Rendezvous with History.* New York: Alfred A. Knopf, 1956. Pp. xi, 547. The opening chapters offer another apologia for the Philippine defeat by a member (from 1943) of MacArthur's staff, presumably reflecting what the general had come to think about things: The lack of support for the prewar Philippine Army was a result of Washington's lack of vision, Europe-firsters and the general's enemies in Washington kept the Philippines from receiving the reinforcements it needed, and Asiatic Fleet commander Admiral Thomas Hart's defeatist and obstructionist attitude further weakened the Philippines' defense. Whitney hardly bothers to disguise his contempt for Wainwright and implies that Wainwright was less than truthful in his memoirs [entry 440].

**104**    Willoughby, Charles A., and John Chamberlain. *MacArthur, 1941–1951.* New York: McGraw-Hill Book Co., 1954. Pp. xiii, 441. The focus of this highly partisan book (more Willoughby memoir than MacArthur biography, James [entry 94] writes) by MacArthur's wartime intelligence chief is on activities in the Southwest Pacific, but one chapter is devoted to a disingenuous defense of MacArthur's actions in the 1941-42 Philippine Campaign. The food problem on Bataan, for example, was mostly a result of the Japanese pushing civilian refugees into the peninsula, knowing that the humanitarian MacArthur would use the army's stocks to feed them.

### Dwight D. Eisenhower

**105**    Ambrose, Stephen E. *Eisenhower: Soldier, General of the Army, President-Elect, 1890–1952.* New York: Simon and Schuster, 1983. Pp. 637. This first volume of the author's "definitive and heroic" (emphasis on the latter) biography of Eisenhower (USMA 1915) includes a brief chapter on the Military Mission, the theme of which is that Eisenhower was miserable in the Philippines and found his work there unrewarding. Ambrose's claim that Mission member James Ord was an instructor at the Army War College when Eisenhower was a student there in 1927-28 is incorrect. At the time, Ord was a battalion commander with the 31st Infantry in Manila.

**106**    Davis, Kenneth S. *Soldier of Democracy: A Biography of Dwight Eisenhower.*

Garden City, NY: Doubleday, Doran & Co., 1945. Pp. x, 566. In what is generally considered to be the first substantive Eisenhower biography, Davis asserts (presumably following Hatch [entry 109]) that while with the Military Mission Eisenhower helped to "work out in detail" the strategy MacArthur later used to defend the islands from Japan, "including the retreat into Bataan." Eisenhower was liked and trusted by Filipinos because "he gave no slightest hint of the 'white supremacy' prejudice which flawed the performance of many another American officer in Manila." His "understanding of the problems of Philippine statehood ... was so profound," Davis claims, that Quezon and American high commissioners "came more and more to rely on" Eisenhower's judgments.

**107** Eisenhower, Dwight D. *At Ease: Stories I Tell to Friends*. Garden City, NY: Doubleday & Co., 1967. Pp. viii, 400. This describes the formation of MacArthur's Military Mission in 1935 and its travails in the Philippines as seen by one of the leading participants. Eisenhower had worked closely with MacArthur in the War Department since 1933 and had been asked to help prepare the written plan for a Philippine military system in late 1934. In 1935, Eisenhower had hoped to return to duty with troops, but MacArthur requested his service with the Military Mission and Eisenhower reluctantly agreed.

**108** Ferrell, Robert H., ed. *The Eisenhower Diaries*. New York: W.W. Norton, 1981. Pp. xvii, 445. Until the publication of Eisenhower's entire Philippine diary [entry 110], this heavily edited version was an essential source for the history of the Military Mission while Eisenhower was associated with it (from October 1935 to December 1939), but the editor had a limited knowledge of the islands. He described the Philippine Scouts as a "native constabulary," rendered the major army camp at Dau as "Davi," and turned the well-known Joseph Stevenot into an unidentifiable Mr. Stevens.

**109** Hatch, Alden. *General Ike: A Biography of Dwight D. Eisenhower*. New York: Henry Holt and Co., 1944. Pp. vii, 288. As Hatch tells the story, the Military Mission was Eisenhower's one-man show. "Ike" collaborated with Philippine officials to write the National Defense Act and get it passed by the assembly; Ike established the Philippine Military Academy, his "pet project"; Ike "laid out airfields" and then hit upon the scheme of building a Philippine Navy; finally, Ike devised a defense plan calling for Philippine and US troops on Luzon to retire into Bataan.

**110** Holt, Daniel D., and James W. Leyerzapf, eds. *Eisenhower: The Prewar Diaries and Selected Papers, 1905–1941*. Baltimore, MD: The Johns Hopkins University Press, 1998. Pp. xxvii, 576. This volume reprints about one-half "of all the prewar Eisenhower documents (diaries aside) known to have survived" and five separate diaries kept by Eisenhower from 1929 to 1941, including the one he maintained while serving with the Military Mission, much of which had never previously been published nor generally available to researchers, as well as letters and other documents written by Eisenhower from Manila. According to the editors (director and archivist at the Eisenhower Library, Abilene, Kansas), copyright restrictions prevented the inclusion of "five very brief segments of the Philippine Diary, which are open at the Eisenhower Library." Two important documents related to the organization of the Philippine Army are reprinted here: 1) "Cost of Defense Plan," a memorandum prepared for MacArthur, dated 15 June 1936, and 2) Eisenhower's "personal observations and convictions with respect to the Philippine Army and the Defense Plan," presented in a memorandum to Quezon, dated 8 August 1940.

**111**    Lyon, Peter. *Eisenhower: Portrait of the Hero*. Boston and Toronto: Little, Brown and Company, 1974. Pp. xii, 935. In the few pages devoted to Eisenhower's Philippine years, the author emphasizes Eisenhower's clash with MacArthur. Lyon dismisses the defense program out of hand as "a shambles." In his opinion (his endnotes show no documentary evidence), the "parasitic politicos" who ruled the Philippines "cared about national defense only as they could make money out of it," and since there was not much money, there was not much interest.

**112**    McCann, Kevin. *Man from Abilene*. Garden City, NY: Doubleday & Co., 1952. Pp. 252. Eisenhower's original Philippine diary was long thought to be lost or destroyed until it turned up in the effects of his friend, Kevin McCann, in 1981. Thus McCann's account of Eisenhower's experiences with the Military Mission was one of the few informed by a knowledge of what Eisenhower had written at the time. McCann asserts that "the original plan [for a Philippine military system] was drawn up by Major James Ord, an instructor at the Army War College … assisted by the faculty there and supervised by MacArthur himself in collaboration with" Eisenhower.

## Other Military Mission–related Biographies

**113**    Casey, Hugh J. *Engineer Memoirs: Major General Hugh J. Casey, US Army*. Washington, DC: Office of History, US Army Corps of Engineers, 1993. Pp. xvi, 276, plus appendices. "Pat" Casey (USMA 1918) reflects on the important events and personalities of his army career in this edited transcript of tape-recorded interviews conducted in 1979-80. He discusses his experiences as a member of the Military Mission in 1937-40, during which he "probably covered more on foot of the Philippines than certainly any other American [and] most Filipinos" and as USAFFE engineer in 1941-42. Appendices include Casey's 22 January 1942 memorandum arguing against withdrawal to the Pilar-Bagac line and his 8 March 1942 report, "Inspection of MLR [Main Line of Resistance], Bataan."

**114**    Fine, Sidney. *Frank Murphy, The New Deal Years*. Chicago: The University of Chicago Press, 1979. Pp. xi, 708. The second of Fine's three-volume biography of Murphy is an often overlooked source yet one of the more detailed studies of the formation and arrival of MacArthur's Military Mission, as seen from the American High Commissioner's hostile perspective. Murphy seems to have been instrumental in forcing MacArthur's retirement from the US Army in 1937 (the outcome of a failed attempt to bring MacArthur back to the US).

**115**   Gopinath, Aruna. *Manuel L. Quezon: The Tutelary Democrat*. Quezon City: New Day, 1987. Pp. xvi, 243. Includes a discussion of criticisms made of the Military Mission's defense plan, although the author confuses the Mission's plan with one written by government adviser L. Siguion Reyna.

**115A**   Hoge, William M. *Engineer Memoirs: General William M. Hoge, US Army*. Washington, DC: Office of History, US Army Corps of Engineers, 1993. Pp. xx, 269. In this edited transcript of tape-recorded interviews conducted in 1974, General Hoge (USMA 1916) discusses some of his experiences as the commanding officer of the 14th Engineers (PS) at Ft. McKinley from July 1935 to November 1937. Hoge also served as chief engineer of the Philippine Army. Hoge describes the Scout barrios at McKinley and claims that he was asked to commence the Alaskan highway project (1942) because of his earlier experience building the "Bataan Highway." Unfortunately, the interviewer was mostly interested in hearing about MacArthur and Eisenhower in the Philippines and not about Hoge's own activities. Although not asked about him, Hoge volunteered that James Ord "was the best man in the entire outfit [MacArthur's Military Mission], had more sense, and knew more about it [the needs of the Philippine Army]" than either MacArthur or Eisenhower.

**116**   Malcolm, George A. *American Colonial Careerist: Half a Century of Official Life and Personal Experience in the Philippines and Puerto Rico*. Boston: The Christopher Publishing House, 1957. Pp. 288. Malcolm arrived in the Philippines in 1906 and served on the supreme court from 1917 until 1939, when he left in fear of an imminent Japanese invasion. Here he offers anecdotes and observations about Philippine and American personalities (from governors general on down) including an assortment of army and constabulary officers, MacArthur, Eisenhower, and Courtney Whitney among them. He devotes a few pages to the issue of national defense and claims to have played an active role in revising the 1935 national defense act.

**117**   Osias, Camilo. *The Story of a Long Career of Varied Tasks*. Quezon City: Manlapaz Publishing Co., 1971. Pp. 376. Representative Osias was one of the few members of the national assembly to speak out publicly against the proposed national defense act in 1935. Here he explains why he opposed the bill.

**118**   Quezon, Manuel Luis. *The Good Fight*. New York and London: D. Appleton-Century Co., 1946. Pp. xxiv, 336. Commonwealth President Quezon appears to have combined two distinct episodes when he recounts obtaining MacArthur's services as military adviser to the Commonwealth in 1934: 1) asking MacArthur if the Philippines could be defended, and 2) asking MacArthur to become military adviser. In reality, it seems that MacArthur agreed during a meeting early in 1934 that the Philippines could be defended and that he would use his authority as chief of staff to prepare an appropriate scheme of defense; it was during a second visit by Quezon to Washington in late 1934 that MacArthur agreed to become military adviser. (See entry 82 for a fuller discussion of the issue.) Quezon also recounts at great length his experiences on Corregidor and reprints communiques that passed between the Philippines and Washington at that time.

**119**   Quirino, Carlos. *Quezon: Paladin of Philippine Freedom*. Manila: Filipiniana Book Guild, 1971. Pp. xvi, 419. In this, the standard Quezon biography, the author relies heavily on Quezon's own words [entry 118] in discussing the acquisition of MacArthur's services as military adviser and the implementation of the military system. He draws attention to differences in various accounts of Quezon's activities and makes use of some personal interviews.

**120**   Smith, Jean Edward. *Lucius D. Clay: An American Life*. New York: Henry Holt and Co., 1990. Pp. xii, 835. During a visit to Washington in 1937, MacArthur asked to have two army engineers assigned "to make a hydroelectric survey of the Philippines." Capt. Pat Casey [entry 113] was one; Clay (USMA 1918) was the other. After arriving in the islands in September 1937, Clay was asked by Eisenhower also to help establish the Philippine Army corps of engineers. Clay was entirely indifferent toward the Philippines and "leapt at the opportunity" to return to the US in mid-1938. In this book, which is largely an oral history, Clay offers extensive comments on MacArthur and Eisenhower in the islands.

Note: The original members of the Military Mission who accompanied MacArthur to the Philippines in October 1935 were Eisenhower, James B. Ord (killed in an airplane crash in Baguio in January 1938), Thomas J. Davis, and army doctor Howard J. Hutter. The Mission then gained the services of American officers and enlisted men who were either already working for the Philippine government (such as William Lee [entry 63], who had been helping to establish a constabulary air arm), or were borrowed from the US Army's Philippine Department, or, like Clay [entry 120] and Casey [entry 113] were brought over later from the United States. Sidney Huff [entry 69] was a retired navy officer living in the Philippines to whom MacArthur offered the job of developing the OSP. Richard Sutherland, later MacArthur's wartime chief of staff, had been serving in China when he was transferred to Manila to replace Ord on the Mission staff in 1938. No complete list of officers assigned to the Military Mission exists. Aside from those cited above, none of the other officers known to have worked with the Mission prior to its incorporation into USAFFE in July 1941 has published memoirs or been the subjects of biographies.

# United States Army
# in the Prewar Philippines

## GENERAL HISTORIES

**121**   Alt, Betty Sowers and Bonnie Domrose Stone. *Campfollowing: A History of the Military Wife*. Westport, CT: Praeger, 1991. Pp. xiii, 164. The authors' brief depiction of "campfollowing" in the Philippines is superficial and entirely without context, but they did interview several army wives who lived in the islands early in the twentieth century and whose stories have not been published elsewhere.

**122**   *Army of the Philippines, Yearbook, 1909*. New Albany, IN, 1909. Pp. 37. The now-defunct "Army of the Philippines" was a fraternal organization founded in Denver, Colorado, in August 1900. Officers and enlisted men who had served ashore or afloat in the Philippines from 1898 to 4 July 1902 were eligible to join. Members formed "camps" in several states and in the Philippines. In 1909 there were camps in Manila, Cavite, and Olongapo. This yearbook includes a brief history of the organization, list of life members, membership rules, a drawing of the society medal, and statements about service in the Philippines by members who attended the tenth annual national reunion in Pittsburgh, Penn., in August 1909. A few other yearbooks (1904, 1907) and society publications can be found in library collections. The 1907 yearbook (86 pp.) included essays about service in the Philippines ("Outpost incident in Luzon," "Fight at Bud Dajo," etc.). The society, or at least some of its camps, later became part of the Veterans of Foreign Wars organization. See also entries 177 and 673.

**123**   Ashburn, P.M. *A History of the Medical Department of the United States Army*. Boston: Houghton Mifflin Co., 1929. Pp. xv, 448. The accomplishments of the army's "Board for the Study of Tropical Diseases" in the Philippines get a brief mention in this history, written by the colonel in charge of the Army Medical Library [see also entries 136, 139, and 153].

**124**   *Board of Review[:] Holdings, Opinions, and Reviews*. Washington, DC: Office of the Judge Advocate General, 1944. Courts-martial hearings can be one of the more revealing sources for the study of the army in the Philippines, less because of the particular crimes committed (which rarely differ from crimes committed in the US) than for the details of military life in the islands that are revealed. The trial transcripts are difficult to access: You must know a trial took place, provide the name of the accused and date of trial to JAG, receive the case file number, and then access the transcript at the US National Archives in College Park, MD. The volumes in this series, however, reprint reviews of selected court-martial cases from the Philippines, China, Hawaii, Canal Zone, and US. Many are very detailed, and all provide the court-martial number allowing access to the full transcript. Volumes I to XII cover the years 1929 to 1941.

**125**    Carter, Thomas. *General History of the Philippines*. Part V, Vol. 4: *Land of the Morning: A Pictorial History of the American Regime*. Manila: Historical Conservation Society, 1990. Pp. xvi, 441. This evocative collection of photographs includes many that are military related, including a section titled "Corregidor: As It Was."

**126**    Carter, William Harding. *The American Army*. Indianapolis: The Bobbs-Merrill Co., 1915. Pp. 294. General Carter (USMA 1873) felt that the army's policies for manning its overseas garrisons were short-sighted. He argued that the Philippine Scouts should be amalgamated with the PC under Philippine government authority and a "new military force of Colonial troops" should be raised.

**126A**    Ciriaco, Conrado F. *Catalogue of Philippine Picture Postcards, American Period: 1898-1941*. N.p.: Privately Published, 1995. Pp. 200. Reprints 1,294 color and black and white postcards (with valuations in pesos) of which over 100 picture army, navy, and marine corps posts, ships, and activities in the Philippines.

**127**    Clymer, Kenton J. *Protestant Missionaries in the Philippines, 1898–1916: An Inquiry into the American Colonial Mentality*. Urbanna and Chicago: University of Illinois Press, 1986. Pp. xi, 267. In their correspondence, mission reports, and publications, American missionaries in the Philippines commented on the army presence in the islands. Missionaries held officers, generally, in high regard but not enlisted men. "In the missionary literature," Clymer writes, "drunkenness, whoring, abusive language, cruelty toward Filipinos, and irreligiosity in general come through strongly as common, if not altogether typical, traits of American soldiers."

**128**    Cordero-Fernando, Gilda, *et al. Turn of the Century*. Quezon City: GCF Books, 1978. Pp. 264. Essays and photographs depict Philippine society and material culture in the early twentieth century. Although the photographer's name is not given, the book includes a number of photographs of soldiers taken by US Army soldier-photographer Harry Whitfield Harnish (1869-1960), whose large and largely unexploited collection of Philippine-related photographs is now found at the University of the Philippines, Diliman.

**129**    Dowlen, Dorothy Dore. *Enduring What Cannot Be Endured: Memoir of a Woman Medical Aide in the Philippines in World War II*. Edited by Theresa Kaminski. Jefferson, NC, and London: McFarland & Co., 2001. Pp. v, 197. The author not only recounts her life on Mindanao during World War II but also discusses the experiences of her father, Victor Dore (1878–1944), in the Philippines as a soldier from 1901 to 1907. Victor Dore lost an arm fighting the Moros at Marawi and remained in the Philippines after his discharge from the army. This book is an excellent source of information on the prejudice confronting American soldiers who married Filipinas.

**130**   Downey, Fairfax. *Sound of the Guns*. New York: David McKay Co., 1955. Pp. xiv, 337. This popular history of the army's artillery arm reprints (from the July 1926 issue of the *Field Artillery Journal*) Edmund Gruber's story of the origin of the song "The Caissons Go Rolling Along," which was inspired by his battery's march from Camp Stotsenburg, Pampanga, to Iba, Zambales, along the Capas Trail in January 1907. Other units marched along the trail, too, perhaps provoked by a contemporary war scare with Japan.

**131**   Flint, Roy K. "The United States Army on the Pacific Frontier, 1899–1939." In *The American Military and the Far East: Proceedings of the Ninth Military History Symposium, United States Air Force Academy*. Edited by Joe C. Dixon. Washington, DC: Office of Air Force History, 1980. Pp. 139-59, 268-71. The author concludes that the army's occupation of the Philippines and other Pacific outposts and the wars it has fought in Asia have historically been a distraction for the army, which in its technology, doctrine, and organization remains focused on potential warfare in Europe.

**132**   Forbes, W. Cameron. *The Philippine Islands*. Vol. 1. New York and Boston: Houghton Mifflin, 1928. Pp. xiv, 620. Given the US Army's prominence in the Philippines during the early years of occupation, the reminiscences of American political figures and others who thought they knew the Islands well invariably discuss the army and constabulary. Governor-General from 1909 to 1913, Forbes devotes an entire chapter to identifying the army's and PC's achievements and problems (although with nothing like the candor revealed in his private papers in the Library of Congress). Forbes includes charts showing the strength figures and casualties of the army and PC. Vol. 2 includes an appendix listing the army commanders in the Philippines to 1928. The one-volume abridgement of Forbes's work (published by Harvard University Press in 1945) is easier to find but far less detailed. Similar books worth consulting for contemporary views on the role of the army in the Philippines are James H. Blount, *The American Occupation of the Philippines, 1898–1912* (New York: G.P. Putnam's Sons, 1913); Charles Burke Elliott, *The Philippines to the End of the Commission Government* (Indianapolis: The Bobbs-Merrill Co., 1917); George A. Malcolm, *The Commonwealth of the Philippines* (New York and London: D. Appleton-Century Co., 1936); and Dean C. Worcester, *The Philippines Past and Present*, Vol. 1 (New York: The MacMillan Co., 1914). Elliott's book includes an appendix that provides "The Cost of the Army in the Philippines" from 1903 to 1914.

**133**   Fritz, David Lawrence. "The Philippine Question: American Civil/Military Policy in the Philippines, 1898–1905." Phd dissertation, University of Texas, Austin, 1977. Pp. xii, 755. This dissertation examines the interaction between the American civilian administrators (primarily William Howard Taft) in the Philippines and their military counterparts. It also includes a discussion of the PC/PS amalgamation issue and evaluates important works dealing with the Philippine-American War, such as J.R.M. Taylor's compilation of insurrection records.

**134**    Funtecha, Henry F. *American Military Occupation of the Lake Lanao Region, 1901–1913*. Marawi City: University Research Center, Mindanao State University, 1979. Pp. x, 127. Overview of US Army campaigns around Lake Lanao and a brief survey of the economic, social, and political responses to American occupation.

**135**    Ghormley, Ralph M., comp. *The Military Order of the Carabao: Centennial History*. N.p. [Washington, D.C.?] Military Order of the Carabao, 2000. Pp. 111. According to Admiral Ghormley, this history of the Order "updates and amplifies" a 1970 history written by Col. F.B. Wiener. Founded in Manila in 1900, the Order once restricted membership to officers who served in the Philippines from 1898 to 1902, but membership has been broadened to encompass virtually any officer who served in Asia through 1975 and anyone who is descended from anyone who ever met the membership criteria. The Order chose "the lowly carabao" as its emblem "to spoof the effete luxury of the golden dragon" emblem of the competing Order of the Dragon, a now-defunct fraternal group composed of officers who had served in the China Relief Expedition in 1900. The book lists past Grand Paramount Carabaos, depicts the order's medals, describes some of the annual "Wallows," including the infamous 1913 banquet that drew President Woodrow Wilson's ire (Ghormley corrects misstatements about that meeting that appeared in Navy Secretary Josephus Daniels's published memoirs), and reprints traditional Carabao songs. Anyone wanting to know the words to forgotten Days of the Empire songs such as "Damn, Damn, Damn the Filipinos" (rechristened "The Soldier's Song") or "The Monkeys Have No Tails in Zamboanga" will find them here. The former, ironically enough, is thought to have been written by an enlisted man who remained in the Philippines as a school teacher in Negros after his discharge from the army. The Order maintains a modest website at www.carabao.org. See also entries 150 and 682.

**136**    Gillett, Mary C. *The Army Medical Department, 1865–1917*. Washington, DC: US Army, Center of Military History, 1995. Pp. xiv, 517. One chapter, "Public Health in the Philippines," depicts the attempts by army doctors to control endemic diseases in the Philippines and improve sanitary conditions in the early years of the twentieth century. Another chapter describes the army's struggle to deal with the alarming level of venereal disease found in the army garrison. See also entries 123, 139, and 153.

**137**    Gowing, Peter Gordon. *Mandate in Moroland: The American Government of Muslim Filipinos, 1899–1920*. Quezon City: New Day, 1983. Pp. xix, 411. The author surveys the impact of American military (1899–1913) and civilian (1914–1920) rule of the Muslim-inhabited regions of Mindanao and the Sulu Archipelago. Includes a lengthy account of Pershing's disarmament campaign and the battles of Bud Dajo (1906) and Bud Bagsak (1913). The bibliography lists numerous unpublished MA and PhD theses that examine the Muslim population in the Philippines and American attempts at governing it.

**138**   Harrison, Francis Burton. *The Corner-Stone of Philippine Independence: A Narrative of Seven Years.* New York: The Century Co., 1922. Pp. xii, 343. In a chapter titled "The American Garrison in the Philippines," Philippine Governor-General (from October 1913 to February 1921) Harrison complained that the US Army's opposition to Philippine self-rule and its freedom from local government oversight complicated relations with the Filipino community and the carrying out of government policies. He was especially concerned about the Philippine Scouts, whose American officers, he claimed, were "in a state of continual dissatisfaction" and whose Filipino enlisted men manufactured "news of Filipino 'unrest'" to justify their employment.

Harrison's unpublished autobiography (found in the Harrison Papers in Special Collections at the University of Virginia's Alderman Library) includes additional information about the army's relationship with the civil government.

**139**   Hume, Edgar Erskine. *Victories of Army Medicine: Scientific Accomplishments of the Medical Department of the United States Army.* Philadelphia and London: J.B. Lippincott Co., 1943. Pp. xiv, 250. Hume mentions the army's efforts to control diseases in the Philippines and the work of the Army Board for the Study of Tropical Diseases. In the early 1930s the board moved from Manila to Panama. See also entries 123, 136, and 153.

**140**   Jornacion, George William. "The Time of the Eagles: United States Army Officers and the Pacification of the Philippine Moros, 1899–1913." Phd dissertation, University of Maine, 1973. Pp. 303. According to the author, "officers of the United States Army created a pattern of military government in Moroland based upon their experience with the Plains Indians." Army officers "sought to maintain peace and order without disrupting native society while encouraging progress through education and economic development," with the emphasis on "keeping the peace."

**141**   Landor, A. Henry Savage. *The Gems of the East: Sixteen Thousand Miles of Research Travel Among Wild and Tame Tribes of Enchanting Islands.* New York and London: Harper & Brothers Publishers, 1904. Pp. xiii, 567. This English author made extensive use of army and other government facilities during a nine-month visit to the Philippines in 1903. His anthropological interests tended toward the remote and exotic, and he includes extensive descriptions of people and scenes in such places as Cuyo Island, Palawan, and Sulu. Includes a lengthy account (that mentions the names of many American enlisted men) of a march made around Lake Lanao under the command of Capt. J.J. Pershing. Landor also visited the islands of Samar and Leyte specifically to see the army posts there, and includes a brief description and photo of Camp Wallace, near San Fernando, La Union.

**142**   Lee, John C.H. *The Manual for Topographers, Philippine Department, United States Army, 1915.* Manila: HPD, Department Engineer, 1917. Pp. 117. Number 52 of the US Army Engineer School's Occasional Papers. This technical manual for carrying out the Military Survey of Luzon also discusses topics such as organizing the survey and relations with the civil government. It includes some of the same information found in the Philippine Department's 47-pp. *Manual of the Military Survey of Luzon* (1916). The Military Survey of Luzon was a long-standing project to map militarily significant portions of Luzon at a scale of 1:63,360. There were forty-four maps in all, covering from Lingayen Gulf in the north to Tayabas in the south.

**143**    Linn, Brian McAllister. "Cerberus' Dilemma: The US Army and Internal Security in the Pacific, 1902–1940." In *Guardians of Empire: The Armed Forces of the Colonial Powers c. 1700–1964.* Edited by David Killingray and David Omissi. Manchester and New York: Manchester University Press, 1999. Pp. 114-36. Argues that neither in Hawaii nor the Philippines could the army decide whether its main mission was to defend against outside aggression or against internal subversion.

**144**    Linn, Brian McAllister. *Guardians of Empire: The U.S. Army and the Pacific, 1902–1940.* London and Chapel Hill: The University of North Carolina Press, 1997. Pp. xvi, 343. This history of the pre-World War II army garrisons in Hawaii and the Philippines is based on an impressive array of primary documents. Curiously, the author says little about the "carabao army's" (an appellation apparently of the author's own concoction) relationship with the civil government and Filipino community. The detailed and insightful discussion of war planning is the book's strongest feature (but see entry 82 for criticism of Linn's conclusions).

**145**    Meixsel, Richard B. "United States Army Policy in the Philippine Islands, 1902–1922." MA thesis, University of Georgia, 1988. Pp. iv, 122. In this study of a largely forgotten period of army history, the author argues that Philippine service was not—contrary to common belief—popular among American soldiers before the 1920s and that the demands of tropical service complicated many aspects of army life and administration [see also entry 291].

**146**    Paulet, Anne. "The Only Good Indian Is a Dead Indian: The Use of United States Indian Policy as a Guide for the Conquest and Occupation of the Philippines, 1898–1905." Phd dissertation, Rutgers, 1995. Pp. 415. From the abstract: US Indian policy "served as a guide for the military conquest and civilian occupation of the archipelago... . A combination of racism and Social Darwinism interacted at the turn of the century to enable Americans to equate Indians and Filipinos."

**147**    Petillo, Carol Morris. "Leaders and Followers: A Half-Century of the U.S. Military in the Philippine Islands." In *The Military and Conflict Between Cultures: Soldiers at the Interface.* Edited by James C. Bradford. College Station, TX: Texas A&M University, 1997. Pp. 183-213. Petillo identifies some aspects of the "culture clash" between soldiers and civilians in the Philippines by examining (using a few secondary sources) the atypical careers of John J. Pershing, Leonard Wood, and Douglas MacArthur.

**148**    *Psychology of the Filipino, [and] Conversation with Major-General Leonard*

*Wood, Governor-General of the Philippine Islands.* Manila: Headquarters Philippine Department, 1925. Pp. 38. According to this study by an anonymous but "acknowledged authority on the subject" of Filipino psychology, only with great difficulty, if at all, could Filipinos be turned into first-rate fighting soldiers. Col. Edward L. Munson of the army medical service was the pamphlet's unnamed author. The appended "conversation" reprints comments Wood made to a *Chicago Daily News* reporter.

**149**   Raines, Rebecca Robins. *Getting the Message Through: A Branch History of the U.S. Army Signal Corps.* Washington, DC: US Army Center of Military History, 1996. Pp. xix, 464. The author devotes a few pages to the activities of the signal corps during the Philippine-American War and early period of occupation. Between 1902 and 1907, the army transferred to the civil government control of over five thousand miles of land lines and inter-island cables.

**150**   Roth, Russell. *Muddy Glory: America's 'Indian Wars' in the Philippines, 1899-1935.* West Hanover, MA: The Christopher Publishing House, 1981. Pp. 281. An "episodic narrative" of the Philippine-American War and subsequent military actions against *ladrones* and Moros in the southern Philippines. In covering these topics, the author believes he has exposed "one of the best-kept secrets of our time," although he relied largely on secondary sources to do so. Interesting asides include accounts of PC officer Leonard Furlong, an attempt by former soldier Herman Miller to acquire the Medal of Honor, and the story of The Military Order of the Carabao.

**151**   Shea, Nancy. *The Army Wife.* New York and London: Harper & Brothers, 1941. Pp. xx, 324. The author, the wife of an air corps officer, explains what needs to be brought aboard the troop transport and what to expect at the army's overseas bases. "A thousand Army wives might spend two years in Manila and it would be interesting to hear their impressions. Be one of those [she advises] who can talk about something besides the servant situation, the marvelous Singapore gin slings at the Army and Navy Club, the tea dances at the Polo Club, and the wonderful Chinese bargains." In this prewar book, Shea also advised officers' wives to prepare for Philippine service by studying Spanish; in the postwar edition, *The Air Force Wife* (New York: Harper & Brothers, 1951), she commented that Philippine-bound wives need not "rush out and buy a Spanish grammar." Rather, "just practice up on speaking English a little slower. Today, the universality of English is very gratifying to the American in the Islands."

**152**   Thompson, Wayne Wray. "Governors of the Moro Province: Wood, Bliss, and Pershing in the Southern Philippines, 1903-1913." Phd dissertation, University of California, San Diego, 1975. Pp. vii, 307. Despite the encouragement they gave to, and personal pecuniary interest they sometimes had in, establishing plantations, building railroads, and encouraging white immigration to Muslim areas of Mindanao, the military governors there (Leonard Wood, 1903-1906; Tasker Bliss, 1906-1909; and John J. Pershing, 1909-13) were ultimately transients whose "future hung more on the impression [they made] in a distant metropolis than on the reality of [their] temporary surroundings."

**153**    Vedder, Edward B. "A Synopsis of the Work of the Army Medical Research Boards in the Philippines." In an unnumbered issue of *The Army Medical Bulletin* (Carlisle, PA: Medical Field Service School, 1929). Pp. vii, 179. This is an extensive annotated bibliography of the published works of the three army medical boards detailed to study tropical diseases in the Philippines and their impact on American and Filipino soldiers. The first board met from 1900 to 1902; a second from 1906 to 1914; and a third was established in 1922 (and still active at time of publication). The first two boards conducted their work from the army's First Reserve (Sternberg) Hospital in Manila; the third worked at the Philippine government's Bureau of Science. Vedder was a member of the second and third boards. See also entries 123, 136, and 139.

Research note: Up to 1913, the published multi-volume *Annual Report* of the US War Department included the reports of the commanding general of the Philippine garrison and subordinate commanders in the islands. Subsequent Philippine Department annual reports were not published and must be sought in the US National Archives.

*Unit Histories, Pre–1941 Garrison*
*The Colonial Regiments*

**154**    Chandler, Melbourne C. *Of GarryOwen in Glory: The History of the 7th U.S. Cavalry*. N.p. Privately Published, 1960. Pp. xv, 458. Until 1912, the army rotated regiments in and out of the Philippines to serve as the islands' garrison force, thus most published unit histories make some mention of the Philippines, because virtually every regiment in the army served there at some point during the decade after the end of the Philippine-American War. (For a published list, see the relevant appendix in William Ganoe, *The History of the United States Army* [New York: D. Appleton-Century Co., 1928]. Later editions deleted this list.) In 1912, the army designated specific regiments as "colonials" to remain permanently in the Philippines. One of these was the famous 7th Cavalry. Chandler's book offers a year-by-year account of the regiment's Philippine service, from 1905 to 1907 in Batangas, Pangasinan, and Leyte, and from 1912 to 1915 at Fort McKinley and Camp Stotsenburg.

The other "colonials" were the 8th Cavalry, and the 8th, 13th, 15th (two battalions of which served in China), and 24th Infantry Regiments. In 1915 the army ordered the 9th and 15th Cavalry Regiments to replace the 7th and 8th, and the 27th Infantry to replace the 24th Infantry as colonial regiments. Along with the 2nd Field Artillery Regiment, these units remained in the Philippines until World War I. The 9th Cavalry returned to the US in 1922. There are published histories of some of these regiments, but they say virtually nothing about the Philippines (see entries below for available titles).

**155**    Daily, Edward L. *From Custer to MacArthur*. Paducah, KY: Turner Publishing, 1995. Pp. 200. Daily's account of the 7th Cavalry's Philippine years is mostly a reprint of Chandler [previous entry], misspelling place names that Chandler spelled correctly.

**156**   Hunt, George A., comp. *The History of the Twenty-Seventh Infantry.* Schofield Barracks, HI: The Twenty-Seventh Infantry Press, 1931. Pp. 204. This otherwise substantial history mentions only in passing the 27th Infantry's assignment to the Philippines as a colonial regiment, from March 1916 to December 1920.

**157**   Muller, William G. *The Twenty-Fourth Infantry Past and Present.* 1923; reprint, Ft. Collins, CO: Old Army Press, 1972. [Pp. 124.] A year-by-year summation of the unit's activities, taken from the monthly regimental returns. The 24th Infantry was in the Philippines from January 1906 to February 1908 and from January 1912 to September 1915.

**158**   [Paul, Frank A.] *Regimental History, Thirty-First U.S. Infantry, July 1916–July 1920.* Manila, 1920. Pp. 36 The Thirty-First—"Manila's Own" (or, irreverently, "The Thirsty-First")—was formed of men from the 8th, 13th, and 15th Infantry Regiments and officers from the 27th Infantry already in the Philippines in late July and early August 1916. The unit's battalions were first assembled in one place in the Philippines in April 1920, at Ft. McKinley, after returning from the Siberia expedition, an account of which is included in this booklet.

**159**   *31st Infantry: History, Lineage, Honors, Decorations and Seventy-Third Anniversary Yearbook.* Ft. Sill, OK: 31st Infantry, 1988-89. [Pp. 74.] Bound typescript. Narrative history of the regiment based largely on secondary sources. Tells the story of the acquisition of the regiment's "Shanghai Bowl" and its recovery on Corregidor in December 1945.

**160**   *Twelfth Organization Day, 1916–1928, Program. Thirty-First Infantry, Manila P.I., August 13, 1928.* Pp. 16. Brief history with roster of officers. Presumably there were similar "Organization Day" booklets issued each year. The USAMHI holds several from the 1930s.

Research note: The 31st Infantry has an active regimental association. The association publishes a newsletter, "Pro Patria Press," and maintains a website at http://www6.brinkster.com/31Regiment.

### The Philippine Scouts

**161**   Coffman, Edward M. "The Philippine Scouts, 1899–1942: A Historical Vignette." In *ACTA* (publication of the International Commission of Military History), no. 3, Bucharest, Romania, 1978, pp. 69–79. The author delivered this paper at an ICMH conference in Teheran, Iran, in 1976. One of the more informed accounts of the Scouts, it is based on archival research and interviews with former officers and their families. Recruited as "Native Scout" auxiliaries to the US Army in 1899 and made a part of the regular army in 1901, during World War I these Filipino soldiers were reformed as provisional regiments, made permanent after the war to take the place of the now-departed "colonial" regiments.

**162**    Endy, Clarence E., Jr. "The Gentlemen from the Philippines." In *Bulletin of the American Historical Collection* 11, no. 3 (July-September 1983): 7-19. Account of the Filipino graduates of the United States Military Academy at West Point, New York, the first of whom was Vicente Lim, class of 1914. Also briefly describes the origin of the foreign cadet program at West Point and provides a capsule history of the Philippine Military Academy.

**163**    *Forty-Fifth Infantry (Philippine Scouts), Fort William McKinley, Rizal, PI, Yearbook, Organization Day, June 4, 1929.* Pp. 36. The 45th Infantry, one of the two Philippine Scout infantry regiments in the garrison after World War I, was formed as an American unit during the war, but its officers were shipped to the Philippines in December 1920 and the regiment filled out with Filipino soldiers. This booklet provides a short history and lists both officer and enlisted personnel in the regiment.

**164**    Franklin, Charles H., comp. *History of the Philippine Scouts, 1899–1934.* Washington, DC: Army War College, 1935. Pp. 188. Bound typescript. The author, an army warrant officer, composed a chronology of events related to the Scouts and compiled lists of officers, laws relating to the Scouts, and similar items.

**165**    Laurie, Clayton D. "The Philippine Scouts: America's Colonial Army, 1899–1913." In *Philippine Studies* 37 (1989): 174-91. Describes the origin of the Scouts during the Philippine-American War.

**166**    *Philippine Scouts.* Ft. Sam Houston, TX: The Philippine Scouts Heritage Society, 1996. Pp. 518. This invaluable resource combines histories, reprinted articles and documents, insignia, and many photographs of Scout units from inception to post-war disbanding. Annexes list Scout officers, awards, and World War II casualties.

**167**    Somera, Ely D. "The Philippine Scouts: Their Early Organization and History, 1899–1903." MA thesis, University of San Francisco, 1959. Pp. x, 190. An able overview of the organization and field activities of the Scouts and their relationship to the constabulary, based largely on published official documents. The author also contrasts the American experience of raising native troops with the experience of other constabulary-like forces. Appendices reprint orders dealing with the formation of the scouts, medals awarded in the Philippine-American War, casualties, and locations of units.

**168**    Tabaniag, Antonio. "The Pre-War Philippine Scouts." In *Journal of East Asiatic Studies* 9, no. 4 (October 1960 [published in 1966]): 7-26. Useful compendium of facts about the Philippine Scouts (rates of pay, description of insignia, unit designations, etc.).

**169**    Woolard, James Richard. "The Philippine Scouts: The Development of

America's Colonial Army." PhD dissertation, The Ohio State University, 1975. Pp. vii, 272. This detailed study of the formative years of the organization (to 1922) based on official records in the US National Archives remains the standard history of the Philippine Scouts.

## BIOGRAPHIES AND MEMOIRS

### Officers

**170**    Anders, Leslie. *Gentle Knight: The Life and Times of Major General Edwin Forrest Harding.* Kent, OH: Kent State University Press, 1985. Pp. x, 384. Harding (USMA 1909) joined the 14th Infantry for the last few months of its tour of duty at Camp Bumpus, Tacloban, Leyte, from November 1909 to February 1910. The author works in considerable detail about Harding's experiences, despite the brief time spent in the islands. The Harding family was in Manila again en route to China in 1923. Harding was sacked as commanding general of the 32nd Division on Buna in World War II and retired in 1946.

**171**    Arnold, H. H. *Global Mission.* New York: Harper & Bros., 1949. Pp. xii, 626. The focus of these memoirs is on flying and World War II, but Arnold (USMA 1907) does not forget his early years as an infantry officer in the Philippines, a first tour in 1907-1909 and a second in 1914-16. He spent much of the time on maneuvers and surveying duty [see also entries 179 and 183].

**172**    Bacevich, A.J. *Diplomat in Khaki: Major General Frank Ross McCoy and American Foreign Policy, 1898–1949.* Lawrence, KS: University Press of Kansas, 1989. Pp. xi, 272. McCoy (USMA 1897) was for many years a close associate of Leonard Wood and usually could be found at the general's side, in the Philippines and elsewhere. McCoy arrived in Manila with Wood in July 1903 and remained in the islands for three years. He returned with Wood in 1921 and stayed until 1925. His Philippine experiences receive extensive coverage although they were hardly those of the typical army officer.

**173**    Binder, L. James. *Lemnitzer: A Soldier for His Time.* Washington and London: Brassey's, 1997. Pp. xiv, 386. Lyman Lemnitzer (USMA 1920) served as a coast artillery officer on Corregidor for five years, 1923-25 and 1931-34, first with the 59th CA Regiment and then with the 92nd CA Regiment (PS). He held a wide array of billets—from battery commander, to barrio officer, to officer assigned to investigate illegal logging on Bataan—and became a protégé of Stanley Embick's during this time.

**174**    Bland, Larry I., ed. *George C. Marshall: Interviews and Reminiscences for Forrest C. Pogue.* Rev. ed. Lexington, VA: George C. Marshall Foundation, 1991. Pp. xvi, 650. This is a "compilation of transcripts and notes made during late 1956 and early 1957 by and for General Marshall's newly appointed official biographer, Forrest C. Pogue." Marshall (commissioned 1902) served a tour in the Philippines from May 1902 to November 1903 and a second from August 1913 to May

1916. Marshall's recollections of these tours are detailed and fascinating. His various activities in the islands included visiting tribesmen in the interior of Mindoro and posting signboards on every island in Manila Bay informing Filipino residents that the government had taken control of the property, and residents had to leave. For the Philippine years, this volume is superior to all of Marshall's (and virtually all other officers') biographies [see also entries 175, 186, and 207].

**175**   Bland, Larry I., ed. *The Papers of George C. Marshall*, Vol. 1, "*The Soldierly Spirit,*" *December 1880–June 1939*. Baltimore and London: The Johns Hopkins University Press, 1981. Pp. xxx, 742. Includes three documents from Marshall's 1902-1903 Philippine tour and six documents from the 1913-16 tour [see also entries 174, 186, and 207].

**176**   Booth, T. Michael, and Duncan Spencer. *Paratrooper: The Life of Gen. James M. Gavin*. New York: Simon & Schuster, 1994. Pp. 494. In this tell-all biography of the famous World War II airborne officer, Douglas MacArthur was "commander of the Philippines" when Gavin (an ex-enlisted man who graduated from West Point in 1929) served under him in an unidentified Philippine Scout regiment (57th Infantry) in 1936-38. Mercifully, these poorly informed authors limit coverage of Gavin's Philippine tour to little more than a page. Bradley Biggs's much shorter biography, *Gavin* (Hamden, CT: Archon Books, 1980), devotes even less space to Gavin's years in the Philippines.

**177**   Buck, Beaumont B. *Memories of Peace and War*. San Antonio, TX: The Naylor Co., 1935. Pp. xiii, 284. Buck (USMA 1885) was in the Philippines in 1899-1900, 1901-1902, 1907, and again in 1912-13, with the 16th and 13th Infantry Regiments. His peacetime tours of duty were spent at Ft. McKinley. This is a compilation of stories about his military experiences which include episodes aboard troopships, hunting, family life in the Philippines, and relations with Filipinos. An appendix includes a photograph of the "Society [of the Army] of the Philippines" medal [see entries 122 and 673].

**178**   Clark, Frank S. *The Chronicle of Aunt Lena*. N.p. Privately Published, 1962. Pp. 488. Clark (commissioned 1909) arrived in the Philippines in July 1911 and remained for three years at Ft. Mills, Corregidor. At the time, the post was being established as a permanent fortification. For both he and his wife ("Aunt Lena" of the title), he writes in this very rare and overlooked book, the Philippine tour of duty was an immensely rewarding experience. They left in May 1914 and, to their regret, never returned. This book is based on a more comprehensive diary that appears to have been lost since Clark's death.

**179**   Coffey, Thomas M. *Hap—Military Aviator: The Story of the U.S. Air Force and the Man Who Built It, General Henry H. "Hap" Arnold*. New York: The Viking Press, 1982. Pp. 416. Famous as the head of the World War II army air force, Arnold nonetheless had seen a great deal of the Philippines early in his career. Arnold (USMA 1907) spent much of a tour with the 29th Infantry Regiment from December 1907 to June 1909 mapping the island of Luzon. A second tour from

January 1914 to January 1916 took Arnold to Corregidor and Batangas for maneuvers, and to Stotsenburg as range officer for machine-gun practice. Arnold's "Philippine Years" cover fifteen pages of text, but no "Philippines" entry is found in the index [see entries 171 and 183].

**180**   Collins, J. Lawton. *Lightning Joe: An Autobiography*. Baton Rouge: Louisiana State University Press, 1979. Pp. xvii, 462. Collins (USMA April 1917) requested, and enjoyed, a three-year tour of duty in the Philippines (1933-36). As executive officer of the 23rd Infantry Brigade at Ft. McKinley, he participated in war planning and annual exercises. His memoirs provide one of the better published accounts of army life in the prewar Philippines.

**181**   Crane, Charles Judson. *The Experiences of a Colonel of Infantry*. New York: The Knickerbocker Press, 1923. Pp. 578. A largely unreflective officer of the old school, Crane (USMA 1877) spent most of his career with the 24th Infantry. After service in the Philippine-American War, he commanded the 9th Infantry at Warwick Barracks, Cebu, from 1910 to 1912. Here he recalls clashes with civilian authority in Cebu and training exercises on Cebu and Guimaras. Crane had nothing positive to say about either the Philippines or Filipinos. He thought the US should get out of the islands "in any honorable manner" and spent his tour of duty anxiously awaiting a return to "God's Country."

**182**   Crosswell, D.K.R. *The Chief of Staff: The Military Career of General Walter Bedell Smith*. Westport, CT: Greenwood Press, 1991. Pp. xxii, 437. Smith (commissioned 1917), best known as Eisenhower's hatchet man during World War II, served with the 45th Infantry at Ft. McKinley from 1929 to 1931. The assignment is briefly discussed with emphasis placed on the social aspects of Philippine duty.

**183**   Daso, Dik Alan. *Hap Arnold and the Evolution of American Air Power*. Washington, DC and London: Smithsonian Institution Press, 2000. Pp. xix, 314. Includes details of Arnold's two tours of Philippine duty based in part on letters held by the Arnold family [see also entries 171 and 179].

**184**   Fletcher, Marvin E. *America's First Black General: Benjamin O. Davis, Sr., 1880-1970*. Forward by Benjamin O. Davis, Jr. Lawrence, KS: University Press of Kansas, 1989. Pp. xix, 226. Davis, commissioned in 1901 after a brief period of enlisted service, served for several years in the Philippines, first with the 9th and 10th Cavalry Regiments on Samar and Panay in 1901-1902 and again with the Ninth at Camp Stotsenburg from July 1917 to March 1920. The author concentrates on Davis's personal life, which centered on a long-distance love affair with the woman who would become his second wife, and says relatively little about life in the Philippines. There were no black-manned units in the islands after the 9th Cavalry left in 1922, and Davis never returned to the Philippines. Davis's work with the Philippine National Guard—admittedly limited—goes unmentioned, as does his attempt to remain in the Philippines.

Davis's son, whose memoirs have been published as *Benjamin O. Davis, Jr.,*

*American: An Autobiography* (Washington, DC: Smithsonian Institution Press, 1991), graduated from the US Military Academy in 1936 and served in the Philippines at Clark Air Base in the 1960s. The younger Davis did not live in the islands when his father was stationed there, however.

**185**   Foulois, Benjamin D., with C.V. Glines. *From the Wright Brothers to the Astronauts: The Memoirs of Major General Benjamin D. Foulois.* New York: McGraw-Hill, 1968. Pp. xi, 306. Foulois's military career began (using his older brother's name) as a private in the 1st US Volunteer Engineers in 1898. He then enlisted in the regular infantry for Philippine service, during which he taught school in Naga. Commissioned in 1901, Foulois's regiment, the 17th Infantry, served again in the islands from 1903 to 1905, and Foulois offers sharp recollections of fighting the Moros. Foulois headed the AEF Air Service during World War I and retired in 1935 without returning to the islands. He held the view that MacArthur was "shipped to the Philippines" in 1935 to get rid of him after an argument with President Franklin Roosevelt over who should determine the size of the army.

**186**   Frye, William. *Marshall: Citizen Soldier.* Indianapolis and New York: The Bobbs-Merrill Co., 1947. Pp. 397. Until the publication of Pogue's [entry 207], this was the standard Marshall biography, written with the approval of—if not a great deal of cooperation from—General Marshall. According to Pogue, veterans who had served with Marshall in the Philippines in 1902-1903 complained of Frye's characterization of their regiment [see also entries 174 and 175].

**187**   Gill, William H., as told to Edward Jacquelin Smith. *Always a Commander: The Reminiscences of Major General William H. Gill.* Colorado Springs, CO: The Colorado College, 1974. Pp. 124. A 1907 graduate of the Virginia Military Academy commissioned in 1912, Gill was stationed with the 8th Infantry at Ft. McKinley in 1915–1917. He performed "the usual garrison and field duties," but his family nearly drowned when a typhoon struck the USAT *Thomas* on the return voyage to the US. Gill left the Philippines with an abiding dislike for George Marshall, who although also a VMI graduate stationed at McKinley, completely ignored Gill. Gill commanded the 32nd Division on New Guinea and Luzon during World War II.

**188**   Hagedorn, Hermann. *Leonard Wood: A Biography.* 2 vols. New York and London: Harper and Bros., 1931. Pp. xii/viii, 436/524. Reprinted by Kraus, NY, 1969. After seven decades, this sympathetic portrayal by a contemporary admirer of one of America's most controversial soldiers remains the standard biography. Wood's experiences in the Philippines—his work in Mindanao (1903-1906), command of the army's Philippine garrison (1906-1908), and governor generalship (1921-1927)—are found in volume two [see also entry 196].

**189**   Hagood, Johnson. *The Services of Supply, A Memoir of the Great War.* Boston and New York: Houghton Mifflin Co., 1927. Pp. xvii, 403. A few paragraphs suffice for Hagood's (USMA 1896) pre–World War I service in the islands, which included working on "the so-called Corregidor Project, a plan to provide everything needful to withstand a long siege."

**190**    Harper, James William. "Hugh Lenox Scott: Soldier-Diplomat, 1876–1917." Phd dissertation, University of Virginia, 1968. Pp. v, 260. One chapter of this biography is devoted to Scott's Mindanao command (1903–1906) based largely on Scott's papers in the Library of Congress [see also entry 210].

**191**    Head, William. *Every Inch a Soldier: Augustine Warner Robins and the Building of U.S. Airpower.* College Station, TX: Texas A&M University Press, 1995. Pp. x, 289. Robins (USMA 1907), the man after whom Warner Robins (now, Robins) AFB, Georgia, was named, arrived at Ft. McKinley in May 1909 with the 12th Cavalry. American acquisition of the Philippines had left "the Filipinos themselves," in Head's words, "not altogether pleased." Therefore, the "Philippines assignment was anything but an easy one." Head's brief coverage of the regiment suggests that Robins fought mostly boredom and homesickness. He did make a bizarre trip to China in 1910 disguised as a "millionaire tourist" to gather military intelligence. Robins returned to the US in 1912, transferred to the air service, and never returned to the islands.

**192**    Heefner, Wilson Allen. *Twentieth Century Warrior: The Life and Service of Major General Edwin D. Patrick.* Shippensburg, PA: White Mane Publishing, 1995. Pp. xvi, 240. Patrick (commissioned in the Indiana National Guard in 1915 and in the army in 1917) stopped in Manila en route to China in 1926. Memories of the Scout "mutiny" of July 1924 were still strong in the army community, for hearing of this event was Patrick's major recollection. "One good white soldier is worth a dozen of the little brown fellows," he concluded, "and the little brown fellows know it." Patrick was commanding general of the 6th Infantry Division when he died of wounds received in action on Luzon in March 1945.

**193**    Holley, I. B. *General John M. Palmer, Citizen Soldiers, and the Army of a Democracy.* Westport, CT: Greenwood Press, 1982. Pp. xviii, 814. Palmer began and Holley completed this unusual mix of biography and memoir. Palmer (USMA 1892) served twice in the Philippines, on Mindanao in 1906-1907 and then with the 24th Infantry on Corregidor in 1914-15. Two chapters describe his actions as governor of Lanao District and a third his service on Corregidor. During the latter tour, he also served with a board of officers who prepared defense plans for the islands. "We correctly anticipated that an enemy would select the Lingayen Gulf area for his main landings," Palmer wrote, but "we rejected a proposal to concentrate the main body of the defense forces in Bataan."

**194**    Howze, Hamilton H. *A Cavalryman's Story: Memoirs of a Twentieth-century Army General.* Washington, DC: Smithsonian Institution Press, 1996. Pp. x, 316. Son of an army general, Howze (USMA 1930) served with the 26th Cavalry at Ft. Stotsenburg from 1938 to 1940. His recollections of a pleasant tour of duty focus on polo, of which he was an avid player. No army regimental team could beat the Elizalde brothers' polo team, he recalled, because no officer could afford the kind of horses the Elizaldes' kept. Howze served with an armored division in Europe in World War II and was later closely associated with the development of army aviation.

**195**    Hurley, Alfred F. *Billy Mitchell: Crusader for Air Power.* Bloomington: Indiana University Press, 1975. Pp. ix, 190 (revision of 1964 edition). Famously court-martialed in 1925, Mitchell (enlisted 1898; commissioned 1901) had like most soldiers spent several years in the Philippines early in his career, but Hurley makes only brief comments on Mitchell's war and peacetime experiences in the islands [see also entry 197].

**196**    Lane, Jack C. *Armed Progressive: General Leonard Wood.* San Rafael, CA: Presidio Press, 1978. Pp. 276. In this scholarly biography, the author's interest, shaped by the concerns of America's Vietnam generation, is with the US in Asia and not with Wood in the Philippines. Despite the book's title, Lane entirely over-looks the "progressive" nature of Wood's activities as commanding general of the Philippine garrison in 1906-1908. The more-aptly titled doctoral dissertation version of this biography, "Leonard Wood and the Shaping of American Defense Policy" (University of Georgia, 1963), includes a chapter on the Subic-Manila naval base controversy that is not found here [see also entry 188].

**197**    Levine, Issac Don. *Mitchell: Pioneer of Air Power.* Cleveland and New York: The World Publishing Co., 1943. Pp. viii, 420. "Billy" Mitchell's experiences in the Philippine-American War are recounted at length in this biography. During a second tour of duty in the Philippines, from 1909 to 1912, Mitchell served as the chief signal officer for the Department of Luzon, during which he traveled to the northernmost islands of Luzon to investigate reports that the Japanese had established wireless stations in the area [see also entry 195].

**198**    Liggett, Hunter. *Commanding an American Army: Recollections of the World War.* Boston and New York: Houghton Mifflin Company, 1925. Pp. 208. General Liggett (USMA 1879) makes a few comments about the impact of the war on the Philippines and the garrison there, which he commanded in 1916-1917. In Liggett's view, the "true defense" of the Philippines "was primarily a function of Sea Power" and required "a first class naval base at Guam."

**199**    Lockerbie, D. Bruce. *A Man Under Orders: Lieutenant General William K. Harrison, Jr.* San Francisco: Harper & Row, 1979. Pp. xii, 194. Harrison (USMA April 1917) was best known as the United Nations Command representative at the Panmunjom talks in 1952-53, but in 1925-27 he served with the 26th Cavalry at Camp Stotsenburg. A story about an officer's wife aboard the troop transport who refused to take a bath if doing so would interfere with her bridge game gets more space than does the "rather routine" garrison life in the islands. The "army wife on troopship refuses to bathe until old Negro porter named George forces her to do so" story is a staple of army memoirs, published and unpublished.

**200**    Maus, L. Mervin. *An Army Officer on Leave in Japan.* Chicago: A.C. McClurg & Co., 1911. Pp. xxi, 413. The book mostly concerns touristing in Japan, but Maus also describes army life in Manila and aboard the troopship from the Philippines to Japan. For some reason Maus, as one unhappy reviewer put it (*New York Times Review of Books*, 21 January 1912), "hit upon the amazing and cumbrous expedient of putting entire chapters dealing with history into the mouths of [two] 'characters' created for the purpose." Both should have been "shot on sight." Maus gave himself the fictional role of a civilian government employee.

**201**    Miles, Perry L. *Fallen Leaves: Memories of an Old Soldier.* Berkeley, CA: Wuerth Publishing, 1961. Pp. 328. Old Army gossip fills every page of this delightful and rare memoir. Miles (USMA 1895) arrived in the Philippines with the 14th Infantry in June 1898 and served in Central Luzon until late 1899, when he was detached for service with the US Army Transport Service. That two-year assignment provided opportunities for traveling throughout much of the Philippines. Miles spent another tour in the islands, again with the 14th Infantry, on Samar from 1903 to 1905 and includes a lengthy account of the regiment's experiences there, during which it constructed Camp Connell, near Calbayog. Miles must have been the only officer in the army who refused an assignment to West Point so that he could accompany his regiment to the peacetime Philippines, and to Samar, no less. The book concludes with chapters on the author's World War I service in France with the black 371st Infantry and an essay, "The Eviction of the Bonus Marchers." Miles commanded the troops which dispersed the so-called Bonus Expeditionary Forces from Washington, DC, in 1932 [see also entry 221].

**202**    Millett, Allan R. *The General: Robert L. Bullard and Officership in the United States Army, 1881-1925.* Westport, CT: Greenwood Press, 1975. Pp. xi, 499. This long-forgotten officer was one of the army's senior commanders in France during World War I. After service in the Philippine-American War, Bullard (USMA 1885) returned to the islands in July 1902 and took a battalion of the 28th Infantry to Mindanao to oversee the building of the Overton-Marahui road and then served as governor of the Lake Lanao district under Leonard Wood. Bullard left the Philippines in July 1904 and did not return. This book, possibly the best American military biography ever written, provides a detailed account of the army's activities in "Moroland."

**203**    Mott, T. Bentley. *Twenty Years as Military Attaché.* New York: Oxford University Press, 1937. Pp. 342. Reprinted by Ayer Publ., Salem, NH, 1979. Mott (USMA 1886) found his two tours of Philippine duty, the first in 1898 and the second in 1913-14 with the field artillery at Camp Stotsenburg, considerably less congenial than his many years in Paris as a military attaché. His brief comments on Philippine service mirror the entire officer corps' outlook in the early years of occupation: In 1898, going to the Philippines, or anywhere, after decades of "the desolate narrowness of life in army garrisons … was like escaping from a cage";

fifteen years later, confronted by the prospect of "rotting away" in the islands, Mott resigned his commission and returned to the United States.

**204**    Nevins, Arthur S. *Gettysburg's Five-Star Farmer*. New York: Carlton Press, 1977. Pp. 155. This is largely a memoir of Nevins's (brother of historian Allan Nevins) friendship with Dwight Eisenhower, the "five-star farmer" of the title, but Nevins (commissioned 1917) briefly recalls Philippine tours of duty in 1920-22 and 1936-38. In the first, he was one of the officers of the Texas-based 57th Infantry sent to the islands "to take over the existing old 2nd Philippine Scout regiment"; in the second, he served as a staff officer with the Philippine Division.

**205**    [Norwood, John Wall.] *Fifty-Thousand Miles with Uncle Sam's Army*. Waynesville, NC: Enterprise Publishing Co., 1912. Pp. 95. Written under the name "Uncle Dudley," this account of army life in the Philippines originally was serialized in a North Carolina newspaper. Norwood (commissioned 1899) draws a particularly good contrast between army service in the Philippines during the "Days of the Empire" and the less rewarding postwar period. Norwood saw service in the islands twice with the 23rd Infantry, in 1900-1901 and again in 1903-1905, both times on Mindanao. Includes considerable detail about life at isolated posts and the hardships families faced.

**206**    Palmer, Frederick. *Bliss, Peacemaker: The Life and Letters of Tasker H. Bliss*. New York: Dodd, Mead & Co., 1934. Pp. ix, 477. One chapter is devoted to "Ruling the Moros," which task Bliss (USMA 1875) attempted from 1906 to 1908 (succeeding Leonard Wood in that role, and preceding Pershing). Palmer briefly notes that Bliss commanded the Department of Luzon for eight months in 1905-1906, which presented "no new problems of administration," in Palmer's view, and that Bliss concluded his islands' service as Philippine garrison commander, from December 1908 to April 1909.

**207**    Pogue, Forrest C. *George C. Marshall: Education of a General, 1880-1939*. New York: The Viking Press, 1963. Pp. xvii, 421. This first volume of the authorized three-volume biography covers both of Marshall's Philippine tours of duty in detail. Marshall was best known for commanding one of the field forces in the 1914 Batangas maneuvers, even though he was only a first lieutenant [see also entries 174, 175, and 186].

**208**    Price, Frank James. *Troy H. Middleton: A Biography*. Baton Rouge: Louisiana State University Press, 1974. Pp. xiv, 416. Middleton (a former enlisted man commissioned in 1912) served as an assistant inspector general of the Philippine Department from his arrival in the islands in November 1936 to his departure in May 1937. He retired from the army to accept a job at LSU. In his brief account of Middleton's six-month tour of duty, Price confuses the Philippine Constabulary with the Philippine Scouts, and both with the Philippine Army.

**209**    Ridgeway, Matthew B. *Soldier: The Memoirs of Matthew B. Ridgeway*. New York: Harper & Brothers, 1956. Pp. 371. Ridgeway (USMA April 1917) served a year in the Philippines (1932-33) as Governor General Theodore Roosevelt, Jr.'s, "technical adviser on military matters." He recounts a trip escorting Roosevelt's mother to Corregidor to view the construction of Malinta Tunnel, but a bad case of diarrhea he contracted while visiting Mindanao left a greater impression on him.

**210**   Scott, Hugh Lenox. *Some Memories of a Soldier*. New York and London: The Century Co., 1928. Pp. xvii, 673. Scott (USMA 1876) served briefly as army chief of staff but was better known as the army's leading authority on the American Indian. He spent the Philippine-American War years in Cuba but governed Sulu from 1903 to 1906. His memoirs include a lengthy (143-pp.) and sympathetic but paternalistic portrayal of the archipelago's people. In a conversation with President Woodrow Wilson in 1913, Scott articulated the unchanging army perspective on Philippine independence: There was no Filipino nation but only "a congeries of tribes ... many [of whom] have been enemies for centuries." America should not leave the islands until Filipinos were "able to walk on their own feet," and that would not be anytime soon, in General Scott's opinion [see also entry 190].

**211**   Smythe, Donald. *Guerrilla Warrior: The Early Life of John J. Pershing*. New York: Charles Scribner's Sons, 1973. Pp. ix, 370. Smythe gives considerable space to Pershing's (USMA 1886) nine years in the Philippines (spent mostly on Mindanao, although Pershing also commanded Ft. McKinley from January 1907 to July 1908 and, very briefly, the Philippines Division in 1910-11). Smythe defends Pershing's actions at Bud Bagsak in 1913 and refutes stories that Pershing fathered several illegitimate children while serving in the islands. Probably Pershing did not (Perret [entry 100] unpersuasively claims to have found the evidence that he did), but by the time he had completed the second volume of Pershing's biography, *Pershing: General of the Armies* (Bloomington: Indiana University Press, 1986), Smythe had come to acknowledge that, as one veteran reminded Pershing, "the course of our lives in the old days was such as to suggest the possibility that the statements rife might have some foundation in truth" [see also entry 213].

**212**   Tuchman, Barbara W. *Stilwell and the American Experience in China, 1911-45*. New York: MacMillan, 1970. Pp. xv, 621. Published by Macdonald Futura Publishers, London, 1981, under the title *Sand Against the Wind*. Tuchman writes that the adventuresome Joseph Stilwell asked for Philippine duty upon graduating from West Point in 1904 and received it because he had finished (just barely) in the top third of his class. But in those days, the growing unpopularity of Philippine duty would have ensured Stilwell's orders to join a regiment proceeding to the islands, even—or especially—had he graduated at the bottom of the class. Stilwell spent from November 1904 to February 1906 with the 12th Infantry, chasing Pulajanes on Samar and leading a less rigorous life at Camp Jossman, on Guimaras Island. There, writes Tuchman, "everything in the native surroundings interested him," but she devotes only a paragraph to the experience. A second tour at Ft. McKinley from February 1911 to January 1912 is mentioned only as a backdrop to

Tuchman's discussion of the 1911 revolution in China. From Manila, Stilwell took leave—a total of seventeen days—to visit the country with which he would later be closely identified.

**213**   Vandiver, Frank E. *Black Jack: The Life and Times of John J. Pershing*. 2 vols. College Station, TX: Texas A&M University Press, 1977. Pp. xxii, 1178 (continuous pagination). Some reviewers thought this biography (eighteen years in the writing) long on fact and short on interpretation, but Pershing's lengthy service in the islands, which began on Thanksgiving Day 1899 and ended (with some interruptions) with his departure on 15 December 1913, is covered in great detail in volume one. As part of his research, the author visited Mindanao and interviewed such luminaries as Emilio Aguinaldo [see also entry 211].

*Enlisted Men*

**214**   Adams, William Llewellyn. *Exploits and Adventures of a Soldier Ashore and Afloat*. Philadelphia: Lippincott, 1911. Pp. 310. Adams served with the Pennsylvania national guard on the Puerto Rico expedition in 1898 and at Cavite and Mindanao as an enlisted man in the marines during the Philippine-American War. The author later (1907-10) served in the army and was with the 29th Infantry regiment at Ft. McKinley in 1907-1909. Includes a good description of the post and of his service with the Military Survey of Luzon project. Also describes antagonism between marines and Filipino Scouts at the 1904 St. Louis Exposition. The marines were angry that the scouts were seen in public with white women.

**215**   Vogel, Victor. *Soldiers of the Old Army*. College Station: Texas A & M University Press, 1990. Pp. xi, 124. This is not a memoir but an account of enlisted service drawing on the author's experiences. (He enlisted in 1934 and later obtained a commission.) Vogel, who did not serve overseas, includes a brief chapter titled "Foreign Service," but it says little about the Philippines. He mentions serving with a Filipino soldier who had previously served in the Philippine Scouts. According to the author, scouts could reenlist into regular army (white) regiments.

**216**   Wheaton, Grace. *"Who Is Alf Thompson?"* N.p. Privately Published, 1996. Pp. 243. At the time this bibliography neared completion, Alf Thompson (born 11 November 1895) was the oldest surviving veteran of the Philippine-based 31st US Infantry. Thompson enlisted in the army in late 1917 and sailed in December for the Philippines, where he was assigned to a machine gun company at Ft. McKinley. Thompson remained in the islands only a short while before the regiment left for Siberia. He never returned to the Philippines, and much of this book reprints his diary entries from Siberia and from World War II, in which he worked as Red Cross official in Europe and North Africa. Thompson's diary entries for the trans–Pacific voyage in 1917 are reprinted as are two letters he mailed from Hawaii and the Philippines. He thought the "native troops ... a fine bunch of men," but "when one gets a glimpse of the real native life, ... one begins to doubt the advisability of their being given free rein in their government affairs as yet."

## Army Dependents

**217**    Armstrong, Charles W., Jr., ed. *Thomasites and the War Generation of Central-Bordner School in the Philippines*. Irvine, CA: Privately Published, 1991. Pp. 239. Includes an account of life as an army dependent in the Philippines by Maj. Gen. John W. Barnes, whose father was stationed with the 14th Engineers in 1923-26 and again in 1933-36. According to Barnes, economy was the "main reason" his family preferred Philippine duty.

**218**    Brandon, Dorothy. *Mamie Doud Eisenhower: A Portrait of a First Lady*. New York: Charles Scribner's Sons, 1954. Pp. viii, 307. Eisenhower's wife only reluctantly followed her husband to the Philippines in October 1936, a year after his arrival with the Military Mission. What did it matter that Manila was the "Pearl of the Orient," Mrs. Eisenhower thought, if one did not wish to live in the Orient to begin with? Includes anecdotes about Eisenhower's mission activities and paints an unpleasant picture of Manila's American community: "Nearly all Americans shunned the company of Filipinos except to win professional and business good will," writes the author, who apparently lived for several years in Manila [see also entries 220 and 222].

**219**    Eisenhower, John S. D. *Strictly Personal*. Garden City, NY: Doubleday & Co., 1974. Pp. xiv, 412. Army dependent John Eisenhower, son of the future president, recalled his years in the Philippines (October 1936–December 1939) "as among the happiest of my life" and devotes ten pages to recollections, including comments about his father and MacArthur not found elsewhere. The author was a student at Brent school in Baguio while living in the Philippines.

**220**    Eisenhower, Susan. *Mrs. Ike: Memories and Reflections on the Life of Mamie Eisenhower*. New York: Farrar, Straus and Giroux, 1996. Pp. xix, 392. According to the author (President Eisenhower's granddaughter), Eisenhower's wife did not accompany him to the Philippines in 1935 because she disliked living in the tropics and anticipated that the Military Mission would soon collapse. The high salary the Commonwealth paid Eisenhower—which put the family "'on easy street for the first time in [their] married life'"—partly reconciled "Mrs. Ike" to life in the islands, but when the Eisenhowers' left in December 1939, Mamie wrote that she had "'left nothing in Manila except some good friends'" [see also entries 218 and 222].

**221**    Fremont, Jessie Benton, as told to Elisabeth Henry Redfield. *Young Ladies Should Marry*. New York: Robert M. McBride & Co., 1936. Pp. x, 286. The more-or-less factual turn-of-the-century adventures of sisters Jessie and Juliet Fremont, in Manila and elsewhere. The Fremonts returned to the United States aboard an army troopship that was bringing 1,300 "short time" soldiers home for discharge. The men mutinied in Nagasaki, a unique occurrence in the history of the army transport service. For a more informed account of the incident, see Perry Miles's *Fallen Leaves* [entry 201]. Miles appears here as "Captain Foote."

**222**    Hatch, Alden. *Red Carpet for Mamie*. New York: Henry Holt and Co., 1954. Pp. viii, 277. The chapter describing the Eisenhowers' life in Manila in 1936-39 is less substantial and more error-filled than Brandon's [entry 218; see also entry 220].

**223**    Lloyd, Olivia Moreland. *Around the World on an Army Transport*. Phoenix, AZ: Privately Published, 1927. Army wife Lloyd traveled to the Philippines via the Atlantic with her husband, an officer assigned to the 2nd Field Artillery Regiment at Ft. McKinley. The only officer named Lloyd shown on the regimental returns is Chaplain Walter K. Lloyd, who arrived in the Philippines in February 1909 aboard the USAT *Kilpatrick*. (The only library in the US that reported holding a copy of this book is the Library of Congress, and its copy is missing.)

**224**    Shunk, Caroline S. *An Army Woman in the Philippines*. Kansas City, MO: Franklin Hudson Publishing Co., 1914. Pp. 183. Shunk's husband, Lt. Col. William Shunk, was assigned to the 1st Cavalry Regiment at Camp Stotsenburg in 1909-10. This collection of letters written by his wife to family members in the US tells of her trip to the Philippines, life in the islands, and of visits to China and Japan. The tone is upbeat and sympathetic to the army and Filipinos, but Shunk makes clear that her year in the Philippines was more than enough.

---

# United States Army Air Corps in the Prewar Philippines

## GENERAL HISTORIES

**225**    Brown, Jerold E. *Where Eagles Land: Planning and Development of U.S. Army Airfields, 1910–1941*. Westport, CT: Greenwood Press, 1990. Pp. x, 220. The title might suggest that the book discusses the development of airfields in the Philippines during this time period, but the author has little to say about the Philippines other than that seaplanes flew from a place he calls "Passy" (should be Pasay) and that an airfield was established on Corregidor in 1916. In fact, the Kindley "Field" placed on Corregidor in 1919 was a seaplane base with an adjacent landing strip and was in a location different from that of the shortlived pre-World War I seaplane base first established in 1913.

**226**   Chandler, Charles DeForest, and Frank P. Lahm. *How Our Army Grew Wings: Airmen and Aircraft Before 1914*. New York: The Ronald Press Co., 1943. Pp. xiii, 333. One chapter discusses "Aviation in the Philippine Islands" from the arrival of Lieutenant Lahm with the 7th Cavalry in late 1911 to the crash of the army's one remaining airplane, near Corregidor, on 12 January 1915. Lahm, who was not sent to the islands specifically to fly, nonetheless had been asked before he left if he would be willing to open a flying school there. He originally flew from the polo grounds at McKinley [see also entry 234].

**227**   Hennessy, Juliette A. *The United States Army Air Arm, April 1861 to April 1917*. USAF Historical Division, 1958. Reprinted by Office of Air Force History, Washington, DC, 1985. Pp. vii, 260. This is the best published account of the air service's introduction to the Philippines, at Ft. McKinley, in 1912 and of the arrival of the 2nd Aero Squadron (a seaplane outfit) at Ft. Mills in February 1916.

**228**   Maurer, Maurer. *Aviation in the U.S. Army, 1919–1939*. Washington, DC: USAF, Office of Air Force History, 1987. Pp. xxxiii, 626. The Chief of Air Service considered the sending of air squadrons to the Philippines to be one of the most pressing needs of the immediate post-World War I period, and the army constructed its three prewar Philippine airfields and developed plans to relocate all air resources to Bataan during the period covered by this book. None of that is discussed here. The author does mention, however, that the army lent a plane and pilot to the Philippine government to spray locusts in sugar cane fields on Mindoro in the 1920s. The book includes a useful discussion of air force-related historical resources.

**229**   Maurer, Maurer, ed. *Combat Squadrons of the Air Force, World War II*. [Maxwell AFB, AL:] Department of the Air Force, Historical Division, Air University, 1969. Pp. ix, 841. Lineages of the prewar USAAF flight squadrons in the Philippines (the 3rd Pursuit, 2nd Observation, and 28th Bombardment) are traced here. Does not include Philippine Army Air Corps units inducted into USAFFE.

**230**   Maurer, Maurer, ed. *The United States Air Service in World War I*, Vol. II, *Early Concepts of Military Aviation*. Washington, DC: Office of Air Force History, 1978. Pp. xv, 460. The place of the Philippines in the army's pre–World War I thinking on the development of military air power can be followed in this collection of primary documents. Includes a photo of a seaplane and air service personnel on Corregidor in November 1913. The other volumes of this series deal with the Air Service in France in World War I.

**231**   Slater, Richard. "'Up and at 'Em': The 4th Composite Group in the Philippines, 1920-1941." In *Friends Journal* (Winter 1987-1988): 8-18. Brief history of the Group (originally established in the Philippines in 1919 as the 1st Observation Group), with many photos. "Up and At 'Em" was the Group's motto.

BIOGRAPHIES AND MEMOIRS

*Officers*

**232**   Beverley, George H. *Pioneer in the U.S. Air Corps: The Memoirs of Brigadier General George H. Beverley.* Manhattan, KS: Sunflower University Press, 1982. Pp. 72. World War I veteran Beverley (commissioned 1918) was the 3rd Pursuit Squadron's engineering officer at Clark Field in 1924-26. He recalls daily rounds of golf, polo against the Elizalde brothers, and air maneuvers to Mindoro and Aparri. This book reprints a charming photograph of the pilots, their wives, and children at Clark Field standing in front of a DH-4B.

**233**   Goddard, George W., with Dewitt S. Copp. *Overview: A Life-Long Adventure in Aerial Photography.* Garden City, NY: Doubleday, 1969. Pp. xiii, 413. English-born Goddard (commissioned 1917) was one of the army's pioneer aerial photographers. (Among other things he directed the photography of the bombing of the *Ostfriedland.*) He commanded the 6th Photo Section at Camp Nichols in 1927-29, during which time he photographed much of north Luzon for map makers at the Coast and Geodetic Survey, and prepared mosaics of Corregidor and Bataan for the army. Goddard's arrival in the Philippines and subsequent photographic missions were thoroughly covered in the Manila press and such journals as *National Geographic.* Goddard collected and photocopied articles about his activities and placed them in a bound volume titled "Pioneering Years in Aerial Photography," a copy of which can be seen in the Library of Congress's rare book room.

**233A**   Hudson, James J. "Captain Field E. Kindley: Arkansas' Air Ace of the First World War." In *The Arkansas Historical Quarterly* 18, no. 2 (Summer 1959): 3-31. Biography of the air service flyer after whom Kindley Field, Corregidor, was named (although the author does not mention that fact) in December 1920. Kindley lived in the Philippines as a boy, where his father was a schoolteacher, and hoped to return to the islands as a squadron commander after the war. Instead, he died in an airplane accident in Texas in 1920, while in command of the famous 94th "Hat-in-ring" Aero Squadron.

**234**   Lahm, Frank. "Early Flying Experiences." In *The Air Power Historian* 2, no. 1 (January 1955): 1–10. Lahm, one of the army's first aviators, found himself stationed with the 7th Cavalry in the Philippines in 1911 and proceeded to open a flying school at Ft. McKinley [see also entry 226].

**235**   Parton, James. *"Air Force Spoken Here": General Ira Eaker and the Command of the Air.* Bethesda, MD: Adler & Adler, in cooperation with the Air Force Historical Foundation, 1986. Pp. xii, 557. Eaker, who piloted one of the first aircraft to land at what would later be known as Clark Field, served in the Philippines from July 1919 to September 1921, at Corregidor, Manila, and Stotsenburg. The author, relying on interviews conducted with Eaker many years after the fact, offers a confused account of Eaker's tour of Philippine duty. (According to Parton, Leonard Wood was the Philippine Department commander in 1920 and later became army chief of staff!) Eaker, Parton writes, led the 2nd Aero Squadron to the Philippines in 1919 and was some months later transferred "to command of the 3rd Aero Squadron" and ordered to establish a flying field at Stotsenburg. This is not the same 2nd Aero Squadron mentioned in Hennessy [entry 227]. Eaker led only one detachment of the squadron to the Philippines, and he did not command the 3rd Aero Squadron.

**236**   Wilson, Donald. *Wooing Peponi: My Odyssey Thru Many Years*. Privately Published, 1973. Pp. 346. Another little-known memoir by an officer who entered the army as an enlisted man with the Maryland National Guard in 1916. Commissioned in 1917, Wilson served with the AEF as an infantry officer until his transfer to the air service in 1918. Wilson was stationed at Nichols Field from 1927 to 1929, during that time visiting Baguio, China and Japan. His comments on service in the Philippines are extensive but about Filipinos he mentions little more than that the servants could be entertaining.

### Enlisted Men

**237**   Arbon, Lee. *They Also Flew: The Enlisted Pilot Legacy, 1912–1942*. Washington and London: Smithsonian Institution Press, 1992. Pp. xxii, 264. Includes a biography of the army's first enlisted pilot, Vernon Lee Burge (enlisted 1907), who learned to fly in the Philippines in 1912. Burge's first tour of duty in the islands, at Forts McKinley and Mills from February 1912 to January 1915, receives an entire chapter, and the author also devotes several paragraphs to Burge's subsequent tours of duty (as a commissioned officer), at Kindley Field on Corregidor in 1923-25 and with the 4th Composite Group at Nichols Field from October 1929 to September 1932. Based on Burge's unpublished memoirs, "Early History of Army Aviation," and documents in the possession of Burge's family. Philippine duty must have agreed with Burge. He once (1915) tried to obtain a commission in the Philippine Scouts but failed the commissioning examination.

**238**   Herron, Don. *Willeford*. Tucson, AZ: Dennis McMillan Publications, 1997. Pp. 469. Study of the writings of the late Charles Willeford, college English instructor and writer of detective fiction whose publications include an account of two years spent as an airman in the Philippines in the 1930s [next entry]. Herron includes additional material on Willeford's Philippine years and reprints several photographs taken in the vicinity of Stotsenburg and Clark Field in 1937.

**239**   Willeford, Charles. *Something About a Soldier*. New York: Random House, 1986. Pp. 255. Ribald look at enlisted life in the Philippines, where the author served from October 1936 to October 1938 with the 3rd Pursuit Squadron, first at Clark and then at Nichols [see also previous entry].

Note: A number of well-known air service officers who have been the subject of biographies, such as Henry Arnold, Benjamin Foulois, and "Billy" Mitchell, also served in the Philippines, but they were not air corps officers at the time. Their biographies are listed under "US Army in the Prewar Philippines."

# United States Naval Forces in the Prewar Philippines

## GENERAL HISTORIES

**240**   Braisted, William Reynolds. *The United States Navy in the Pacific, 1897–1909.* Austin, TX: University of Texas Press, 1958. Pp. xii, 282. The author's comprehensive treatment of the navy's role in shaping American policy in the Far East includes a look at the navy's plans for placing a fleet in Philippine waters. Early in the century, one-third of the navy's capital ships were found in the Asiatic Fleet, but within a few years the "fleet" had been reduced to a collection of smaller craft capable of patrolling Philippine waters or "showing the flag" in China. Navy efforts to establish a well-fortified base in the islands (initially at Guimaras and then at Subic Bay) fared no better.

**241**   Braisted, William Reynolds. *The United States Navy in the Pacific, 1909–1922.* Austin, TX: University of Texas Press, 1971. Pp. xii, 741. In this sequel to the previous entry, the author focuses more broadly on naval activities on both sides of the Pacific Ocean, but controversies concerning defense of the Philippines and pre and postwar plans for relieving (or consigning to its fate) the army and navy garrisons in the islands are covered in depth.

**242**   Carlisle, Sheila, ed. *U.S. Naval Cryptographic Activities in the Philippines Prior to World War II.* Laguna Hills, CA: Aegean Park Press, [1994]. Pp. v, 102. This history of the navy's radio-interception of Japanese naval radio traffic is a commercial publication of an unclassified 1981 navy document titled "U.S. Naval Pre-World War II Radio Intelligence Activities in the Philippine Islands." Using extracts from official reports, it traces the activities of intercept station "C" [Cast] from its establishment in Olongapo in 1930, to a specially built tunnel on Corregidor in October 1940, to the evacuation of the remaining members of the intercept unit by submarine on 8 April 1942. The navy had first raised the idea of locating the station on Corregidor in 1933, but the army had refused, contending that the sailors' higher pay would lower the soldiers' morale. Appendices include a list of personnel assigned to radio intelligence activities in the Philippines from 1934 to 1942, equipment used, and diagrams of the "Cast" tunnel on

Corregidor, drawn from memory by a sailor who served there, since no official diagrams appear to exist in navy records.

**243**    Lewis, Graydon A., ed. *Intercept Station "C": From Olongapo Through the Evacuation of Corregidor, 1929–1942*. Denver, CO: Naval Cryptologic Veterans Association, 1983. Pp. v, 83. The navy established a unit at Olongapo to intercept Japanese radio transmissions in 1929. Station "C," as the Olongapo station was known ("A" was in Shanghai and ceased operating in December 1940; "B" was on Guam), relocated to Mariveles in 1935, to Cavite the following year, and to Corregidor at the end of 1939. (Dates given by Lewis for the unit's establishment and relocations differ slightly from Carlisle [previous entry], because Lewis used dates of authorization, while Carlisle provides the dates events actually took place.) This booklet provides a short history of the unit interspersed with veterans' reminiscences. It includes a diagram of the now-destroyed navy communications tunnel on Corregidor's Monkey Point.

**244**    Miller, Edward S. *War Plan Orange: The U.S. Strategy to Defeat Japan, 1897–1945*. Annapolis, MD: Naval Institute Press, 1991. Pp. xv, 509. Comprehensive history of the war plan to defeat Japan ("Orange") focusing on the evolution of navy thinking toward the defensibility of the Philippines and the Philippines' place in defeating Japan. Miller does not examine local defense plans in any detail, however, and his cursory discussion of WPO-3 is based on the army's official published histories.

**245**    Packard, Wyman H. *A Century of U.S. Naval Intelligence*. Washington, DC: Department of the Navy, 1996. Pp. xxi, 498. The author, a retired naval officer, worked on this encyclopedic history of naval intelligence (classified editions of which first appeared in the 1970s) for three decades. Because "the records of DIO-16ND [District Intelligence Office, 16th Naval District] were lost during the Japanese occupation," there is little here on the Philippines, but a close reading reveals some Philippine-related details: a list of Japanese-language officers in the 1920s and 1930s who were later assigned to 16th ND and Cast; an account of the submarine effort to supply guerrillas forces in 1943-45; and the fact that in 1938, 16ND had only one part-time intelligence officer assigned to it. Presumably, in keeping with Office of Naval Intelligence directives, like the other naval districts the Sixteenth increased its intelligence-gathering activities in 1940-41.

**246**    Williams, Vernon Leon. "The U.S. Navy in the Philippine Insurrection and Subsequent Native Unrest, 1898–1906." PhD dissertation, Texas A & M University, 1985. Pp. 353. From the abstract: "The Navy that emerged during the first decade of the Twentieth Century was quite different than that of the Nineteenth Century. The Philippine Insurrection was the crucible of this, the New Navy."

## Biographies and Memoirs

### Officers

**247**    Bartlett, Merrill L. *Lejeune: A Marine's Life, 1867–1942*. Columbia: University of South Carolina Press, 1991. Pp. xix, 214. John Archer Lejeune (USNA 1888), perhaps the best-known and most respected marine commandant (1920-29), commanded the Marine Barracks, Cavite, from April 1907 to May 1909 and briefly assumed the duties of marine brigade commander in Manila. Lejeune's decision to bring his family to the islands was, the author writes, unusual at the time, and "the harsh climate and primitive living" made their tour an unrewarding one [see also entry 251].

**248**    Brownson, Willard Herbert. *From Frigate to Dreadnought*. Compiled by Caroline Brownson Hart. Sharon, CT: King House, 1973. Pp. x, 294. Brownson (USNA 1865) commanded the Asiatic Fleet in 1906-1907, during which time he inspected Manila, Iloilo, and army posts on Mindanao. Compiler Hart (his daughter and wife of Admiral Thomas Hart [entry 458]), includes extracts from his letters home describing his Philippine adventures and appends an account of her own visit to Manila in January 1907.

**248A**    Duncan, Francis. *Rickover: The Struggle for Excellence*. Annapolis, MD: Naval Institute Press, 2001. Pp. xviii, 364. The author devotes only a few pages to Rickover's Cavite assignment but does offer some interesting insights about Philippine duty. For example, Rickover, in charge of overseeing ship repairs, discovered that officers typically padded the repair list so that they could have longer shore leaves in Manila. Duncan writes of Polmar's and Allen's book [entry 253] that it suffered "because Rickover refused to have anything to do with it and discouraged others from helping the authors."

**249**    Dyer, George Carroll. *The Amphibians Came to Conquer: The Story of Admiral Richmond Kelley Turner*. 2 vols. Washington, DC: Director of Naval History, 1969. Pp. xxv/ix, 1278 (continuous pagination). Turner's biography offers a rare published account of joint army-navy operations in the prewar Philippines. Turner (USNA 1908) joined the Asiatic Fleet in January 1928 to oversee development of the Fleet's air arm, which dated to the arrival at Cavite of six Douglas DT-2 seaplanes in early 1924. Under Turner's direction, naval aviators made numerous reconnaissance flights over the Philippines to gather the information needed to defend the archipelago and participated in air maneuvers with local army air units.

**250**    Forrestel, E.P. *Admiral Raymond A. Spruance, USN*. Washington, DC: Director of Naval History, 1966. Pp. xxv, 275. The famous World War II fleet commander first saw the Philippines while sailing with the Great White Fleet in 1908 and commanded an Olongapo-based destroyer in 1913-14. At that time, according to the author, Spruance (USNA 1907) took a keen interest in "Filipino politics and legislative affairs" which stood him in good stead when he served as ambassador to the Philippines in 1952-55. Few details of that interest appear here.

**251**   Lejeune, John A. *The Reminiscences of a Marine*. Philadelphia: Dorrance & Co., 1930. Pp. 488. Lejeune found his two year tour (1907-1909) at Cavite and in Manila mostly "quiet and unexciting," although a sudden decision to mount guns at Olongapo in July 1907 shook-up the normally somnolent marine garrison there [see also entry 247].

**252**   Mannix, Daniel P., III. *The Old Navy*. Edited by D.P. Mannix, IV. New York: MacMillan, 1983. Pp. ix, 294. Mannix's adventures with what he calls "The Bamboo Fleet" in 1907-1908 receive a full chapter in this memoir. Mannix (USNA 1900) explored the country around Subic Bay, saw the sights in Manila, and traveled from Camp Overton to Lake Lanao. "Americans were abysmally ignorant about everything foreign," wrote Mannix, who himself had had an unusually cosmopolitan upbringing for those days. He had lived in China where his marine officer father had been a military adviser.

**253**   Polmar, Norman, and Thomas B. Allen. *Rickover*. New York: Simon and Schuster, 1982. Pp. 744. In 1937-39, Hyman G. Rickover (USNA 1922), postwar czar of the US Navy's nuclear submarine program, was assistant planning officer at the Cavite naval yard. The authors stress the base's limitations as a ship repair facility and repeat an anecdote about Cavite's radio call sign, "BARN," which, Rickover thought, aptly symbolized how the navy brass regarded an assignment there. Rickover later had published his wife's fascinating account of a trip she made through Southeast Asia in 1938-39 while her husband was assigned to Cavite. Unfortunately, she wrote almost nothing about the Philippines. See Ruth Masters Rickover, *Pepper, Rice, and Elephants* (Annapolis, MD: Naval Institute Press, 1975).

**254**   Potter, E.B. *Nimitz*. Annapolis, MD: Naval Institute Press, 1976. Pp. xiii, 507. The World War II Pacific Fleet commander's (USNA 1905) naval career began in the Philippines, where for nearly three years (1905-1908) he captained the gunboat *Panay* and the destroyer *Decatur* in the Southern Islands and Mindanao. Nimitz was reprimanded for grounding his ship near Batangas, but his career did not suffer. Potter briefly describes Nimitz's experiences in the islands and includes extracts from letters Nimitz wrote at the time.

**255**   Regan, Stephen D. *In Bitter Tempest: The Biography of Admiral Frank Jack Fletcher*. Ames, Iowa: Iowa State University Press, 1994. Pp. xvi, 288. Fletcher (USNA 1906) commanded task forces at Coral Sea and Midway before his unsteady performance in the Solomons in August 1942 led to reassignment to a shore billet for the remainder of the war. Earlier (1909-11, 1924-25, and 1931-33) Fletcher served on several ships in the Asiatic Fleet, normally "the dead-end street of naval careers," and commanded Cavite naval station. As commander of the gunboat *Sacramento*, Fletcher assisted the Philippine Constabulary in 1924 in the suppression of a *colorum* uprising in Mindanao. Regan describes the incident using Fletcher's personal letters.

**256**   Richardson, James O., as told to Vice Admiral George C. Dyer. *On the Treadmill to Pearl Harbor: The Memoirs of Admiral James O. Richardson*. Washington, DC: Department of the Navy, Naval History Division, 1973. Pp. xiv, 558. According to this insider's view of the navy high command in the 1930s, one of the navy's "problems" was President Franklin Roosevelt. Richardson (USNA 1902) was relieved as Commander-in-Chief, US Fleet, in early 1941 because he opposed FDR's decision to base the fleet at Pearl Harbor. Here, he briefly recalls his service aboard the *Quiros* (captured from the Spanish in 1898), which patrolled the waters off Mindanao and Sulu in 1902-1903.

**257**   Schmidt, Hans. *Maverick Marine: General Smedley D. Butler and the Contradictions of American Military History*. Lexington, KY: University Press of Kentucky, 1987. Pp. x, 292. The marines' most colorful and controversial officer, Butler (commissioned in 1898 at age 16) first served in the Philippines in 1899-1900. He returned for duty at Cavite and Olongapo from October 1905 to August 1907. In his brief coverage of Butler's Philippine period, Schmidt displays little interest in the major issues of the day, the "bases controversy" (the army wanted Manila Bay to be the major fortified base in the Philippines, while the navy preferred Subic) and the war scare with Japan but describes Olongapo naval yard and concludes that duty there was "pleasant enough" for Butler and his young bride. Butler's own letters [entry 260] suggest otherwise.

**258**   Shoup, David M. *The Marines in China, 1927–1928*. Edited by Howard Jablon. Hamden, CT: Archon Books, 1987. Pp. viii, 155. Although Shoup (commissioned 1926 and commandant of the Marine Corps from 1960 to 1963) was detoured to Olongapo in 1927 for only five weeks before continuing a voyage to China, his observations on the islands and their people are more extensive (if ill-informed) than those found in most memoirs or biographies. Two chapters describe life at Olongapo, a hike to a Negrito village, and a week-end excursion to Manila's cabarets, where sailors drank until the "color line had vanished" and "'swinging the baboons'" became socially acceptable.

**259**   Spector, Ronald. *Admiral of the New Empire: The Life and Career of George Dewey*. Baton Rouge: Louisiana State University Press, 1974. Reprinted, with a new introduction by the author, by University of South Carolina Press, Columbia, SC, 1988. Pp. xx, 220. Scholarly account of Dewey and the navy's role in seizing the Philippines in 1898 and the subsequent naval bases controversy. Dewey championed a navy base at Subic Bay, to no avail. (Dewey's *Autobiography*, New York, 1913 [many editions], says nothing about his Philippine-related activities after his departure from the islands in 1899.)

**260**   Venzon, Anne Cipriano, ed. *General Smedley Darlington Butler: The Letters of a Leatherneck, 1898–1931*. Westport, CT: Praeger, 1992. Pp. xii, 357. Four letters Butler sent from the Philippines in 1906 included in this collection say little about the country or its inhabitants. Butler's main concern was the poor accommodations at Olongapo for both officers and enlisted men [see also entry 257].

**261**   Willock, Roger. *Unaccustomed to Fear: A Biography of the Late General Roy S. Geiger*. Princeton, NJ: Privately Published, 1968, Reprinted by the Marine Corps Association, Quantico, VA, 1983. Pp. xxvii, 321. Geiger (enlisted 1907; commissioned 1909), an early marine aviator who later followed General Simon Buckner as 10th Army commander on Okinawa in 1945, served with the 2nd Regiment of the marines' Philippine brigade at Cavite in 1913. The author describes service conditions at that time, when about one-fifth of the Marine Corps, some 1,700 officers and men, was stationed in the Philippines. Cavite was home to one regiment and brigade headquarters; a second regiment served at Olongapo.

*Navy Dependents*

**262**   Yates, Margaret Taylor. *"Via Government Transport."* Manila: Philippine Education Co., 1926. Pp. 76. Impressions of the ocean voyage by the young wife of a naval officer who sailed to the Philippines aboard the *Chaumont* in July–August 1924.

---

# Military Posts and Naval Bases

## GENERAL GUIDES

**263**   Call, Lewis W., comp. *United States Military Reservations, National Cemeteries, and Military Parks*. Washington, DC: US Army, Office of the Judge Advocate General, 1910. Pp. 508. Describes the area of and the laws by which every US Army post was acquired. There are also editions of 1904, 1907, and 1916 that list Philippine posts.

**264**   Coletta, Paolo E., ed. *United States Navy and Marine Corps Bases, Overseas*. Westport, CT: Greenwood, 1985. Pp. xvii, 459. A five-page entry for Subic Bay Naval Base includes one paragraph on the prewar years. More extended prewar material can be found in the entries for Cavite and Sangley Point. There is also a confusing entry labeled "Cañacao, or Bilibid Prison, Manila, Philippine Islands, U.S. Naval Hospital."

**265**   Gleeck, Lewis E., Jr. *The Manila Americans, 1901–1964*. Manila: Carmelo & Bauermann, 1977. Pp. xviii, 445. Describes Ft. McKinley, Ft. Mills (Corregidor), the Post of Manila, and Military Plaza, home of the commanding general of the Philippine Department.

**266**   Sullivan, Charles J. *Army Posts and Towns: The Baedeker of the Army*. 2nd Edition. Burlington, VT: Privately Published, 1935. Pp. vii, 255. A marine enlisted man turned army officer who retired in 1935, Sullivan first published this compilation of information about living conditions at army posts in 1926. A third edition appeared in early 1942. Each edition included general information about each overseas department followed by details (housing, schooling, transportation, etc.) of each post within the department. The fourth and most easily found edition, published in September 1942, left out all material dealing with posts outside the continental United States. Sullivan served in the Philippines with the 31st Infantry in 1929-32.

**267**   World War I Group, Historical Division, U.S. Army. *Order of Battle of the United States Land Forces in the World War (1917-19), Zone of the Interior.* Vol. 3, pt. 2. Washington, DC: Department of the Army, 1949. Reprinted by the US Army's Center of Military History, Washington, DC, 1992. Pp. xv, 549-992 (pagination continued from previous volumes). Brief histories of the posts, camps, and stations of the Philippine Department are found in one chapter. A fold-out map of Manila shows the military property in the city. This volume also includes accounts of the Philippine Department's activities during World War I and the Philippine National Guard.

## Post/Base Histories

### Army and Navy Club

**268**   Gleeck, Lewis E., Jr. *Over Seventy-Five Years of Philippine-American History: The Army and Navy Club of Manila.* Manila: Carmelo and Bauermann, 1976. Pp. v, 78. History of the once-famous club, based largely on newspaper accounts. Originally located at 238 Calle Palacio, Intramuros, the club moved to its present location in April 1911.

### Cavite/Cañacao/Sangley Point

**269**   Gleeck, Lewis E., Jr. "Sangley Point, Cavite, and the U.S. Navy." In *Bulletin of the American Historical Collection* 21, no. 2 (April-June 1993): 7-29. Brief account of the former naval air station at Sangley Point, concentrating on its postwar history and turnover to the Philippine government in 1971. Includes list of postwar commanding officers, maps, and photographs.

**270**   *Navy Guide to Cavite and Manila.* Manila, 1908. Pp. 130. This guide to things to do in and around Manila was prepared for distribution to sailors of the battleship fleet that was scheduled to visit the city in 1908. In addition to assorted tourist information, timetables (for tram, ferry, and rail), a fold-out map of Manila, and many advertisements, it includes a description of Cavite navy yard and how it had changed since Spanish days.

### Clark Field (see "Stotsenburg, Fort")
### Drum, Fort (see "Fortified Islands")
### Fortified Islands of Manila Bay

**271**   Allen, Francis J. *The Concrete Battleship: Fort Drum, El Fraile Island, Manila*

*Bay.* Missoula, MT: Pictorial Histories Publishing Co., 1989. Pp. 52. Brief text with numerous photos and drawings.

**272**   Aluit, Alfonso J. *The Galleon History of Corregidor.* 2nd rev. ed. Manila: Galleon Publications, 1970. Pp. 86, plus 40 pages of maps and photographs. First published in 1968, this popular tourist-oriented history of the island and battle based on a few secondary sources is in its sixteenth edition (1997). For a critical discussion of this work, see the relevant author entries in Netzorg [entry 19].

**273**   Belote, James H. and William M. Belote. *Corregidor, The Saga of a Fortress.* New York: Harper & Row, 1967. Pp. xii, 274. This is the standard account of the Japanese attack on the fortified islands of Manila Bay, based on interviews with many veterans of the battle. The authors gathered considerable material on pre-war Corregidor and intended it to comprise a significant portion of the book, but the publisher objected. The interwar material is now part of the "Belote Collection" at USAMHI. A portion of it was published under the title, "The Rock in the 'Tween Wars Years,'" in *BAHC* 19, no. 1 (January-March 1991): 26-43.

**274**   Bogart, Charles H. "Carabao Island's Fort Frank." In *Periodical: Journal of the Council on America's Military Past* 12, no. 1 (May 1982): 3-18. Like the author's other articles [following entries], this one is well-researched and illustrated with photographs and a map of the island.

**275**   Bogart, Charles H. "The Concrete Battleship—Fort Drum." In *Periodical: Journal of the Council on America's Military Past* 9, no. 4 (Winter 1977-78): 13-16. Brief account concentrating on the fort's armaments.

**276**   Bogart, Charles H., ed. "Corregidor, The Last Month of Peace: The Letters of Captain John D. Wood." In *Virginia Magazine of History and Biography* 93, no. 4 (1985): 435-55. Excerpts letters CAC officer Wood sent to his wife in the United States from Corregidor in November 1941. Wood died when the "Hell Ship" transporting him to Japan was sunk by a US submarine.

**277**   Bogart, Charles H. "Fort Hughes: Philippine Outpost Duty." In *Periodical: Journal of the Council on America's Military Past* 15, no. 3 (October 1987): 25-40. For this article, the most detailed published description of Fort Hughes, the author corresponded with eighteen enlisted men, officers, and wives who had lived on the island.

**278**   Bogart, Charles H. "Letters from Corregidor—and the Aftermath." In *Periodical: Journal of the Council on America's Military Past* 18, no. 2 (October 1991): 33-44. Extracts of letters written to family members by Major Joseph V. Weaver, MD, and wife from Corregidor, where Weaver was assigned from April 1939 to November 1941. Weaver toured Corregidor again in September 1945 and reported that he could not recognize his former home on Middleside.

**279**   Kennedy, Milly Wood. *Corregidor: Glory, Ghosts, and Gold.* N.p. Privately Published, 1970. Pp. A-J, 211. (Philippine-published softcover edition. There is also a hardcover edition published in the US in 1971 with different pagination.) A tourist-oriented account based upon the standard secondary sources and concentrating on the war years. Includes a discussion of the veracity of the many stories about gold on the island. Many photos, details of armaments, and maps.

**280**    Lewis, Emanuel Raymond. *Seacoast Fortifications of the United States: An Introductory History.* Annapolis, MD: Naval Institute Press, 1993. Pp. xiii, 145. Originally published by the Smithsonian Institution Press in 1970, this short history of America's evolving coast defense systems from 1794 to World War II remains the standard for this topic. It includes coverage (with photographs) of the fortifications of Manila and Subic Bays.

**281**    McGovern, Terrance C. "Manila Bay: The American Harbour Defences." In *International Journal of Fortification and Military Architecture* 23 (1995): 65-109. Detailed guide to the batteries and weapons found on the fortified islands with 1930s-vintage maps, engineering drawings and many "before and after" the war photographs.

**282**    Small, Charles S. *Rails to Doomsday: The U.S. Army's Corregidor and Manila Bay Railroads.* Greenwich, CT: Railroad Monographs, 1980. Pp. 70, S1-6. Knowledgeable account of the fortified islands' railroads and gun batteries by a retired naval officer and railroad enthusiast. Includes reprints of once-classified maps of Corregidor, dated 1936.

**283**    Stirling, N. B. *Treasure Under the Sea.* Garden City, NY: Doubleday & Co., Inc., 1957. Pp. 354. One chapter, "Operation Sunken Pesos," based on official documents, interviews, and published accounts, tells the story of the destruction of currency on Corregidor, the disposal of silver peso coins at sea, and the attempts by the American government and civilian firms after the war to recover the pesos.

Research note: Details of gun batteries of the Harbor Defenses of Manila and Subic Bays can be found at www.cdsg.org, the webpage of The Coast Defense Study Group. For more on Corregidor's history, see the extensive collection of articles and photographs posted at the Corregidor Historical Society website, http://corregidor.org/ct&n_index.html.

> *Frank, Fort (see "Fortified Islands")*
> *Hughes, Fort (see "Fortified Islands")*
> *John Hay, Camp*

**284**    Laubenthal, Sanders A. *A History of John Hay Air Base.* Hickam AFB, Hawaii: Office of PACAF History, 1981. Pp. 199. This hard-to-find history of the army's and air force's recreation camp (more commonly referred to as "Camp John Hay") at Baguio was serialized in the *Bulletin of the American Historical Collection*, in 6 parts: Part 1, vol. 21, no. 4 (October-December 1993): 7-42; part 2 (published out of order), vol. 22, no. 4 (October-December 1994): 73-96; part 3, vol. 22, no. 1 (January-March 1994): 44-79; part 4, vol. 22, no. 2 (April-June 1994): 50-88; part 5, vol. 22, no. 3 (July-September 1994): 84-112; and part 6, vol. 23, no. 2 (April-June 1995): 42-64.

**285**   Reed, Robert R. *City of Pines: The Origins of Baguio as a Colonial Hill Station and Regional Capital*. Berkeley, CA: Center for South and Southeast Asian Studies, University of California, 1976. Pp. xx, 189. Reprinted by A-Seven Publishing, Baguio, 1999. Includes a brief discussion of the establishment of Camp John Hay.

**286**   Resurreccion-Andrada, Bona Elisa. *Camp John Hay[:] How It All Began ... Where It Is Bound*. Edited by L. C. Agnir-Paraan and Alice Buenviaje-Wilder. Baguio City, 2000. Pp. 230. Coffee-table style book with brief text and many photos. Although the name has remained, most of the army-built structures at John Hay have been destroyed since the departure of American military forces from the Philippines.

*Sangley Point (see "Cavite")*
*San Pedro, Fort (Cebu) (see "Warwick Barracks")*
*San Pedro, Fort (Iloilo)*

**287**   Rich, Albert T. *Fort San Pedro 22, Iloilo, Panay, Philippine Islands, 1616–1909: A History of the Ancient Spanish Fort at Iloilo, Panay*. Iloilo: US Army, Department of the Visayas, 1909. Pp. 24. Bound Typescript. The Spanish constructed this fort, which no longer exists, in 1616-17 and used it for many years as a prison. After occupying the fort in 1899, the US Army continued to use it as a prison. According to the author, who was the department intelligence officer, the army added the number "22" to the fort's title to distinguish it from Ft. San Pedro in Cebu. A brief narrative history is followed by extracts from historical works concerning the fort and from documents supplied to the author by local officials. Includes three fold-out blueprints of the fort dated 1892.

*Santiago, Fort*

**288**   Daugherty, Martha Oliver. "The Romance of Living in Old Fort Santiago." In *Philippine Magazine* 29, no. 7 (December 1932): 303-304. Ft. Santiago in Manila's Intramuros served as US Army headquarters during the period of American occupation of the Philippines. A few army families lived there, too. Army wife Daugherty enjoyed the "cozy privacy" shared by the "thirteen young officers and their families" who inhabited the fort. A portion of this article is reprinted in Lewis E. Gleeck, Jr., *The American Half-Century* (Manila: Historical Conservation Society, 1984), p. 319.

*Stotsenburg, Fort/Clark Field*

**289**   Fletcher, Harry R. *Air Force Bases, Vol. II: Air Bases Outside the United States of America*. Washington, DC: USAF, Center For Air Force History, 1993. Pp. xxi, 219. Pages 21-29 cover "Clark Air Base," although the air force had given up the base by the time this book was published. Includes a list of units assigned to Clark before the war and (mis)names the airfield commanders in 1939, 1940, and 1941.

**290**   *Heritage: A Brief History of Fort Stotsenburg and Clark Air Base.* Clark AB: 13th Air Force (DXI), 1968. Pp. vi, 26. This frequently reprinted pamphlet contains short biographies of army officers John M. Stotsenburg and Harold M. Clark in addition to a very brief account of the post's founding. Best for its collection of photos and other reprinted documents.

**291**   Meixsel, Richard B. "Camp Stotsenburg and the Army Experience in the Philippines: A Brief History." In *Bulletin of the American Historical Collection* 22, no. 3 (July-September 1994): 5-36. Based largely on the author's MA thesis [entry 145], this history of the well-known cavalry post focuses on Stotsenburg's founding years. "Camp" Stotsenburg became "Fort" Stotsenburg on 1 April 1929.

**292**   Richardson, Evelyn W. "The History of Clark Air Force Base in the Philippines." MA thesis, University of the Philippines, 1955. Pp. 247. This thesis is a story of opportunities lost. William Lee, "Father of the Philippine Air Force," was assigned to the US 13th Air Force when the author lived at Clark, but she did not interview him nor any of the many Filipinos and Americans who could have served as historical resources. Instead, most of this thesis covers only the years 1946 to 1954 and reads like an air force public affairs guide to the base. About ten pages deal with the prewar period.

**293**   Rosmer, David L., ed. *An Annotated Pictorial History of Clark Air Base, 1899-1986.* Special ed. Clark AB: Ft. Stotsenburg Historical Foundation, 1986. Pp. viii, 608. This fourth and undoubtedly final edition of the book (the first appeared in June 1984 and was published by the 13th Air Force Office of History) is larger than earlier ones, encompassing "the cataclysmic events of 1986" and adding appendices listing units assigned to Clark over the years. Some of the textual material must be used with caution, but the book is an excellent source of photographs. The extensive 13th Air Force history office photograph collection on which this book was largely based was destroyed or discarded as nonessential by departing air force employees in 1991.

Research note: A selection of photographs taken in 1935 of Fort Stotsenburg and Mount Pinatubo can be viewed on-line at www.dreamtrekspampanga.com/stotsenburg.htm.

### Subic Bay Naval Base

**294**   Anderson, Gerald R. *Subic Bay, from Magellan to Mt. Pinatubo: The History of the U.S. Naval Station, Subic Bay.* Dagupan City: Privately Published, 1991. Pp. 98, with 13 pages of appendices (maps, poems, songs relating to Subic, photographs). Engagingly written account of the bay from pre-Spanish times to present, concentrating on its role as a US Naval Base. The author seems well-informed but cites no sources.

**295**   Bogart, Charles H. "Subic Bay and Fort Wint—Keys to Manila." In *Periodical: Journal of the Council on America's Military Past* 11, no. 1 (Spring 1979):

26-37. Despite its objection to the navy's desire to give priority to the defense of Subic over Manila Bay, the army purchased and began fortifying Grande Island (Fort Wint) in 1905. Bogart describes the fort's armaments and its controversial abandonment in December 1941.

### Warwick Barracks

**296**    Quisumbing, Jose R. *The American Occupation of Cebu: Warwick Barracks, 1899–1917*. Quezon City: Progressive Printing, 1983. Pp. xiii, 114. This history of Cebu during the Revolution and under American rule includes an account of the US Army garrison at Camp Warwick (Warwick Barracks from 1905), named after an officer killed in the Philippine-American War. It was occupied by American troops until 1912 and by Philippine Scouts until its abandonment in November 1917. Appendices include units assigned to the post, strength reports, and commanding officers.

The army owned two separate properties in Cebu City. *Order of Battle* [entry 267] makes a distinction between Ft. San Pedro, Cebu, and Warwick Barracks, but the post "returns"—monthly reports listing post activities and garrisoning units—from the army garrison at Cebu City are labeled Warwick Barracks. Some editions of *Call* [entry 263] list Ft. San Pedro and Warwick Barracks as separate posts; other editions combine them.

### Wint, Fort (see "Subic Bay Naval Base")

Research note: Monthly post returns (to December 1916) for all army posts, including those in the Philippines, are available on National Archives and Records Administration microfilm publication no. M617 (1,550 reels). For post names listed by microfilm reel number, *see Military Service Records: A Select Catalog of National Archives Microfilm Publications* (Washington, DC: National Archives Trust Fund Board, 1985 [several editions]).

# Philippine Campaign, 1941–1942

## GENERAL HISTORIES

**297**    Agoncillo, Teodoro A. *The Fateful Years: Japan's Adventure in the Philippines, 1941-45*. 2 Vols. Quezon City: R.P. Garcia Publishing Co., 1965. Pp. xvi/ix, 1075 (continuous pagination). Volume 1 contains a lengthy account of Japan's attack, the battles of Bataan and Corregidor, the Death March and O'Donnell (Capas). The author used many standard sources, such as Morton [entry 334] and

Toland [entry 351], but also relied on unpublished memoirs and knowledge gathered through interviews conducted during the war with "scores of soldiers and civilians on the subject of Bataan and Capas." He purposely did not read Falk's book [entry 530], he writes, because he wanted to see how his conclusions about the Death March might differ. (They were much the same.)

**298**    *Alab Ng Puso: The Filipinos in World War II.* [Quezon City: Department of National Defense, c1996] Pp. 192. Text and editorship credited to Cesar P. Pobre and Juanito T. Rimando. Brief text supplemented by numerous photos that cover defense preparations, the Japanese invasion, the resistance movement, and (mostly) liberation. Includes in addition to contemporary photos, photos of war memorials, Philippine stamps and paper money that depict World War II events and personalities, and ceremonial events relating to the celebration of the 50th anniversary of the liberation of the Philippines (1995). Appendices include a roll of honor (Filipinos awarded medals for heroism) and "wartime heroes," short biographies and sketches of persons ranging from Jose Abad Santos (chief justice of the supreme court who refused to cooperate with the Japanese and was executed) to Luis Taruc (a founder of the Hukbalahap).

**299**    Ancheta, Celedonio A., ed. *Triumph in the Philippines, 1941–1946.* Metro Manila: National Bookstore, Inc., 1978. Pp. xiii, 343. Although some writers have asserted that Ancheta authored this book, it is a published version of a previously unpublished history of the war in the Philippines prepared in 1946 by the Combat History Division, G-1, US Army Forces Western Pacific, Manila. The manuscript's obeisance to Douglas MacArthur made it a source of ridicule to others and may explain why it was never published by the army, although its authors had hopes that it would be. Several pages outline the "pre-war military history" of the Philippines (emphasizing the Philippine Scouts) and tell the early history of Corregidor. Philippine Army officer and historian Ancheta appended an essay titled "a reassessment of the history of the Second World War in Bataan from the viewpoint of a Filipino."

In 1946, the army published the portion dealing with Corregidor separately under the title *Corregidor of Eternal Memory* for distribution to soldiers visiting the island fortress. Another portion of the original report appeared in the Philippine Historical Association's *Historical Bulletin* 14, nos. 1-2 (March-June 1970): 136-80, under the title "The Story of the Philippine Guerrillas during the Second World War."

**300**    Ancheta, Celedonio A., ed. *The Wainwright Papers: Historical Documents of World War II in the Philippines.* Quezon City: New Day, 1980-82. 4 vols. While still POWs, senior American officers of the surrendered Philippine forces began writing unit histories and after-action reports. These were gathered together in 1946 under the title "Report of Operations of USAFFE and USFIP in the Philippine Islands, 1941-1942," by General Jonathan Wainwright. Subordinate officers wrote the histories of their commands, which were included as annexes to Wainwright's report. Researchers owe editor Ancheta and his publisher a debt of gratitude for making these invaluable reports accessible to the public. Volume 1 includes reports of USAFFE, North and South Luzon Forces, and I/II Philippine Corps on Bataan; volume 2 reprints Harbor Defense, Fort Drum, Provisional Coast Artillery Brigade, and Provisional Tank Group reports; reports of the Mindanao-Visayan forces are found in volume 3; and volume 4 reprints reports of the operations of the Philippine Division, the Quartermaster Corps, the Signal Corps, and Finance Department. Morton discusses the genesis of these documents in *Fall of the Philippines* [entry 334].

**301**    Anderson, Duncan. "Douglas MacArthur and the Fall of the Philippines, 1941-42." In *Fallen Stars: Eleven Studies of Twentieth Century Military Disasters.* Edited by Brian Bond. London: Brassey's, 1991. Pp. 164-87. Anderson argues that reinforcement of the Philippines in mid-1941 was a decision "imposed" on MacArthur by Washington, where political and military leaders had faith in the ability of air power to ward off the Japanese. MacArthur's "assurances about the efficiency of his [Filipino] troops" made no impression. The author, a lecturer in the Department of War Studies at Sandhurst whose expertise is the nineteenth-century English militia, has little use for the Philippine Army: "The Philippine 'artillery regiments' were little more than gangs of curious peasants playing with obsolete guns," is a typical insight. Based on a handful of secondary and published primary sources and with too many errors of fact but nonetheless thought-provoking.

**302**    Astor, Gerald. *Crisis in the Pacific: The Battles for the Philippine Islands by the Men Who Fought Them.* New York: Donald I. Fine Books, 1996. Pp. xiii, 478. The author strings together reminiscences of the Philippine Campaigns of 1941-42 and 1944-45, based on interviews with several dozen veterans of the war (civilians as well as military but only one Filipino, described as a "guerrilla section leader") and a few published sources. The Philippine Army suffers its usual fate: 41st Division commander Vicente Lim (his name spelled two different ways) is mentioned three times, two of those to illustrate the incompetence of Filipino soldiers. The sum of this book is less than its parts: not much that is new is revealed here, but there are some interesting stories.

**303**    Baclagon, Uldarico S. *Heroes of World War II.* Metro Manila: Agro Printing and Publishing, 1980. Pp. viii, 344. Similar to entry 305, with an addendum describing Chinese participation in the resistance movement, listing Filipino medal recipients, and documenting the "medal of valor for the hero" (i.e. Ferdinand Marcos).

**304**    Baclagon, Uldarico S. *Last 130 Days of the USAFFE.* Makati, Metro Manila: Privately Published, 1982. Pp. xiii, 277. Day-by-day account of events on Bataan, emphasizing the experiences of Filipino soldiers on the front line. A strength of this book is the author's use of many unpublished or hard-to-obtain first-hand accounts by Filipino soldiers of the action on Bataan.

**305**    Baclagon, Uldarico S. *They Served with Honor: Filipino War Heroes of World War II.* Quezon City: D.M. Press, 1968. Pp. viii, 304. Stories of the bravery of Filipino soldiers during the 1941-42 Campaign and the resistance movement, told largely through postwar medal citations [see also entry 303].

**306**   Bailey, Jennifer L. *Philippine Islands.* Washington, DC: US Army Center of Military History, 1992. Pp. 24. One of the "US Army Campaigns of World War II" series published on the occasion of the war's 50th anniversary. In her account of the 1941-42 Campaign, the author concludes that MacArthur appeared to be attempting to follow both WPO and his own beach-defense plan. (This pamphlet has been placed on the web at http://metalab.unc.edu/hyperwar/USA/USA-C-Philippines.html.)

**307**   Beck, John Jacob. *MacArthur and Wainwright: Sacrifice of the Philippines.* Albuquerque, NM: University of New Mexico Press, 1974. Pp. xix, 302. Using official documents (many of which are reprinted in the text) and interviews with senior officers and former aides of MacArthur and Wainwright (such as chief engineer Hugh Casey, MacArthur's deputy chief of staff Richard Marshall, and Wainwright's senior aide-de-camp John Pugh), the author offers a detailed history of the Philippine Campaign focusing on decisions made by the high command. MacArthur, Beck concludes, was "primarily a strategist" who "aroused professional admiration"; Wainwright "a tactician," who "aroused personal affection." Had MacArthur remained in command in the Philippines, "it is doubtful that he would ever have surrendered." Beck believes that "the decision to give Wainwright complete command of all forces in the Philippines was one of the greatest errors that the War Department committed in its handling of the war in the Philippines." Includes an annotated bibliography.

**308**   Birdseye, James Haven. "Japanese and Philippine-American Logistics: The Philippine Dilemma, 1935-1942." PhD dissertation, University of Alabama, 1993. Pp. x, 456. The Philippine Campaign could use an in-depth study of logistics, but despite its title this dissertation is essentially a retelling of the Philippine Campaign of 1941-42, relying heavily on the Morton Collection [entry 334] and a few secondary sources.

**308A**   Clodfelter, Micheal. *Warfare and Armed Conflict: A Statistical Reference to Casualty and Other Figures, 1618–1991.* Jefferson, NC: McFarland & Company, 1992. 2 Vols. Pp. xxxiv, 1414 (continuous pagination). In volume 2, the author gives the following casualty figures for the 1941-42 Philippine Campaign: More than 5,000 US and Filipino troops died in battle on Luzon; Japanese casualties numbered more than 10,000; total US Army killed and wounded in the campaign was 3,331. See also entries 352A and 356.

**309**   Condon-Rall, Mary Ellen, and Albert E. Cowdrey, *Medical Service in the War Against Japan.* Washington, DC: Center of Military History, United States Army, 1998. Pp. xx, 485. One chapter briefly describes medical preparations for war in the Philippines and problems faced by army doctors on Bataan and Corregidor, and another addresses the medical problems of guerrilla units and prisoners of war. The latter's footnotes serve as a useful bibliography of POW literature. Most accounts state that only one US Army nurse accompanied the *Mactan* [see entries 326, 337, 546, and 609], not two as these authors claim.

**310**    Conroy, Robert. *The Battle of Bataan: America's Greatest Defeat.* New York: MacMillan, 1969. Pp. 85. Brief, stirring account of the battle, with many photos. The author's understanding of army terminology and organization could be improved: He writes of the 57th Philippine Scout "Division" (he means "regiment") and credits the 51st Division, PA, with numbering 25,000 men (it had perhaps one-third that number).

**311**    *Defenders, 40th (Ruby) Anniversaries, 1941–1981 [and] 1942–1982, The.* Manila: Defenders of Bataan and Corregidor, Inc., 1981. Pp. 32. There are at least two versions of this folio-sized souvenir brochure. Both include detailed battle maps and lists of American and Filipino military and naval officers who participated in the 1941-42 campaign, as well as information about activities of the DBC.

**312**    Dod, Karl C. *The Corps of Engineers: The War Against Japan.* Washington, DC: Office of the Chief of Military History, United States Army, 1966. Pp. xv, 759. Military and civilian engineering resources in the Philippines were woefully inadequate for supporting the arms buildup that began in 1941, but airfield and other construction plans were accelerated with arrival of engineering units from the US and a USAFFE chief engineer, Hugh Casey, in October 1941 [entry 113]. On Bataan, engineering problems included poorly trained troops and division commanders who used their engineer resources improperly.

**313**    Drea, Edward J. *MacArthur's ULTRA: Codebreaking and the War Against Japan, 1942–1945.* Lawrence, KS: University Press of Kansas, 1992. Pp. xv, 296. This examination of the process by which army and navy personnel intercepted and decoded Japanese radio traffic and how MacArthur then used the information includes a brief discussion of prewar radio intelligence activities in the Philippines. The army's Signal Intelligence Service operated an intercept station near Ft. McKinley, known as Station 6, and the navy operated a larger facility, known as "Cast," on Corregidor [see entries 242 and 243]. Six enlisted men of Station 6 were left behind to be captured, only one of whom survived the war. This book is also an essential source for the Philippine Campaign of 1944-45.

**314**    Firth, Robert H. *A Matter of Time: Why the Philippines Fell.* Walnut, CA: Privately Published, 1981. Pp. iii, 139. Revised and enlarged edition of the author's *Why the Philippines Fell: The Japanese Invasion, 1941–1942* (1962). Brief, well-written, study based on secondary sources that asks the usual questions about the Philippine Campaign. The author concludes that despite errors in judgment (such as believing his troops could stop the Japanese on the invasion beaches), unlike some other commanders in the darkest days of the war, MacArthur "did not lose his courage or will-power."

**315**    Green, Michael. *MacArthur in the Pacific, from the Philippines to the Fall* *of Japan.* Osceola, WI: Motorbooks International, 1996. Pp. 160. Picture history of MacArthur and his armies during the war. The 200 photos in this book illustrate the American and Japanese land and naval weapons (tanks, half-tracks, guns, landing craft, ships) used in the 1941-42 and 1944-45 Philippine Campaigns.

**316**   Griffin, Marcus, and Eva Jane Matson. *Heroes of Bataan, Corregidor and Northern Luzon.* 2nd and enlarged ed. Carlsbad, NM: Privately Published, 1989. Pp. 230. The first edition appeared in 1946. Includes hundreds of unit and individual photographs of American veterans of the Philippine Campaign, concentrating on the 200th CAC.

**317**   Hanson, John F. "Bataan: A Critical Study." MA thesis, Mississippi State University, 1975. Pp. vii, 140. The author evaluates the conduct of operations by American and Japanese forces in the Bataan campaign in light of "the principles of war" as given in US Army Field Manual 100-105.

**318**   Hartendorp, A.V.H. *The Japanese Occupation of the Philippines.* Manila: Bookmark, 1967. 2 Vols. Pp. xvi/vii, 662/682. This is a detailed account of the experiences of the civilian internees at the University of Santo Tomas in Manila during the war, but volume one also includes sections describing the experiences of civilian refugees on Bataan and of the US Army nurses on Bataan and Corregidor. Also reprints portions of a diary kept by a nurse at Ft. Stosenburg from 8 to 14 December 1941.

**319**   Hersey, John. *Men on Bataan.* New York: Alfred A. Knopf, 1943. Pp. 314. General MacArthur, who was not much in evidence on Bataan, wages a one-man war against the Japanese. Hersey's book, which James [entry 94] thought to be one of the best of the early MacArthur biographies, includes much on MacArthur's prewar years, too.

**320**   *History of the Defenders of the Philippines, Guam and Wake Islands, 1941-1945.* Paducah, KY: Turner Publishing, 1991. Pp. 256. Short histories of army and navy units in the Philippines in 1941-42 are followed by "special stories" in which veterans of the campaign recall events of the war and imprisonment. Biographical sketches and photos of all members of the American Defenders of Bataan and Corregidor who cared to submit them conclude the book (pp. 105-237), which is richly illustrated with photos and maps.

**321**   Holbrook, Stewart H. *None More Courageous: American War Heroes of Today.* New York: The Macmillan Co., 1942. Pp. x, 245. Recounts deeds of valor of American heroes on Bataan, including medals of honor winners Lt. Alexander Ninninger and Sgt. Jose Calugas, and Bataan's "One Man Army," Capt. Arthur Wermuth (leaving out the detail that the war began with military police officer Wermuth in an army stockade awaiting court martial).

**322**   Jamboy, Evelyn M. *The Resistance Movement in Lanao, 1942–1945.* Edited by Luis Q. Lacar and Gabino T. Puno. Iligan City: MSU-Iligan Institute of Technology, 1985. Pp. 124. (This author's name is variously given as Evelyn M. Jamboy or Evelyn Mallillin-Jamboy.) This book, the published version of the author's MA thesis (University of the Philippines, 1982), describes the mobilization and training of the 101st PA Division and the Japanese attack on the Lake Lanao region. Includes information about Guy Fort not found elsewhere.

**323** Jose, Ricardo T. *et al. The Japanese Occupation.* Metro Manila: Asia Publishing and Reader's Digest, 1998. Pp. 303. This is volume seven of the ten-volume series *Kasaysayan: The Story of the Filipino People.* Jose wrote the main text and other authors contributed brief essays in their areas of expertise. The profuse illustrations depict preparations for war, the fighting, and Japanese occupation.

**324** Jose, Ricardo T., and Lydia Yu-Jose. *The Japanese Occupation of the Philippines: A Pictorial History.* Makati, Metro Manila: Ayala Foundation, Inc., 1997. Pp. vii, 258. Includes dozens of photographs of preparations for war and of the 1941-42 Campaign, some of which are common but many others rare or seldom seen in English-language publications. One aerial photo shows bombs exploding on Clark Field on 8 December 1941.

**325** Katz, Phillip P. *World War II in the Philippines: A Pictorial Review.* Edited by Eugene J. Adams. Makati: Privately Published, c1994. Pp. viii, 140. Includes a few, mostly common, photographs of the 1941-42 campaign.

**326** Korson, George. *At His Side: The Story of the American Red Cross Overseas in World War II.* New York: Coward-McCann, Inc., 1945. Pp. xiv, 322. One chapter describes the voyage of the *Mactan* [see also entries 309, 337, 546, and 609].

**327** Leighton, Richard M., and Robert W. Coakley. *Global Logistics and Strategy, 1940–1943.* Washington, DC: Office of the Chief of Military History, Department of the Army, 1955. Pp. xxii, 780. The decision to reinforce the islands in 1941, the authors conclude, was made without much thought given to the logistical problems involved in the context of a global military buildup.

**328** *"Magic" Background to Pearl Harbor.* 5 vols. (in 8 parts). Washington, DC: Department of Defense, United States of America, 1977. Intelligence obtained from the interception and decrypting of Japanese world-wide diplomatic messages was given the code name "Magic." The published version of a once-classified study completed in 1946, these volumes "contain a major part of the communications intelligence which the US derived from intercepted Japanese communications during World War II." The volumes summarize (in chronological order) intercepted message traffic dealing with intelligence gathering activities of the Japanese consul in Manila, and other Japanese agents. Accompanying appendices reprint the original messages.

**329** Manikan, Gamaliel L. *Guerilla [sic] Warfare on Panay Island in the Philippines.* Manila: Sixth Military District Veterans Foundation, 1977. Pp. lxii, 756. This exhaustive history of the guerrilla war on Panay, Guimaras, and Romblon Islands (6th Military District) fought by forces under the command of Lt. Col. Macario Peralta, Jr., includes a good general overview of Commonwealth-era military developments, mobilization of the 61st PA Division in 1941, and the Japanese invasion. Of particular interest is the lengthy account of the refusal of Peralta (and most Filipino officers and men) to surrender when ordered to do so in May 1942. Peralta recalled that the refusal to surrender and commence guerrilla war was based, in part, on MacArthur's authorization to wage a guerrilla war and on knowledge that most Japanese troops had been redeployed outside the Philippines. Includes "situation maps" of Filipino, American, and Japanese troop positions on Panay.

**330**   Masi, Anthony. "MacArthur's Defense of the Philippines in the Perspective of the United States Press." MA thesis, University of Maryland, 1968. Pp. iii, 142. Interesting juxtaposition of the events of the Philippine Campaign with press response in the United States, drawing on sixty-three newspapers from virtually every state. Reprints the "order to kill Bataan captives" given in Jimbo Nobuhiko [entries 522 and 584], a letter to the author from Stanley Falk [entry 530] questioning the authenticity of the order, and a letter from Clifford Bluemel explaining how he came to know of the order. In this letter, Bluemel also defends the conduct of the Philippine Army which, he states, did better under the circumstances than its critics would have done.

**331**   Matloff, Maurice, and Edwin M. Snell. *Strategic Planning for Coalition Warfare, 1941–1942*. Washington, DC: Office of the Chief of Military History, Department of the Army, 1953. Pp. xvi, 454. Includes a brief discussion of Pacific war plans and the decision to reinforce the Philippines in late 1941.

**332**   Morris, Eric. *Corregidor: The End of the Line*. New York: Military Heritage Press, 1982. Pp. xviii, 528. Also published by Stein and Day, NY, 1981. This account of the fighting on Bataan and Corregidor (mostly Bataan) is based on interviews with forty American veterans and several civilians. Two served with Philippine Army units: Maj. Paul Ashton as a surgeon with the 21st Division and Capt. Winston Jones with the 41st Division's field artillery. The first three chapters describe prewar army life in "A Soldier's Paradise" and the preparations for war.

**333**   Morton, Louis. "The Decision to Withdraw to Bataan." In *Command Decisions*, ed. Kent Roberts Greenfield, 110-28. New York: Harcourt, Brace and Co., 1959. An edition of this book was published under the same title by the Office of the Chief of Military History, Washington, DC, in 1960 (subsequently reprinted), and the individual chapters were reprinted as pamphlets by the US Army Center of Military History, Washington, DC, in 1990. This article consists of extracts from *Fall of the Philippines* [next entry] and a conclusion contrasting MacArthur's actions in 1941-42 with General Tomoyuki Yamashita's defense strategy in 1944-45. (This chapter has been placed on the web at http://www.army.mil/cmh-pg/books/70-7_06.htm.)

**334**   Morton, Louis. *The Fall of the Philippines*. Washington, DC: Office of the

Chief of Military History, Department of the Army, 1953. Pp. xvii, 626. Confronting a dearth of official documents (either destroyed in 1941-42 or kept beyond Morton's reach by MacArthur), Morton and other army researchers gathered documents, questionnaires, diaries, and other first-hand accounts from officers who had served in the Philippine Campaign to prepare this comprehensive and still unsurpassed account of the war in the Philippines in 1941-42. Morton's book serves as the basis for virtually all other histories of the Philippine Campaign but has not been without its critics. While concluding that Morton's book was "the most detailed, informative, and scholarly history" yet written of the Philippine Campaign, Beck [entry 307] thought that Morton's "conclusions concerning the Clark Field disaster and Quezon's neutralization proposal [were] incomplete and misleading" and that Morton hesitated to address "controversy and human blunders." The documents Morton collected now form the "Morton Collection" at USAMHI. The original manuscript copy of the history, critiques of the book by army historians and senior veterans of the campaign, and additional primary source material can also be found in Background Papers for the U.S. Army in World War II (see appendix 2), which form part of Record Group 319 at the US National Archives, College Park, Maryland. (This book has been placed on the web at http://metalab.unc.edu/hyperwar/USA/USA-P-PI.htm.)

**335**     Morton, Louis. *Strategy and Command: The First Two Years.* Washington, DC: Office of the Chief of Military History, Department of the Army, 1962. Pp. xxii, 761. Portions of this book consist of a synopsis of the author's *Fall of the Philippines* [previous entry], with some additional research carried out after *Fall's* publication.

**336**     Mullins, Wayman C., ed. *1942: "Issue in Doubt."* Austin, TX: Eakin Press, 1994. Pp. xx, 310. Collection of first-person and historians' accounts of the first year of the Pacific war presented at a 1992 "Symposium on the War in the Pacific" sponsored by the Admiral Nimitz Museum, San Antonio, Texas. Includes recollections by Philippine veterans Donald Wills (26th Cavalry), Joseph Moore (20th Pursuit Squadron), Wallace Fields (co-pilot of one of the B-17s that evacuated Quezon's party from Mindanao), Hattie Brantley (army nurse captured on Corregidor), Thomas Moorer (Patrol Wing 10), and Cecil King, Jr. (Admiral Hart's staff).

**337**     Noyer, William L. *Mactan: Ship of Destiny.* Fresno, CA: Rainbow Press, 1979. Pp. vi, 114. The *Mactan* was a small, forty-two years' old inter-island steamer hired by the Red Cross at the army's behest to carry 224 seriously wounded American and Filipino soldiers from Manila to Australia (about half of whom would return to active duty). For this day-by-day account of the journey (31 December 1941 to 27 January 1942), the author interviewed many of the persons who made the trip including Filipino nurses and crewmen. Appendices include a list of passengers and reprints official correspondence relating to the hiring of the ship and its journey [see also entries 309, 326, 546, and 609].

**338**     Office of the Chief Engineer, General Headquarters, Army Forces, Pacific.

*Engineers of the Southwest Pacific, 1941–1945*. Washington, DC, 1948-59. 8 Vols. Each volume in this series (except volume four, "Amphibian Engineer Operations") devotes a chapter or appendix to engineer activities in the defense of the Philippines in 1941-42. They include excellent maps and photographs. According to the Office of History, US Army Corps of Engineers, the proposed volume five of this series, "Combat Engineer Operations," was never written.

**339**   *Reports of General MacArthur*. 2 vols., in 4 parts. Published by the army in 1966, and reprinted by the Center of Military History, Washington, DC, in 1994. Maj. Gen. Charles Willoughby oversaw the preparation by the General Staff, GHQ, in Tokyo between 1945 and 1951 of this "official history" of MacArthur's Pacific campaigns. The study remained unpublished for fifteen years at MacArthur's behest, according to the army, "because he believed [it] needed further editing and correction of some inaccuracies." Others, such as Edward Drea [entry 313] suggest that the work's "uncritical approach and selective use of documentation" prevented its publication. Two of the four parts are pertinent to study of the Philippine Campaign of 1941-42:

1) *The Campaigns of MacArthur in the Pacific*, Vol. 1, Pp. xv, 490. Commences with "The Japanese offensive in the Pacific" and concludes with "Japan's Surrender." A few pages on the Philippine Campaign are included in chapter one, and a separate chapter describes guerrilla activities in the Philippines.

2) *Japanese Operations in the Southwest Pacific Area*, Vol. 2, pt. 1. Pp. xiii, 363. Based on Japanese demobilization bureau records, this volume begins with prewar Japanese military preparations and concludes with Japanese defense plans for the Philippines on the eve of the 1944 Leyte landing. There are a few comments on Japanese intelligence activities in the Philippines in 1940-41 and a lengthier discussion of the Philippine Campaign from Japanese records and interrogation of Japanese officers. Includes detailed maps of the Japanese advance and reproductions of Japanese battle paintings, showing the attack on Clark Field, fighting on Corregidor, and Wainwright surrender ceremony.

The two remaining parts of *Reports* do not include information about the first Philippine Campaign. They are 1) Vol. 1, supplement, *MacArthur in Japan: The Occupation, Military Phase*; and 2) Vol. 2, pt. 2, *Japanese Operations in the Southwest Pacific Area* (from October 1944 to the end of the war).

**340**   Rutherford, Ward. *Fall of the Philippines*. New York: Ballantine Books, Inc., 1971. Pp. 160. Campaign book no. 16 in Ballantine's "Illustrated History of the Violent Century" series. Brief account of the Philippine Campaign, copiously illustrated with photographs, drawings of weapons, and maps.

**341**   Salazar, Generoso P., Fernando R. Reyes, and Leonardo Q. Nuval. *Defense, Defeat and Defiance*. Manila: Veterans Federation of the Philippines, 1994. Pp. xvi, 792. This was the first in a six-volume series published by the VFP under the general title, *WW [sic] II in the Philippines*. To quote from the introduction: "This is the first Philippine attempt to write about World War II in the Philippines with special emphasis on the role that the Filipino people played." Volume one includes a lengthy chronology of events and reprints USAFFE/USFIP reports [see entry 300]. Appendices include a list of prisoners at New Bilibid (Muntinglupa), Villamor's 1943 report of Philippine activities [see entry 64], and a list of submarine voyages to the Philippines during the war. The other volumes in the series are (listed next):

**342**   Salazar, Generoso P., Fernando R. Reyes, and Leonardo Q. Nuval. *The Last Journey*. Manila: Veterans Federation of the Philippines, 1994. Pp. xii, 897. Volume two lists the names of 25,803 Philippine Army soldiers who died at Capas (O'Donnell) prison camp in 1942 and were reinterred at the Philippine military cemetery at Fort Bonifacio (*Libingan ng mga Bayani*).

**343**   Salazar, Generoso P., Fernando R. Reyes, and Leonardo Q. Nuval. *Batanes and North Luzon*. Manila: Veterans Federation of the Philippines, 1994. Pp. 500. This was the third volume in the series but was unnumbered. It deals largely, though not exclusively, with guerrilla activities in 1944-45 and includes a reprint of Volckmann's 1945 "After Battle Report" [see entry 439] and a list of guerrillas killed in action.

**344**   Salazar, Generoso P., Fernando R. Reyes, and Leonardo Q. Nuval. *Manila, Bicolandia, and the Tagalog Provinces*. Manila: Veterans Federation of the Philippines, 1995. Pp. ix, 476. Volume four also deals mostly with guerrilla activities but includes a reprint of the Report of the South Luzon Force [see entry 300].

**345**   Reyes, Fernando R., and Leonardo Q. Nuval. *The Luzon Central Plain, Zambales, Bataan, and Corregidor*. Manila: Veterans Federation of the Philippines, 1996. Pp. xi, 366. Volume five provides an overview of the war in Central Luzon based on published accounts and reprints Wainwright's USAFFE/USFIP report [see entry 300]. The authors state that there are no Philippine Army casualty rosters available for the period December 1941 to April 1942. However, "Japanese Monograph no. 1" [see entry 517], estimated that 2,098 officers and enlisted men of the Philippine Army were killed in action on Bataan and Corregidor.

**346**   Reyes, Fernando R., and Leonardo Q. Nuval. *The Visayas, Palawan, Mindoro, Masbate, Mindanao, and Sulu*. Manila: Veterans Federation of the Philippines, 1996. Pp. xi, 489. Volume six largely deals with guerrilla activities but also includes lists of officers assigned to various administrative and tactical units in the 6th, 7th, 8th, 9th, and 10th Military Districts and a list of soldiers killed in action in the 6th and 7th Military Districts.

**347**   Simmonds, Ed, and Norm Smith. *Echoes Over the Pacific: An Overview of Allied Air Warning Radar in the Pacific from Pearl Harbor to the Philippines Campaign*. Banora Point, Australia: E.W. & E. Simmonds, 1995. Pp. viii, 275. This history of the development and use of radar in Australia, New Zealand, and the New Guinea Campaign (emphasizing Royal Australian Air Force activities) repeats a few paragraphs from one of the US Army's official history volumes [entry 350] describing the availability of radar in the Philippines in 1941.

**348**    Stauffer, Alvin P. *The Quartermaster Corps: Operations in the War Against Japan.* Washington, DC: Office of the Chief of Military History, Department of the Army, 1956. Pp. xv, 358. The first chapter discusses quartermaster dilemmas in the Philippine Campaign, relying mostly on USAFFE quartermaster Brig. Gen. Charles C. Drake's post-campaign reports and his unpublished memoirs. The inability to provide adequate food and other supplies to the troops on Bataan and Corregidor was a result of the last-minute decision to "'fight it out on the beaches,'" the Philippine government's unwillingness to allow provinces to be denuded of foodstuffs needed by the civilian population, the hurried and chaotic retreat into Bataan, and, the author concludes, too little prewar thinking about the food needs of a garrison isolated in the distant Pacific.

**349**    Taylor, Frank. *Bataan [and] Corregidor.* San Fernando, La Union: Malayan Printery, 1992. Pp. 88. Brief, straightforward account of the campaign with many photographs (some well known but others less so), based partly on interviews with veterans.

**350**    Thompson, George Raynor, Dixie R. Harris, Pauline M. Oakes, and Dulany Terrett. *The Signal Corps: The Test (December 1941 to July 1943).* Washington, DC: Office of the Chief of Military History, Department of the Army, 1957. Pp. xv, 621. Describes the radar and other army signals equipment (radio, telephone, teletype) available in the Philippine Campaign (including a brief mention of the marine corps' radar at Nasugbu). The authors also point out errors and misunderstandings about the use of radar found in other official histories of the campaign [see also entry 515].

**351**    Toland, John. *But Not in Shame: The Six Months After Pearl Harbor.* New York: Random House, 1961. Pp. xv, 427. Based on interviews with many of the surviving principals—Filipino, American (including some who had not cooperated with Morton in preparing the US Army's official history [entry 334]), and Japanese—as well as lesser lights, Toland's remains the most evocative retelling of the Philippine Campaign.

**352**    Toland, John. *The Rising Sun: The Decline and Fall of the Japanese Empire, 1936–1945.* New York: Random House, 1970. Pp. xxxv, 954. Toland broadens, reprises, and corrects the story he told in *But Not in Shame* [previous entry] based on additional research and interviews. In his earlier work, Toland concluded that "the atrocities committed on the [Bataan] Death March had not been 'purposefully planned and executed.'" Here, he concludes otherwise. Toland's much-repeated claim that 2,330 Americans died on the March is far in excess of Falk's figure [entry 530].

**352A**    United States Army, Statistical and Accounting Branch, Office of the Adjutant General. *Army Battle Casualties and Nonbattle Deaths in World War II,*

*Final Report, 7 December 1941-31 December 1946.* June 1953. Pp. 118. This official army report gives the following casualty figures for the Philippine Campaign, 7 December 1941 to 10 May 1942. The numbers presumably include Philippine Scouts but not Philippine Army. Air Corps losses are included in totals and shown separately in parenthesis: killed in action 1,909 (316); died of wounds 120 (26); declared dead from missing in action status 1,168 (94); captured 25,580 (5,560); died while captured 10,650 (2,951); total deaths among battle casualties 13,847 (3,387). See also entries 308A and 356.

**353**    Varias, Antonio, comp. *WW-II (1941-42) in the Philippines.* Manila: Defenders of Bataan & Corregidor, Inc., 1979. Pp. 361. The author, an officer with the 71st Division, PA, during the Philippine Campaign, attempted to compile a complete list of officer personnel of the Philippine Army and US Army units in the islands and to prepare detailed chronologies for each unit. Many gaps remain, but this book is a mine of information.

**354**    Walker, James A. "The Decision to Reinforce the Philippines: A Desperate Gamble." Phd dissertation, Temple University, 1996. Pp. xvii, 210. From the abstract: "The author contends that the decision to reinforce the Philippines in 1941 was made in order to support America's military strategy of Europe first.... A decision based in large part on the misleading reports of General Douglas MacArthur and in the prowess of the B-17 Flying Fortress" [sic]. A chapter titled "MacArthur and the Philippine Army" summarizes MacArthur's 1936 report on Philippine defense.

**355**    Watson, Mark Skinner. *Chief of Staff: Prewar Plans and Preparations.* Washington, DC: Historical Division, Department of the Army, 1950. Pp. xx, 551. One chapter discusses the decision to reinforce the Philippines, a decision made abruptly and for no readily discernable reason, according to the author.

**356**    Whitman, John W. *Bataan: Our Last Ditch.* New York: Hippocrene Books, 1990. Pp. xiv, 754. The author labels this a "true campaign study" of the Battle of Bataan based on eighteen years of research and hundreds of interviews. He draws no new conclusions and deliberately avoids placing the battle in a larger context, but this otherwise exhaustive account will probably remain unsurpassed in thoroughness. Includes a lengthy bibliography. Whitman does not hazard a guess about the number of casualties suffered in the campaign, but according to "Japanese Monograph no. 1" [see entry 517], the "American Army" (probably includes Philippine Scouts) lost 365 soldiers killed in action on Bataan from 9 January to 9 April 1942; the Philippine Army lost 1,938 officers and men.

**357**    Whitman, John W. "US Army Doctrinal Effectiveness on Bataan, 1942: The First Battle." MA thesis, Command and General Staff College, Fort Leavenworth, KS, 1984. Pp. iii, 134. The author matches battlefield performance of US and PS units (not Philippine Army) on Bataan against then-current army doctrine. Doctrine, he concludes, was generally appropriate but not always applicable to conditions on Bataan, nor, when applicable, effectively applied. Sometimes this reflected the lack of material resources but was also a result of the "defensive mind set" of American commanders and lack of training.

**357A** Worth, Roland H., Jr. *Secret Allies in the Pacific: Covert Intelligence and Code-Breaking Prior to the Attack on Pearl Harbor.* Jefferson, NC: McFarland & Company, 2001. Pp. viii, 214. Following the insight that historians sometimes reinvent the wheel by ignoring long-published material, the author uses the many volumes of *Pearl Habor Attack: Hearings Before the Joint Committee on the Investigation of the Pearl Harbor Attack* (1946) to write a history of the code-breaking activities of the navy's station Cast and the army's Station 6. He demonstrates that some of the intelligence "secrets" made public in the 1970s had been revealed in the Pearl Harbor hearings long before. Also includes an account of the activities of the British intelligence agent in the Philippines, Gerald Wilkinson. See also entries 242, 243, 313, and 379A.

**358** Young, Donald J. *The Battle of Bataan.* Jefferson, NC: McFarland, 1992. Pp. xiii, 381. This is another book by an army officer who thought available studies of the Bataan Campaign inadequate. The resulting work does not approach in depth Whitman's *Bataan* [entry 357] but does complement it with unique photographs, excellent maps, and histories of organizations on Bataan that get short shrift in other accounts.

## Air Campaign

**359** *Army Air Forces in the War Against Japan, 1941–1942.* Washington, DC: HQ, Army Air Forces, August 1945. Pp. 171. A bare-bones narrative describing the reinforcement of the islands and the air campaign over Luzon and Mindanao is provided in this once-restricted publication. This book is presumably the published version of "Army Air Force [or USAF] Historical Study" no. 34 of the same title, the authorship of which is credited to Kathleen Williams. For the two other officially sponsored wartime histories of the air force in the Philippine Campaign of 1941-42, see entries 360 and 361.

**360** Assistant Chief of Air Staff, Intelligence, Historical Division. *Army Air Action in the Philippines and Netherlands East Indies, 1941–1942.* Washington, DC, March 1945. Pp. 300. Bound typescript. No named author but credited to Richard L. Watson, Jr. [see entry 365]. Narrative of events indicated in the title, with considerable attention given to the United States' changed attitude toward the defensibility of the Philippines and the development of ferry routes for aircraft across the Pacific. Useful appendices include "Personnel in first flight of B-17s to the Philippines"; "Characteristics of airplanes in, and to go to, the Philippine Islands"; "Relief of the Philippines," memo. for the Chief of Staff by Brig. Gen. L.T. Gerow, 3 January 1942; "Report[s] on Airdromes under jurisdiction of Visayan-Mindanao Force, USAFFE," 2 February and 1 March 1942 (descriptions of airfields on Cebu, Bohol, Leyte, Negros, and Mindanao); and "An account of probably the last aircraft to fly out of Bataan" by Stewart Robb. His story differs from that given by Romulo [entry 403], one of the plane's six passengers. Romulo mentions only the pilot, Roland J. Barnick, who had discovered and fixed up the old amphibian aircraft. Robb stated that he and several others had started working on the plane late on 8 April and that later "a Lt. Barnick" showed up and said that he was to be the pilot, "provided we could get it going." The last attachment is a copy of Walter Edmonds' [entry 366] interview with Lt. Gen. R.K. Sutherland (dated 4 June 1945) in which Sutherland claimed that MacArthur decided early on the morning of 8 December 1941 that beach defense troops should "`remove immediately on Bataan'" once the Japanese landed. Sutherland explained that MacArthur only planned "to fight it out" on the beaches if the troops had had sufficient time to train, and the USAFFE commander realized that they had not.

**361**    Assistant Chief of Air Staff, Intelligence, Historical Division. *Summary of Air Action in the Philippines and Netherlands East Indies, 7 December 1941 to 26 March 1942*. Washington, DC, January 1945. Pp. 266. Bound typescript. No named author but credited to Juliette Abington. Number 29 of the wartime "Army Air Forces Historical Studies" provides a day-by-day account of air missions conducted, "a record of the units participating, of the bases from which they flew, of the time, the type of planes, estimated results, and where known the names of the crews."

**362**    Bartsch, William H. "Was MacArthur Ill-Served by his Air Force Commanders in the Philippines?" In *Air Power History* 44 (Summer 1997): 44-63. Methodical attack on the claims made by Perret [entry 100] that senior USAFFE air officers were alcoholic and incompetent, and that they and not MacArthur were to blame for the Clark Field debacle.

**363**    Brownstein, Herbert S. *The "Swoose," Odyssey of a B-17*. Washington, DC: Smithsonian Institution Press, 1993. Pp. ix, 212. The "Swoose," now in the Smithsonian's collection, was one of the nine B-17s of the 14th Bombardment Squadron flown from Hawaii to Clark Field in September 1941. The flight and subsequent adventures in the Philippines are covered in considerable detail. Reprints prewar maps of Clark and Del Monte Fields.

**364**    Caidin, Martin. *The Ragged, Rugged Warriors*. New York: E.P. Dutton & Co., 1966. Pp. 384. For two chapters devoted to the air war in the Philippines in 1941-42, the author relied on interviews and "personal recollections kindly made available to the author by participants in the events described," both Japanese and American. Of ground crew at Clark on 8 December 1941, Caidin writes that "many of the men assigned to the air base had bolted in terror for the hills when the first shriek of falling Japanese bombs split the air," which made it difficult to launch missions from the base. Of MacArthur's postwar denial of Brereton's claim to have asked permission to attack Taiwan, Caidin writes that "there are some remarkable phrases in the special statement issued by General MacArthur which reflect not only a conflict with conclusions drawn by other military officials *but also a complete disregard of the facts!*" (Caidin's emphasis). Includes a lengthy extract from Obert's diary [see entries 368 and 453].

**365**   Craven, Wesley Frank, and James Lea Cate, eds. *The Army Air Forces in World War II*, Vol. 1, *Plans and Early Operations, January 1939 to August 1942*. Published for the Office of Air Force History by the University of Chicago Press, Chicago, 1948. Pp. xxxi, 788. Reprinted by the Office of Air Force History, Washington, DC, 1983, with a new forward by Richard H. Kohn. Despite the title's chronological parameters, this volume of the air force's official history of the war includes chapters on the air service in World War I and interwar developments. The reinforcement and reorganization of the army air forces in the Philippines from late 1940 is comprehensively treated in a series of articles written by Richard L. Watson.

**366**   Edmonds, Walter D. *They Fought with What They Had: The Story of the Army Air Forces in the Southwest Pacific, 1941–1942*. Forward by General George C. Kenney. Boston: Little, Brown and Co., 1951. Pp. xxiii, 532. Reprinted by Zenger Publishing Co., Washington, DC, 1982, and by the Center For Air Force History, Washington, DC, 1992. This detailed account of the air force in the Philippines in 1941-42, based on published works and numerous interviews conducted in 1944-45, remains the standard. Includes some material on PAAC activities during the campaign.

**367**   Futrell, Robert F. "Air Hostilities in the Philippines: 8 December 1941." In *Air University Review* 16, no. 2 (January-February 1965): 32-45. This article is held by some to be the most thorough examination of why the debacle at Clark Field occurred.

**368**   Haugland, Vern. *The AAF Against Japan*. New York and London: Harper and Brothers, 1948. Pp. xvii, 515. According to Caidin [entry 364], no journalist spent more time in the Pacific than Haugland. The author, who witnessed MacArthur's arrival in Australia, had access to veterans and official air force documents but has little to say not found in the official histories. Haugland brooks no criticism of MacArthur. The highlight of this history is a lengthy extract from Obert's "diary of fighter operations" [see entries 364 and 453].

**369**   Salecker, Gene Eric. *Fortress Against the Sun: The B-17 Flying Fortress in the Pacific*. Conshohocken, PA: Combined Publishing, 2001. Pp. 464. Detailed look at the aircraft and the experiences of its crews in the Philippines and elsewhere in Asia. The portion dealing with the 19th Bomb Group in 1941-42 draws heavily on Edmonds (misspelled Edmunds) [entry 366]. An appendix lists by number and model the B-17s assigned to the Pacific theater and tells what happened to them.

**370**   Slater, Richard R. "And Then There Were None!: The American Army Air Corps' Last Stand in the Philippines." In *Airpower Magazine* 17, no. 6 (November 1987): 10-25. This article includes photographs of virtually every type—and every variety of every type—of American military aircraft used in the Philippine Campaign of 1941-42.

## Naval Campaign

**371**   Blair, Clay, Jr. *Silent Victory: The U.S. Submarine War Against Japan.* Philadelphia and New York: J.B. Lippincott, 1975. Pp. 1072. Exhaustive, torpedo-by-torpedo, account of the submarine defense of the Philippines, which was, the author concludes, "on the whole, abysmally planned and executed." Includes maps showing locations of submarines at crucial times during the campaign. Abridged and published in paperback as *Combat Patrol* (New York: Bantam Books, 1978).

**372**   Bulkley, Robert J., Jr. *At Close Quarters: PT Boats in the United States Navy.* Washington, DC: Naval History Division, 1962. Pp. xxiv, 574. This history of the development of the PT boat and its use in the Pacific war describes what happened to the six patrol torpedo boats of Squadron 3 (established August 1941) in the Philippine Campaign (with details of MacArthur's escape aboard PT 41 and Quezon's journey aboard the same boat from Negros to Mindanao). Includes a few mentions of the Philippine Army's Q boats. This author's name should not be confused with that of PT boat commander John D. Bulkeley [entry 457].

**373**   Gugliotta, Bobette. *Pigboat 39: An American Sub Goes to War.* Lexington, KY: University Press of Kentucky, 1984. Pp. xii, 224. This story of a Cavite-based submarine and its crew gives one of the few looks at navy social life in prewar Manila. The S-39 went aground on the coastal reef of Rossell Island (east of Papua New Guinea) in August 1942. It is, according to the author, there still.

**374**   Hoyt, Edwin P. *The Lonely Ships: The Life and Death of the U.S. Asiatic Fleet.* New York: David McKay Co., 1976. Pp. xi, 338. Popular and prolific naval historian Hoyt offers an anecdote-filled history of the US Navy in the Far East, from the 1820s to the destruction of the Asiatic Fleet in 1942. Much of the action takes place in China, but there are chapters on Dewey in the Philippines, and the second half of the book recounts the Fleet's (including the personnel left behind on Bataan and Corregidor) trials in the 1941-42 Campaign.

**375**   Karig, Walter, and Welbourn Kelley. *Battle Report.* Vol. 1. *Pearl Harbor to Coral Sea.* New York and Toronto: Farrar & Rinehart, 1944. Pp. xii, 499. Officially sponsored history of the destruction of the Asiatic Fleet in 1941-42 and of the activities of PATWING 10 and the Naval Defense Battalion on Bataan. Includes a photograph and history of the Marsman Building and explains how Fleet headquarters ended up there; list of medals awarded to sailors and marines in the Philippine Campaign; and list of naval service casualties (killed in action, wounded, missing, and prisoners of war) during the first six months of the war, organized by state and territory (but does not include those who were from the Philippines).

**376**   Messimer, Dwight R. *In the Hands of Fate: The Story of Patrol Wing Ten, 8 December 1941–11 May 1942.* Annapolis, MD: Naval Institute Press, 1985. Pp. xv, 350. To provide the Asiatic Fleet with air reconnaissance capability, the navy transferred a squadron (VP-21) of PBYs, large "flying boats," from Hawaii to the

Philippines in September 1939. When VP-26 joined it in December 1940, the squadrons were renumbered VP-101 and VP-102, the former at Sangley Point and the latter at Olongapo. Together they formed Patrol Wing Ten. This is the story of what happened to the men and their aircraft, based largely on interviews and correspondence with survivors. Includes aerial photos of naval facilities at Sangley Point, Mariveles, and Olongapo.

**377**   Messimer, Dwight R. *Pawns of War: The Loss of the USS Langley and the USS Pecos.* Annapolis, MD: Naval Institute Press, 1983. Pp. x, 228. The *Langley*, originally a collier, was made into the navy's first aircraft carrier in 1922. In 1936 it was converted to a seaplane tender and as such served with the Asiatic Fleet from 1939. In what the author calls "possibly the most accurate or the luckiest high-level bombing attack made on a moving ship during World War II," Japanese airplanes crippled the ship on 27 February 1942, while it was ferrying airplanes from Australia to Java. (No one remained in the area to watch the abandoned ship sink, which created something of a stir in the navy at the time.) The *Pecos*, a fleet oiler, was taking the *Langley*'s survivors to Australia when it was sunk by Japanese carrier aircraft. Fearful of being attacked by an enemy submarine, the destroyer that arrived to rescue the *Pecos*' survivors soon fled toward Australia, leaving two-thirds of the men behind in the water to perish.

**378**   Morison, Samuel Eliot. *History of United States Naval Operations in World War II*, Vol. III, *The Rising Sun in the Pacific, 1931–April 1942*. Boston: Little, Brown, and Co., 1948. Pp. xxviii, 411. (Many editions.) Morison describes America's Asiatic Fleet, the Pacific in the navy's war plans, and the fleet's disposition in the Philippines on the eve of war. The author does not mention the Philippine Army OSP's motor torpedo boats but suggests that the accomplishments of the US Navy's PT boats in the campaign have been exaggerated. The author's views are summarized in *The Two-Ocean War: A Short History of the United States Navy in the Second World War* (Boston: Little, Brown and Co., 1963), a one-volume abridgement of the fifteen-volume *History of United States Naval Operations*. Dull [entry 518] writes in his book's annotated bibliography that subsequent editions of Morison's volumes were corrected as more information from Japanese naval records became available; Netzorg [entry 19] writes of one Morison volume: "Frequently reprinted, apparently never revised or checked for accuracy."

**379**   Mullin, J. Daniel. *Another Six-Hundred.* N.p. Privately Published [c1984]. Pp. x, 262, plus appendices. This is a detailed, almost day-by-day, account of the actions of the four destroyers (USS *Peary, Pope, Pillsbury,* and *Ford*) of the Asiatic Fleet's Destroyer Division 59, during 1941-42, based on interviews, official reports, and secondary sources. The author, who served aboard the USS *John D. Ford*, also describes navy life in the prewar Philippines. Appendices include detailed maps of the Division's movements and a list of its 666 sailors, of whom 273 were killed in action and another 160 captured, of whom twenty-eight died.

**379A**   Prados, John. *Combined Fleet Decoded: The Secret History of American*

*Intelligence and the Japanese Navy in World War II.* New York: Random House, 1995. Pp. xxvi, 832. Includes a history of the navy's station "Cast": its relocation to Corregidor in 1939 (with a map and diagram of the station tunnel at Monkey Point), wartime activities, and evacuation of its personnel in early 1942. Based in part on interviews with veterans of the organization. See also entries 242 and 243.

**380**    Roscoe, Theodore. *United States Destroyer Operations in World War II.* Annapolis, MD: Naval Institute Press, 1953. Pp. xviii, 581. The Asiatic Fleet included "thirteen venerable destroyers of the 1917-18 class," known as "four pipers" from their distinctive silhouettes. The author says little about their actions in the Philippine Campaign. This book is most useful for its drawings and technical information about destroyers.

**381**    Roscoe, Theodore. *United States Submarine Operations in World War II.* Annapolis, MD: Naval Institute Press, 1949. Pp. xx, 577. This book, based on the submarine service's unpublished "Operational History," includes a lengthy account of the actions of the Asiatic Fleet's twenty-nine submarines during the Philippine Campaign. Abridged and published in paperback as *Pigboats* (New York: Bantam Books, 1958).

**382**    Schultz, Duane P. *The Last Battle Station: The Story of the U.S.S. Houston.* New York: St. Martin's Press, 1985. Pp. 271. Known as the "Little White House" (or "Roosevelt's personal yacht"), because the President sailed on it often in the mid–1930s, the Asiatic Fleet's flagship was at Iloilo on 8 December 1941. It and most of the Fleet's other surface ships left at once for the Dutch East Indies. Its subsequent adventures are told here largely through the recollections of survivors of the ship's sinking by the Japanese at the Battle of Sunda Strait (where it and an Australian ship escaping the Java Sea happened across a large enemy landing force and its covering fleet). Includes maps, drawings, and photos [see also entries 386 and 463].

**383**    Underbrink, Robert L. *Destination Corregidor.* Annapolis, MD: United States Naval Institute, 1971. Pp. xiv, 240. Tells the story of attempts to bring supplies in (and personnel out) of Bataan and Corregidor and other parts of the Philippines through Japanese-controlled sea lanes and air space by freighter, submarine, and PBY flying boat until the surrender of Corregidor [see also entry 420].

**384**    White, W.L. *They Were Expendable.* New York: Harcourt, Brace and Co., 1942. Pp. vii, 209. Exploits of the US Navy's PT boats in the Philippine Campaign, as related by Lts. John Bulkeley and Robert Kelly, and Ensigns Anthony Akers and George Cox. Concludes with a list of officers and enlisted men assigned to PT Squadron 3 (which included four Filipinos: Serafin Gines, Severo Orate, and Benjamin Licodo of Pangasinan, and Clemente Gelito of Capiz).

**385**    Winslow, W.G. *The Fleet the Gods Forgot: The U.S. Asiatic Fleet in World War II.* Annapolis, MD: Naval Institute Press, 1982. Pp. xiii, 327. The author, who served aboard the cruiser *Houston*, tells the fate of the Asiatic Fleet. Although there is little here about the Filipino war effort, Winslow mentions that the OSP MTBs had the mission of staging "a diversionary raid off Subic Bay, to give the impression that Squadron 3 boats were still on the prowl" on the night of 11 March 1942 when in fact they were carrying MacArthur's party to Mindanao.

**386**    Winslow, Walter G. *U.S.S. Houston: Ghost of the Java Coast.* [Bethesda, MD]: Winslow Books, 1971. Pp. 30. Commissioned in 1930, the *Houston* was flagship of the Asiatic Fleet in 1931-33 and again from November 1940 until its destruction in battle. This is a brief history, with photographs, a line drawing of the ship, and a roster of final crewmembers [see also entries 382 and 463].

## Campaign Biographies and Memoirs

### Philippine Army

**387**    Andrade, Pio, Jr. *The Fooling of America: The Untold Story of Carlos P. Romulo.* Rev. Edition. Manila: Ouch Publisher, 1990. Pp. x, 247. Andrade maintains that Romulo's *I Saw the Fall of the Philippines* [entry 403] "is a collection of invented war stories" and has equally harsh things to say about Romulo's other books [see also entries 404 and 407].

**388**    Apalisok, Simplicio M. *Bohol's Wartime Years, 1937–1947.* Manila: Privately Published, 1992. Pp. xvii, 126. This is book one of a three-volume series, titled *Bohol Without Tears*, dealing with the history of the island of Bohol in the central Philippines. Much of this book describes the guerrilla war, but the author also provides some details of his trainee experience in 1940 and his USAFFE service on Bohol.

**389**    Atienza, Rigoberto J. *A Time for War: 105 Days in Bataan.* N.p. Privately Published (printed by Vera-Reyes), 1985. Pp. viii, 235. Atienza, a regular officer in the prewar Philippine Army (commissioned 1938), served with the 41st Division (PA) on Bataan. After the war, he served as AFP Chief of Staff. Atienza penned these memoirs, which remained unpublished during his lifetime, in 1942 after his release from POW camp. Includes a roster of officers of the 41st Division.

**390**    Bernido, Esteban. *Wartime Recollections.* Cubao, Quezon City: Privately Published, 1981. Pp. 132. The author served with the 61st Infantry Regiment on Mindanao. His battalion commander was Lt. Clyde Childress, 31st US Infantry. When Childress escaped into the interior of the island to avoid capture, Bernido disbanded the remnants of the unit and returned home to Bohol. Much of the book describes guerrilla activities on Bohol.

**391**    Casillan, Marcelo G., Sr. *My Life and Times.* Dagupan City: Privately Published, 1999. Pp. iii, 115. A school teacher, Casillan completed military training with the Reserve Officers Service School at Camp Dau (del Pilar) in 1939 and served with the 31st Infantry (PA) on Bataan. He provides some details of the

Bataan experience (such as how the men augmented their meager official rations) and, quite unusually, of his service with the Japanese-sponsored constabulary bureau, for which he was imprisoned in Bilibid after the war.

**392**   De Leon, Sixto O. *The Jamila Story*. Quezon City: Don Sergio N. Jamila, Sr., Foundation, [c1990]. Pp. 160. Recounts Jamila's ROTC experiences at Far Eastern University, an infantry officer's training course at Camp Murphy (now Camp Aguinaldo) in late 1941, and service with the army finance section on Bataan and Corregidor. Jamila escaped to Panay aboard the *Legaspi* in February 1942 and spent much of the war as a guerrilla on his native Bohol.

**393**   De Veyra, Manuel E. *Doctor in Bataan, 1941–1942*. Quezon City: New Day, 1991. Pp. 102. After five weeks of training at Camp Murphy in late 1941, the author was called to active duty and served in the Philippine Army hospital on Bataan. There, Dr. De Veyra and his colleagues improvised medical treatments for sick and wounded soldiers. He includes an account of service on Bataan and Corregidor by a Philippine Army nurse, Juana Ranada. De Veyra survived the Death March and was released from prison in June 1942.

**394**   Doreza, Primo M. *From Panay to Laos and Beyond: A Soldier's Memoir*. Pasig, Metro Manila: Privately Published, 1994. Pp. 223. The author served for several months in 1941 as an enlisted man with the Philippine Scouts (45th Infantry Regiment and 12th Military Police Company), before being released from service to accept a commission in the Philippine Army's 61st Division.

**395**   Gasendo, Nepali L., Sr. *Vignettes from WW II*. N.p. n.d. Pp. 31. Anecdotes about service on Bataan by a senior enlisted man with the 71st Field Artillery Regiment.

**396**   Gumban, Edgardo T. *Bataan Company Commander*. N.p. n.d. Pp. 119. The author commanded Company G, 2nd Battalion, 42nd Regiment, 41st Division (PA) on Bataan. According to Baclagon [entry 304], Gumban was the only company-level officer on Bataan "who maintained and was able to preserve his diary."

**397**   Jalandoni, Venicio. *A Silent Sacrifice*. Edited by Debbie Lozare-Santiago. N.p. Privately Published, 1998. Pp. 86. Jalandoni, a company commander in the 72nd Infantry, 71st Division, provides a lengthy account of training at Tanjay, Negros Occidental, in late 1941 and some details of fighting on Bataan and of the POW camp experience at Capas (O'Donnell).

**398**   Magtoto, Amado, B. "Rock of Bataan." Pp. 298. Bound typescript. Magtoto, a prewar reserve officer, served as a battalion commander in the 42nd Infantry, 41st Division. He authored this account of its prewar formation and battlefield experiences, considered by some 41st Division veterans to be the best recounting of the division's experiences on Bataan. Reported by Netzorg [entry 19] as serialized in *Mr. and Ms.* magazine in April-June 1981.

**399**   Marquez, Alberto T. *War Memoirs of the Alcala Veterans*. Quezon City: New

Day, 1992. Pp. vi, 157. Brief stories of World War II experiences by veterans from Alcala, Pangasinan Province. Several were serving with the Philippine Scouts in 1941 and others with the 21st Division, the local reserve division. One veteran served with the US Navy in both World Wars. Marquez himself remembers watching General Wainwright's command post being established near Alcala in mid-December 1941. When the army retreated, Marquez scoured the site for souvenirs. A few reminiscences are by veterans of the "Huks and Bandits Campaign," Korea, and Vietnam.

**400**   Nieva, Antonio A. *The Fight for Freedom: Remembering Bataan and Corregidor.* Quezon City: New Day Publishers, 1997. Pp. x, 229. The author, who served with the 32nd Infantry Regiment, 31st Division (PA), during the war, offers anecdotes and reflections about Bataan, Corregidor, and guerrilla life, seen through the prism of fifty years of disappointment and disillusionment over the failure of wartime sacrifices to lead to postwar benefits.

**401**   Ongpauco, Fidel L. *They Refused to Die: True Stories about World War II Heroes in the Philippines, 1941-1945.* Gatineau, Quebec: Levesque Publications, 1982. Pp. 368. Collection of brief articles about Filipinos who saw action on Bataan that appeared over many years in Philippine publications. A strength of the book is the author's depiction of life at Capas (Camp O'Donnell) POW camp, where he was given the task of writing and illustrating the camp's history. The original drawings and surviving prison camp muster roles are now found in the Ongpauco Papers at the Philippine National Library.

**402**   Rio, Eliseo D. *Rays of a Setting Sun: Recollections of World War II.* Manila: De La Salle University Press, 1999. Pp. x, 261. Extensive account of fighting on Bataan by a junior officer who was a member of the PMA Class of 1942 (commissioned December 1941) assigned to the 1st Division (PA).

**403**   Romulo, Carlos P. *I Saw the Fall of the Philippines.* Garden City, NY: Doubleday, Doran & Company, Inc., 1943. Pp. viii, 323. (Also published under the title *Last Man Off Bataan.*) A prominent prewar journalist who became well-acquainted with MacArthur during the general's service as military adviser, Romulo began the war as a Philippine Army reserve officer and was brought to Corregidor on New Year's Day 1942 to broadcast to troops, civilians, and Japanese over the "Voice of Freedom" radio. The book is predictably propagandistic (quoting Quezon as urging the soldiers on Bataan to fight on, for example, and saying nothing of Quezon's request to return to Manila to seek terms from the Japanese), but there are many anecdotes of life in Malinta Tunnel and on Bataan [see also entries 387, 404, and 407].

**404**   Romulo, Carlos P. *I Walked with Heroes.* New York and Chicago: Holt, Rinehart and Winston, 1961. Pp. 342. CPR, best known in the Philippine Campaign as "the voice of the 'Voice of Freedom'" [previous entry] says relatively little about his experiences on Corregidor but credits himself with convincing Quezon not to surrender to the Japanese. Much of the book recounts his prewar experiences as a journalist and editor of the *Philippines Herald*, which became "the voice of … support of Quezon and MacArthur in all they hoped to do for the Philippines." Romulo also has some interesting things to say about the impact of the army's racial attitudes in prewar Manila and their effect on Fil-American relations [see also entries 387, 403, and 407].

**405**   Segura, Maunuel F. *Tabunan*. Cebu City: MF Segura Publications, 1975. Pp. 354. This detailed history of the guerrilla war on Cebu also describes the prewar mobilization of the 81st PA Division and the Japanese invasion of the island. The author, commissioned in 1940 after completing the ROTC advanced course at the University of the Philippines, served with the division's 82nd Regiment.

**406**   Sevilla, Victor J. *Bataan Odyssey*. Manila: Salesiana Publishers, 1988. Pp. 91. (According to the author, a shorter first edition of this book appeared in 1952.) A brief, detached, recollection of fighting on Bataan by a lieutenant with the 3rd Infantry Regiment, 1st Regular Division (PA). An appendix provides a history of the division without mentioning controversial episodes, such as the relief of the division's first commanding general.

**407**   Spencer, Cornelia. *Romulo, Voice of Freedom*. New York: The John Day Company, 1953. Pp. 256. Despite his prominence as a newspaperman and public servant (and despite leaving behind an extensive public collection of documents), Carlos P. Romulo has yet to receive a significant biography. Spencer's is typical of the few that exist, relying heavily and uncritically on Romulo's own books [see also entries 387, 403, and 404].

**408**   Tagarao, Silvestre L. *All This Was Bataan*. Quezon City: New Day, 1991. Pp. vii, 141. The author effectively recreates the feeling of being at the front on Bataan, as a sergeant with the 42nd Infantry, 41st Division. Tagarao served with the sniper unit organized by Maj. Gaylord Frazer (referred to as "Major Roberts," here), an American adviser with the 41st Division who was killed in action.

**409**   Villarin, Mariano. *We Remember Bataan and Corregidor*. Baltimore: Gateway Press, 1990. Pp. xvii, 335. The author, a prewar reserve officer in the Philippine Army who later served with the 2nd Division on Bataan, draws on extensive reading, interviews, and personal knowledge for this insightful account of the preparation for war, the fighting on Bataan, and life as a prisoner of war.

**410**   Viloria, Benjamin Nisce. *They Carried On! Silliman University Men and Women in the Negros Resistance Movement, 1941–1945*. Manila: Veterans Federation of the Philippines, 1998. Pp. 289. The bulk of this book describes guerrilla actions on Negros Island, but the author, a reserve officer assigned to the 73rd Infantry (one of the regiments of the 71st Division, PA, that remained on Negros while others went to Luzon), comments on prewar training and describes the unit's mobilization in December 1941, movement to Mindanao, and combat activities until the order to surrender. Includes lists of American and Filipino officers assigned to the regiment and of Americans at Silliman University.

### Ferdinand Marcos–related Books

**411**   Crisol, Jose M., and Uldarico S. Baclagon. *Valor: World War II Saga of Ferdinand E. Marcos.* Quezon City: Development Academy of the Philippines, 1983. Pp. 115. The authors, both World War II veterans, defend the former-Philippine president's controversial version of what he did during the war. Includes full-page color photos of every medal Marcos was given.

That Ferdinand Marcos goes unmentioned in those histories of the war published before his rise to power in the mid-1960s and in those published after the collapse of his dictatorship in the mid-1980s says a great deal about what he really did from 1941 to 1945.

**412**   *Documents on the Marcos War Medals.* Manila: Office of Media Affairs, Republic of the Philippines, 1983. Pp. iv, 108. This is the Philippine government's refutation of the claims made (and some not made) by journalist John Sharkey in a *Washington Post* article (18 December 1983) calling into question Marcos' medal-winning wartime heroics. It consists mostly of after-the-war affidavits by Filipino, American, and Japanese veterans who confirm Marcos' deeds of valor.

**413**   Europa, Prudencio R. *A Warrior's Rendezvous with Destiny.* San Francisco: Privately Published, 1989. Pp. xii, 127. This thin attempt to rehabilitate the ex-dictator is mostly a reprint of *Documents on the Marcos War Medals* [previous entry].

**414**   Gray, Benjamin A. *Rendezvous with Destiny.* Manila: Philippine Education Co., 1968. Pp. 383. In this telling of Marcos' bravery on Bataan (keyed to Marcos' successful bid for reelection in 1969) as a junior officer in the 21st Division, General MacArthur "insisted on presenting the Distinguished Service Cross to Lt. Marcos in a foxhole" on Bataan, an event not described in MacArthur's own biographies. MacArthur's single visit to Bataan took place before the supposed heroics that led to Marcos becoming the Philippines' most highly decorated soldier. The book reprints many of Marcos' official medals citations (all dated after the war). According to Seagraves [entry 418], Gray's book is "sprinkled with accuracies."

**415**   Hamilton-Paterson, James. *America's Boy: A Century of Colonialism in the Philippines.* New York: Henry Holt and Company, 1998. Pp. xvi, 462. American officialdom accepted Marcos' "self-assessment" as a war hero, the author asserts, because it wanted Philippine support for the war in Vietnam. Filipinos accepted Marcos' claims for more complex reasons involving ambiguity about the nature of collaboration during the war, cynicism about Philippine politics, and of course the danger involved in questioning his claims. (Too, Marcos may well have done at least some of the brave deeds he claimed to have done on Bataan.) Includes an account of Bonifacio Gillego's original exposé of Marcos' fraudulent claims to medals in 1982.

**416**   McDougald, Charles C. *The Marcos File: Was He a Philippine Hero or a*

*Corrupt Tyrant?* San Francisco, CA: San Francisco Publishers, 1987. Pp. x, 345. In part one "Soldier," the author sorts out the conflicting claims concerning Ferdinand Marcos' wartime activities and the legitimacy of the medals he received or for which he claimed to have been recommended. The author concludes that "Marcos the soldier was an illusion" and that Marcos' claims of wartime bravery "appear to be part of an elaborate hoax."

**417**   Mella, Cesar T., and Gracianus R. Reyes. *Marcos: The War Years.* 2nd ed. Manila: Word Experts, 1981. Pp. 190. Marcos wages a one-man war on Bataan, winning every medal from the "Congressional Medal of Honor (Medal for Valor)" on down. Illustrated with photographs of the "Marcos War Murals" and photographs of people who testified to Marcos' wartime exploits.

**418**   Seagraves, Sterling. *The Marcos Dynasty.* New York: Harper and Row, 1988. Pp. 485. Some reviewers took the author to task for seeming to swallow every bit of coffee-shop gossip he picked up about the Marcoses, but Seagraves tells a riveting story. Of Marcos' war years, Seagraves writes that there are two versions from which to choose: "Marcos as one-man army, and Marcos as looter and scrounger (and possible double agent)." He proceeds to lay out the damning evidence for the latter. According to Seagraves, US Army records that undermined Marcos' claims of wartime heroics had been "mischievously [buried] for decades in a midwestern vault" (he apparently means the National Personnel Records Center in St. Louis, MO) until being placed in the US National Archives in the mid-1980s.

**419**   Spence, Hartzell. *Marcos of the Philippines: A Biography.* New York and Cleveland: The World Publishing Co., 1969. Pp. 365. A shorter version of this book was published in 1964 as *For Every Tear a Victory*, supposedly commissioned by Marcos to further his presidential campaign and liberally distributed to American officials and agencies. (Raymond Bonner, *Waltzing with a Dictator* [New York: Times Books, 1987] stated that the text was essentially narrated to Spence by Marcos.) This is the former Philippine president's version of how he came to be the Philippines' most decorated soldier of World War II as a result of his bravery as an officer with the 21st Division on Bataan and as a guerrilla. The author quotes General MacArthur as saying that without Marcos' "exploits, Bataan would have fallen three months sooner than it did" (a statement no MacArthur biographer has been able to confirm). In one part of the text providing the context for mobilizing the Philippine Army in 1941, Spence, a prolific author and founder of the wartime army weekly, *Yank*, achieves the distinction of making a factually inaccurate statement in every single sentence.

## United States Army

**420**   Chynoweth, Bradford Grethen. *Bellamy Park.* Hicksville, NY: Exposition Press, 1975. Pp. 301. The author (USMA 1912) commanded the 61st Division (PA) on Panay and later the forces on Cebu. This memoir of thirty years' military service includes several chapters on the Philippines, including the author's life as an army dependent on Mindanao early in the century. One chapter describes the resupply efforts of the *Legaspi*, an episode "grossly distorted" by Underbrink in *Destination Corregidor* [entry 383], according to Chynoweth, who seems to have felt that the wrong people received credit for supplying the Corregidor garrison. Chynoweth recalls his command of the 61st Division on Panay and then of the Visayan Force on Cebu. He is very, very critical of many of his superior and subordinate officers. This memoir is also filled with information about prominent Filipinos the author met.

**421**   Comello, Jerome Joseph. "Jonathan M. Wainwright: Planning and Executing the Defense of the Philippines." PhD dissertation, Temple University, 1999. Pp. 244. From the abstract: "The author contends that the examination of the experiences of Jonathan Wainwright as they relate to his contributions to planning and executing the defense of the Philippines will further illuminate key considerations in United States strategic planning from the American occupation of the Philippines to the present." Based largely on a few secondary sources.

**422**   Harkins, Philip. *Blackburn's Headhunters*. New York: W.W. Norton, 1955. Pp. ix, 326. First Lieutenant Donald Blackburn arrived in the Philippines in October 1941 and was assigned to instruct Ilocano soldiers of the 12th Infantry (PA), in communications and motor transportation. Later, he took command of the regiment's headquarters battalion and made his way to Manila and Bataan when his unit disintegrated in the face of Japanese attacks. Blackburn escaped with Volckmann [entry 439] to Northern Luzon when Bataan fell, and most of this book describes his experiences as a guerrilla, based on interviews and Blackburn's diary.

**423**   Harrington, Joseph D. *Yankee Samurai: The Secret Role of Nisei in America's Pacific Victory*. Detroit, MI: Pettigrew Enterprises, Inc., 1979. Pp. 383. Another rendition of the Richard Sakakida and Arthur Komori saga who like Sakakida had been recruited in March 1941 in Hawaii by army intelligence and sent to Manila. Unlike Sakakida, Komori escaped to Australia [see also entries 434 and 435].

**424**   Hieb, Harley F. *Heart of Iron*. Lodi, CA: Pacifica Publ., 1987. Pp. xvii, 411. The author comments briefly on life in the peacetime 31st Infantry Regiment, with which he served as an enlisted man 1935-37 and 1939-41. Commissioned and assigned as an instructor with the 71st Infantry, 71st Division (PA), on Negros, Hieb served with his unit on Bataan, escaped from the Death March, and spent the remainder of the war as a guerrilla in the Cagayan Valley (with the 15th Infantry, USAFIP-NL). Most of the book describes his guerrilla activities.

**425**   Hill, Milton A. *Lessons of Bataan*. Ft. Shafter, HI: Headquarters Hawaiian Department, October 1942. Pp. 46. Reprinted from *The Infantry Journal*. The Bataan campaign held useful lessons for troop training, use of tanks, infantry-artillery coordination, and so on. Colonel Hill, who was evacuated from the Philippines due to ill health just before the surrender of Corregidor, also thought it worth noting that

Philippine Scouts could make "beautiful insignia out of aluminum—better than you buy in some shops—and colonel's eagles out of 20 centavo pieces."

**426**   Holt, Thaddeus. "King of Bataan." In *No End Save Victory: Perspectives on World War II*. Edited by Robert Crowley. New York: G.P. Putnam's Sons, 2001. Pp. 155–171. This article original appeared in *MHQ: The Quarterly Journal of Military History* 7, no. 2 (Winter 1995). Brig. Gen. Edward P. King, Jr., commanded Ft. Stotsenburg in 1941 (he had been stationed at the post in 1915-17, as well) and then became USAFFE's chief of artillery. King took command of troops on Bataan when Wainwright moved to Corregidor following MacArthur's flight in March 1942. As such, it fell to King's lot to surrender Bataan, on 9 April 1942. According to the author, when King met MacArthur again in Washington in 1951, MacArthur pretended not to know who King was.

**427**   Mallonée, Richard C., ed. *The Naked Flagpole, Battle for Bataan: From the Diary of Richard C. Mallonée*. San Rafael, CA: Presidio Press, 1980. Pp. xiii, 204. Reprinted with a new forward in 1997 under the title *Battle for Bataan: An Eyewitness Account*. Mallonée (the editor is the son of the diary's author) served in the Philippines in 1926-29. He returned in October 1941 and was to his dismay assigned as "senior instructor" to the 21st FA, 21st Division (PA). This is an abridgement of the two-volume diary he kept of his wartime experiences. When Teodoro Agoncillo requested a copy of this diary after the war, Mallonée refused, explaining that the entries had been written at a time of great bitterness and no good would come of publicizing the opinions he held at that time. Perhaps Mallonée was overly sensitive. His opinions of Filipino soldiers were generally high, but he did feel that officers of the 2nd Regular Division assigned to safeguard the southeastern coast of Bataan were more concerned about their personal comfort than about the state of defense preparations—and says so at some length in the unpublished diaries [copies at USAMHI]. Most of this book—the first 150 pages—details the 21st's part in the Philippine Campaign.

**428**   Lapham, Robert, and Bernard Norling. *Lapham's Raiders: Guerrillas in the Philippines, 1942–1945*. Lexington, KY: The University Press of Kentucky, 1996. Pp. xii, 292. Lapham's "Luzon Guerrilla Armed Forces" was one of the larger and better organized guerrilla organizations on Luzon. This detailed and candid account of the guerrilla war includes a chapter describing the organization of army forces in the islands in 1941 and the shortcomings of American preparations for war. The main one was "psychological": Americans could not believe that they faced a serious threat from a non-white people. The book has some curious errors: Did Lapham (who was initially assigned to the 45th Infantry, PS) really believe the PS had been established only in the 1920s?

**429**   Meixsel, Richard B. "Major General George Grunert, WPO-3, and the Philippine Army, 1940-1941." In *The Journal of Military History* 59 (April 1995): 303-24. Argues that contrary to the usual depiction of WPO-3 as one in a series of war plans calling for an immediate withdrawal of American forces into Bataan,

Grunert, the last prewar commander of the Philippine Department, rewrote the department Orange plan in 1940-41 to make use of Philippine Army troops for a more comprehensive defense of Luzon. Based largely on a chapter in the author's dissertation [entry 81].

**430**    Miller, Ernest B. *Bataan Uncensored*. Long Prairie, MN: Hart Publications, 1949; reprint, Little Falls, MN: Military Historical Society of Minnesota, 1991. Pp. [xi] 403. The author, a prewar national guard officer who commanded the 194th Tank Battalion in the Philippine Campaign, makes little secret of his disdain for USAFFE's senior commanders, whom he felt understood nothing of tank warfare, and the nation's senior leadership, whom he felt had been inexcusably lax in readying the nation for war. A few chapters of the book describe Miller's imprisonment in Japan at Zentsuji and Roku Roshi.

Miller and the tank group commander, Brig. Gen. James R.N. Weaver, gave sometimes impossible-to-reconcile versions of tank group actions in the Philippine Campaign to army historians after the war. Their conflicting views of the campaign can best be followed in the *Fall of the Philippines* file in Background Papers for the U.S. Army in World War II, in Record Group 319, U.S. National Archives.

**431**    Norling, Bernard. *The Intrepid Guerrillas of North Luzon*. Lexington, KY: The University Press of Kentucky, 1999. Pp. xiv, 284. This account of guerrilla forces in northern Luzon in the early part of the war focuses on the activities of Capt. Ralph Praeger (USMA 1938) and Lt. Thomas Jones. Praeger arrived in the Philippines in July 1939 and commanded Troop C, 26th Cavalry, at Ft. Stotsenburg. At Baguio when the Japanese attacked at Lingayen, Praeger led his men north to Cagayan and Apayao provinces, picked up stragglers from other army and constabulary units, and began fighting the Japanese. "Of the original [guerrilla] commanders in North Luzon," the author writes, "Praeger lasted the longest and kept his troop together to the end." Praeger was captured in August 1943 and executed by the Japanese in August 1944. Thomas Jones, an officer of the 26th, was captured and sentenced to death by the Japanese but survived the war. Norling also examines the actions of Col. John Horan, the controversial commander of Camp John Hay at the start of the war, and other guerrilla leaders.

**432**    Ramsey, Edwin Price, and Stephen J. Rivele. *Lieutenant Ramsey's War*. New York: Knightsbridge, 1990. Pp. 333. Reprinted by Brassey's (US), 1996. Ramsey, a reserve officer called to active duty in early 1941, arrived in Manila in June for service with the 26th Cavalry. He later escaped from Bataan and spent the war with guerrilla organizations in Central Luzon. A few pages of the book describe Ramsey's life at Ft. Stotsenburg and sojourns to Manila in the six months before the war. The portrait Ramsey paints of himself as chief of a Luzon-wide guerrilla network is one that not all fellow guerrillas claim to recognize.

**433**    Rogers, Paul P. *The Good Years: MacArthur and Sutherland*. New York: Praeger, 1990. Pp. 381. When newly enlisted Private Rogers arrived in Manila in late October 1941, there happened to be a vacancy for a stenographer at USAFFE headquarters, and Rogers was the only stenographer available. He held this job—talking dictation from MacArthur and Sutherland—for the rest of the war. His observations on the office personalities, albeit as the junior-most member of the "Bataan Gang," make this the most fascinating memoir of anyone who served on the USAFFE staff.

**434**   Sakakida, Richard, as told to Wayne Kiyosaki. *A Spy in Their Midst: The World War II Struggle of a Japanese-American Hero*. Lanham, MD: Madison Books, 1995. Pp. 199. Hawaii-born Sakakida was one of several Japanese-Americans enlisted by the army and sent to the Philippines in summer 1941 to perform intelligence work in the Manila Japanese community. After the outbreak of war, Sakakida interrogated prisoners on Bataan and was captured on Corregidor. Japanese soldiers pointed him out as the "Sergeant Sakakida" who had interrogated them on Bataan, but he convinced the Japanese that he had been wanted by the army as a civilian linguist and had had little choice but to agree. He was eventually made a servant of a Japanese officer, retreated north with the Japanese army, and was discovered by an American army patrol in September 1945. Sakakida retired from the air force as a lieutenant colonel in 1975. The prewar and fighting periods (how he was recruited in Hawaii, the contacts he made in the Manila Japanese community, and so on) receive extended coverage. Sakakida's obituary in the *Washington Post* (26 January 1996) repeated accusations by some that he had been a collaborator [see also entries 423 and 435]. On Sakakida's role during the war, see also Alfredo Roces, *Looking for Liling: A Family History of World War II Martyr Rafael R. Roces, Jr.* (Manila: Anvil Publishing, 2000). Sakakida tells more about his wartime ordeal at www.javadc.org, the website of the Japanese-American Veterans' Association.

**435**   Sayer, Ian, and Douglas Bottin. *America's Secret Army: The Untold Story of the Counter Intelligence Corps*. New York and Toronto: Franklin Watts, 1989. Pp. x, 400. Includes a chapter on the ordeal of Army intelligence agent Richard Sakakida [see entries 423 and 434].

**436**   Schultz, Duane. *Hero of Bataan: The Story of General Jonathan M. Wainwright*. New York: St. Martin's Press, 1981. Pp. xii, 479. Wainwright (USMA 1906) arrived in the Philippine on 31 October 1940 to command the Philippine Division. One chapter examines the year before the war, with the emphasis on war preparation. An earlier Philippine tour of duty (1908-1910) gets only a brief mention in this hagiography [see also entry 440].

**437**   Selleck, Clyde. *The War Diary of Gen. Clyde Selleck, Commanding General, 71st Division, USAFFE*. Manila: Historical Conservation Society, 1985. Pp. 28. Selleck (USMA 1910) prepared these notes on the division's mobilization and subsequent combat service on Bataan, emphasizing the organizational, personnel and equipment shortcomings confronting the division, presumably with an eye toward having the star he lost (when relieved of command on Bataan) returned to him.

**438**   Sorley, Lewis. *Honorable Warrior: General Harold K. Johnson and the Ethics of Command.* Lawrence, KS: University Press of Kansas, 1998. Pp. x, 364. For future army chief of staff (1964-68) Johnson's (USMA 1933) experiences in the Philippines with the 57th Infantry (PS) in 1940-42, the author mostly repeats what Johnson said years later in his official army oral history interview (copy at USAMHI), even though some of those recollections are not credible. Johnson remembered that most Philippine Scout recruits in 1941 were college graduates, for example. Also describes Johnson's experiences as a POW.

**439**   Volckmann, R.W. *We Remained: Three Years Behind the Enemy Lines in the Philippines.* New York: W.W. Norton, 1954. Pp. xi, 244. Volckmann (USMA 1934) served as senior instructor of the 11th Infantry Regiment, 11th Division (PA) and retreated with it from Dagupan to Bataan. He did not surrender but made his way north with several other officers and eventually assumed command of guerrilla forces in North Luzon. The guerrilla motto, "we remained," is a rejoinder to MacArthur's "I shall return."

**440**   Wainwright, Jonathan M. *General Wainwright's Story.* Edited by Robert Considine. Garden City, NY: Doubleday & Co., 1946. Pp. 314. Reprinted by Greenwood Press, Westport, CT, 1970. Wainwright recounts his wartime and prisoner experiences, with a brief discussion of preparation for war in 1940-41. Morton [entry 334] opined that, with the exception of Miller's memoir [entry 430], the publication of Wainwright's account of the Philippine Campaign "very possibly forestalled the publication by other commanders and staff officers of their own versions of the campaign" [see also entry 436].

**441**   Whitehead, Arthur Kendal. *Odyssey of a Philippine Scout.* Tucson, AZ: Privately Published, 1989. Pp. xv, 319. An officer with the 26th Cavalry, Whitehead arrived at Ft. Stotsenburg in February 1941. He was separated from his regiment during the fighting around Lingayen Gulf, made his way to Panay, surrendered and was sent by the Japanese to contact other units that had yet to surrender, escaped to Cuyo Island, where he found members of the 48th Materiel Squadron [entry 509] sitting out the war, and finally succeeded in sailing to Australia with several Filipinos in January 1944.

## United States Army Air Corps

**442**   Brereton, Lewis H. *The Brereton Diaries: The War in the Air in the Pacific, Middle East and Europe, 3 October 1941–8 May 1945.* New York: William Morrow and Co., 1946. Pp. 450. Brereton (US Naval Academy 1911) took command of USAFFE's Far East Air Force, and this diary is his recreated-after-the-fact version of what happened next. Brereton claimed to have repeatedly and futilely requested permission to bomb Formosa early on the morning of 8 December 1941; MacArthur responded that he knew nothing of such requests. Brereton, who mentions that he had served in the Philippines in 1916-17, arrived in Manila on 4 November 1941 (he gives the incorrect date of 3 November in his book) and departed on 24 December 1941 for Java and Australia. Historians have given the book a mixed reception. For a scathing denunciation of both Brereton and his diaries, see Perret [entry 100]. See also entry 452.

**443**   Burt, William R. *Adventures with Warlords: Insight into Key Events of World War II*. New York: Vantage Press, 1994. Pp. xii, 283. As a reserve officer with the Air Corps Plans Division in 1940-41, Burt was involved in the decision-making that sent air corps reinforcements to the Philippines just before the war. He writes that air corps officers paid close attention to the lessons learned by the RAF in the Battle of Britain (and even suggests that Hugh Dowding would have made an excellent air force advisor to the Philippine government in 1941) and appreciated the need to build up adequate support facilities and install an air warning system before sending bombers to the Philippines. However, Secretary of War Henry Stimson and chief of staff George Marshall seemed suddenly mesmerized by the B-17 in late 1941, early enough to rush aircraft to the Philippines but too late to build the necessary support structure to protect the planes and sustain bombing operations. Appendices include Carl Spaatz's 1 September 1939 memorandum for General Arnold recommending the "expansion and improvement of air base facilities in Luzon" and a 1946 statement by E. O'Donnell on "Air Defense of the Philippine Islands in December 1941."

**444**   Fields, John Wallace. *Kangaroo Squadron: Memories of a Pacific Bomber Pilot*. Privately Published, 1982. Pp. 194. Bound typescript. Transcript of an interview with B-17 pilot Fields of the 19th BG's 435th Squadron, conducted by his son, Kenneth Wallace Fields. Fields flew fifty-one missions from Australia to the Philippines, New Guinea, and the Solomons between February and November 1942. He co-piloted one of the three B-17s that evacuated members of Quezon's party (his plane carried 17 passengers, including Valdes and Romulo) from Del Monte on 17 March 1942 and provides a few details of that flight. One particularly interesting item is a ten-page (typed, single-spaced), history of the 19th BG compiled in 1943 by a Major John H. M. Smith, who had joined the group in 1940 and served with the 93rd BS in the Philippines. Smith concludes: "One of the principle shortcomings of the Group during its period of combat was the desperate measure of the Higher Command to attempt to stop the advances of the Japanese [which] resulted in many futile, ill-advised, wholly inadequate attacks carried out by this Group."

**445**   Gause, Damon, with an introduction by Damon L. Gause. *The War Journal of Major Damon "Rocky" Gause*. New York: Hyperion, 1999. Pp. xxxiii, 183. Gause, a pilot with the 27th Bombardment Group, arrived in Manila on 27 November 1941. The group's aircraft never arrived, and Gause found himself serving as an infantryman on Bataan. He was briefly a prisoner of the Japanese before escaping to Corregidor, where he was assigned to the 4th Marines for beach defense. He escaped from Corregidor (with a PAAC officer, Lt. Alberto S. Aranzaso, PMA 1940, who did not survive) to the mainland and then to Lubang Island. There, he met Capt. William Lloyd Osborne, an infantry officer who had also escaped from Bataan. Together they sailed for Australia, where they arrived safely in mid–October 1942. Gause was killed in an aircraft accident near London, England, in March 1944. This book consists of a lengthy biographical introduction and conclusion by Gause's son and the diary Gause kept from the beginning of 1942 until his arrival in Australia, which he edited and polished in 1943 in hope of having it published. Gause's remarkable story is a testament to many Filipinos who stood by the Americans under the most difficult circumstances.

**446**   Godman, Henry C., with Cliff Dudley. *Supreme Commander*. Harrison, AR: New Leaf Press, 1980. Pp. 125. Godman, son of an army pilot killed during World War I, piloted one of the B-17s flown from Hawaii to Clark Field in September 1941 and was MacArthur's personal pilot in Australia and New Guinea. This book is mostly a testament to Godman's religious faith, but it includes some anecdotes of wartime service. Godman claims that another twenty people could have been crowded aboard the plane that flew MacArthur from Mindanao, but Sutherland, who "didn't know anything about B-17s," refused to overload the aircraft. Later, on New Guinea, Sutherland had Godman reassigned to a combat squadron after Godman had an argument with Sutherland's Australian girlfriend.

**447**   Hunt, Ray C., and Bernard Norling. *Behind Japanese Lines: An American Guerrilla in the Philippines*. Lexington, KY: The University Press of Kentucky, 1986. Pp. xiii, 258. Hunt, who had enlisted in the army in 1939, arrived with the 21st Pursuit Squadron in Manila in mid-November 1941 and devotes a few paragraphs to his impressions of the prewar Philippines. Captured on Bataan, Hunt escaped during the Death March and eventually joined up with the guerrillas. Norling, a retired professor of history, authored this book (written in the first person) based on Hunt's adventures and other research.

**448**   Ind, Allison. *Bataan: The Judgment Seat*. New York: Macmillan, 1944. Pp. 395. Ind was a former naval reserve officer who later obtained a commission in military intelligence. He was called to active duty in 1940 and sent to the Philippines in April 1941 to direct air corps intelligence activities. He flew to Mindanao on 10 March 1942 and then escaped to Australia. His book is a richly detailed account of air corps personalities and the activities of the high command. The original manuscript for this book was reportedly much longer than the published version, but no copy of the original appears to exist.

**449**   Kenney, George C. *The Saga of Pappy Gunn*. New York: Duell, Sloan and Pearce, 1959. Pp. viii, 133. Paul Irvin "Pappy" Gunn was a former enlisted naval aviator (on active duty 1917-37) who went to the Philippines in 1939 as Andres Soriano's personal pilot and then became the operations manager of Philippine Air Lines. Recalled to active duty and commissioned a captain in the army air corps on 8 December 1941, Gunn had the job of transporting personnel and supplies wherever they were needed. He flew to Australia in early 1942 but participated in several air missions back to the Philippines until the surrender. General Kenney met Gunn in Australia late in 1942, where Gunn had attached himself to a bomber outfit. This book is filled with anecdotes about the colorful and unconventional Gunn's exploits in the Philippines and Southwest Pacific Area during the war. Once again a civilian, Gunn died in an airplane crash in the Philippines in 1958.

**450**  McClendon, Dennis E., and Wallace F. Richards. *The Legend of Colin Kelly.* Missoula, MT: Pictorial Histories Publishing Co., 1994. Pp. iv, 68. The authors attempt to separate fact from fiction in the much mythologized story of the death of "America's first hero of World War II," B-17 pilot Capt. Colin P. Kelly, Jr. (USMA 1937), near Clark Field on 10 December 1941. The book is based on interviews with surviving crew members and includes accounts by Filipinos who witnessed the plane's crash.

**451**  McKee, Philip. *Warriors with Wings.* New York: Thomas Y. Crowell Co., 1947. Pp. 266. Relates short stories told by three pilots of the 19th Bomb Group who served in the Philippines in 1941: Fred T. Crimmins, Jr., Alvin J.H. Mueller, and Emmett O'Donnell.

**452**  Miller, Roger. "A 'Pretty Damn Able Commander': Lewis Hyde Brereton." Two parts. In *Air Power History* 47, no. 4 (2000): 4-27; and 48, no. 1 (2001): 22-45. Using a rich array of sources, including Brereton's 201 (personnel) file, the author concludes that despite the debacle at Clark Field, Brereton was "neither a star performer nor mediocre failure," no more nor less competent than most general officers in the war. See also entry 442.

**453**  Obert, David L. *Philippines Defender: A Fighter Pilot's Diary, 1941–1942.* Norman, OK: Levite of Apache, 1992. Pp. 160. A P-40 pilot of the 17th Squadron, 24th Pursuit Group, at Nichols Field, Obert flew from Bataan to Del Monte on 4 January 1942, where he remained for two weeks before being ordered back to Bataan (the pilots drew cards to determine who would have to return). He describes conditions at Del Monte; and recalls a Philippine air unit at Cebu—"one old P-12 without guns and two or three primary training planes with two 30-cal. machine guns mounted on them"—the local citizenry angry because the pilots would not take the planes up against the Japanese. Obert escaped to Australia and ended the war with the air force in Europe. His wife, whom he had met and married in the islands, spent the war in Santo Tomas.

**454**  St. John, Joseph F., as told to Howard Handleman. *Leyte Calling.* New York: The Vanguard Press, 1945. Pp. 220. An enlisted man with the 14th Bombardment Squadron, St. John arrived in the Philippines in September 1941. At Clark Field on 8 December, St. John moved with his unit to Malabang, Mindanao, in early January 1942. He decided not to surrender when organized resistance to the Japanese collapsed in May, and most of this book recounts his experiences as a guerrilla in the Butuan area of Mindanao and as a radio operator on Leyte in 1943-44.

**455**  Valencia, Jerry, ed. *Knights of the Sky.* San Diego, CA: Privately Published, 1980. Pp. 216. This compilation of first-hand accounts of aerial combat by American aces of World War I and II includes that of I.B. Jack Donalson of the 21st Pursuit Squadron, who flew one of the last P-40s off Bataan and later escaped to Australia. This book is labeled "volume 1," but the editor apparently never completed a planned volume 2.

**456**    White, W. L. *Queens Die Proudly*. New York: Harcourt, Brace and Company, 1943. Pp. 273. Tells the story of Lt. Col. Frank Kurtz and other officers of the 19th Bomb Group, from the attack on Clark Field to the retreat from Java to Australia, interspersed with recollections of Kurtz's wife, Margo. Margo Kurtz gives a fuller account of her side of the story, adds more biographical details about her husband (who, in addition to being an air corps pilot, was a bronze medalist in platform diving in the 1932 Olympics), and reprints brief excerpts from letters her husband sent her from the Philippines in *My Rival, the Sky* (New York: G.P. Putnam's Sons, 1945), pp. 218.

## United States Naval Forces

**457**    Breuer, William B. *Sea Wolf: A Biography of John D. Bulkeley, USN*. Novato, CA: Presidio, 1989. Pp. x, 318. This medal-of-honor winning PT boat commander's naval career started off on the wrong foot. He graduated so near the bottom of his 1933 USNA class that he was not offered a commission until the following year. He then happened across a Japanese diplomat and stole the man's briefcase. Confronted with this intelligence coup, an embarrassed navy snuck Bulkeley out of the country aboard the next China-bound transport. Breuer, author of a number of popular military histories, is more recorder of Bulkeley's tales than biographer. Adventures in the Philippines as commander of PT boat Squadron 3 are related strictly from Bulkeley's point of view. As Bulkeley saw it, his "rescue" of Quezon from Negros was more like a kidnapping. He had orders from MacArthur to bring Quezon to Mindanao whether "the son-of-a-bitch" wanted to come or not and, by his account, brow beat the recalcitrant Commonwealth president until Quezon agreed to board the PT boat. Bulkeley also claims to have been contacted by several army generals on Bataan who wanted to use the PT boats to escape to China. When they learned that MacArthur was leaving aboard the boats, "they had an added fear," Bulkeley recalled: "That I had told General MacArthur" about their plans.

**458**    Leutze, James. *A Different Kind of Victory: A Biography of Admiral Thomas C. Hart*. Annapolis, MD: Naval Institute Press, 1973. Pp. xi, 362. "Tough Tommy" Hart (USNA 1897) was one of the navy's senior admirals when he was refused command of the US Fleet in 1939 because FDR did not like him, and was instead offered the decrepit Asiatic Fleet in the hope, so he believed, that he would retire. MacArthur's contemptuous view of Hart dominates the Philippine Campaign literature, but Leutze (making use of Hart's unpublished diaries) argues that with little aid or guidance from Washington, Hart tried to prepare the navy's forces in the Philippines for war and formed close ties with US Army garrison commanders in order to further local defense efforts. When MacArthur took command of army forces in July 1941, he rejected Hart's offers to collaborate on defense preparations but promptly blamed Hart and the navy for the subsequent debacle.

**459**   Mason, John T., ed. *The Pacific War Remembered: An Oral History Collection.* Annapolis, Maryland: Naval Institute Press, 1986. Pp. xix, 373. Extracts from thirty-one oral histories given by enlisted and officer veterans, covering the navy's war in the Pacific from Pearl Harbor to the surrender ceremony in Tokyo Bay. Includes Admiral Thomas C. Hart's strategic view of conditions in Asia on the eve of war and accounts of prewar army-navy relations in the Philippines by Kemp Tolley, assigned to the Asiatic Fleet, and Robert Lee Dennison, Hart's "ambassador" to General MacArthur. The latter provides useful insights into MacArthur's defense strategy for the Philippine Campaign.

**460**   Morrill, John, and Pete Martin. *South from Corregidor.* New York: Simon and Shuster, 1943. Pp. x, 252. Morrill's (USNA 1924) ship, the minesweeper *Quail*, was undergoing repair in Cavite when the Japanese struck. During the campaign, it cleared paths through the minefield south of Corregidor, and the men then served as a gun crew on Caballo. Morrill did not wait to be told to surrender. On 6 May 1942 he gathered his men together and set sail (not on the *Quail*, which had been scuttled) for Australia. This book, one of the wartime "Books for Victory" series, is largely an account of his and seventeen crewmens' 2,000 mile voyage.

**461**   Tolley, Kemp. *Cruise of the Lanikai: Incitement to War.* Annapolis, MD: Naval Institute Press, 1973. Pp. xiii, 345. On 1 December 1941, President Roosevelt ordered that the Asiatic Fleet send "three small vessels" to form a "defensive information patrol" along the coast of French Indochina. One of these ships was to be the two-masted schooner *Lanikai*. Its commander, Tolley (USNA 1929) argues that FDR expected that the Japanese would attack the ships, thus providing the excuse needed to bring the US into the war Japan was preparing to wage against the British, to whom FDR had made secret pledges of support. According to Tolley, FDR insisted on the presence of Filipino crews (which were to be drawn from an "Insular Force" of 1,000 navy-employed Filipino sailors) aboard the ships to encourage Filipino outrage against Japan when the ships were attacked. Only one vessel, the *Isabel*, was sent on this mission. (It returned safely.) Lanikai was to be the second, but it had sailed no further than the mouth of Manila Bay when war broke out. Its "cruise" took it to Java and then Australia, where Tolley left the ship to become assistant naval attaché in Moscow. Manila-born Tolley had been assigned to Cavite in the early 1930s and intersperses his story with recollections of those happier times in the Philippines, as well.

**462**   Williams, Ted. *Rogues of Bataan.* New York: Carlton Press, 1979. Pp. 144. An account of a marine air warning (radar) unit in the Philippine Campaign, first established near Nasugbu and then on Bataan. Cpl. Williams, whose two-year tour in the islands was about to end in December 1941, served as driver, engine repair man, and guard. Includes roster of personnel assigned to the unit. Williams was captured in April 1941 but says nothing about his POW experiences, some details of which are recounted in entry 606.

**463**    Winslow, W.G. *The Ghost That Died at Sunda Strait*. Annapolis, MD: Naval Institute Press, 1984. Pp. xx, 244. Winslow, pilot of one of the USS *Houston*'s four seaplanes, describes his experiences and that of the Asiatic Fleet's flagship, the heavy cruiser *Houston*, from the months before World War II up to its sinking in the Battle of Sunda Strait, in the Dutch East Indies, on 1 March 1942, taking to the bottom 655 of its 1,015-man crew. Appendices list the ships of the Asiatic Fleet and the *Houston*'s crew. An earlier, shorter version of this book was published as *The Ghost of the Java Coast* (Satellite Beach, FL: Coral Reef Publication, 1974) [see also entries 382 and 386].

**464**    Wolfert, Ira. *American Guerrilla in the Philippines*. New York: Simon and Schuster, 1945. Pp. x, 301. Recounts the experiences of Iliff D. Richardson, executive officer of PT-34. Richardson had been with the Asiatic Fleet for over a year before the war's start but here relates only the last encounters of PT-34 before its destruction at Cebu in May 1942. Richardson then took up life as a guerrilla under Ruperto Kangleon on Leyte.

*Army/Navy Nurses*

**465**    Danner, Dorothy Still. *What a Way to Spend a War: Navy Nurse POWs in the Philippines*. Annapolis, MD: Naval Institute Press, 1995. Pp. ix, 215. The author, who joined the nurse corps in 1938, remembers prewar life at Cañacao naval hospital, followed by internment at Santo Tomas and Los Baños. Includes photographs of the prewar naval hospital complex.

**466**    Fessler, Diane Burke, ed. *No Time for Fear: Voices of American Military Nurses in World War II*. East Lansing, MI: Michigan State University Press, 1996. Pp. xv, 280. One chapter includes brief statements by eight army and navy nurses who were captured in the Philippines. "Orders to leave Manila with General MacArthur and the other military didn't come for the navy nurses," recalled nurse Dorothy Danner [see previous entry], "and we've never known what happened. We were still in Manila waiting for orders when the Japanese took over."

**467**    Flikke, Julia O. *Nurses in Action: The Story of the Army Nurse Corps*. Philadelphia: J.B. Lippincott, 1943. Pp. xiii, 239. Part history of the army nurse corps and part handbook for wartime volunteers, this book recounts the experiences of army nurses in the Philippine Campaign based on stories told by the army nurses who escaped to Australia.

**468**    Jopling, Lucy Wilson. *Warrior in White*. San Antonio, TX: The Watercress Press, 1990. Pp. 133. The author's anecdotes of service on Bataan at Hospital no. 2 are more graphic than most. Jopling (née Wilson) later (1943-45) served in the Southwest Pacific as one of the first "flight nurses" and was a military wife in occupied Japan. Includes a list of army and navy nurses who served in the 1941-42 Philippine Campaign.

**469**    McKay, Hortense E., as told to Maxine K. Russell. *Jungle Angel: Bataan Remembered*. Brainerd, MN: Privately Published, 1988. Pp. 104. Army nurse McKay arrived in Manila in February 1941, was assigned to Stotsenburg and witnessed the attack on Clark Field, then served on Corregidor. She could say more about "upbringing, selfishness and personal hygiene," she writes of her month in Malinta tunnel, but "that would be unprofessional." She then went to Hospital no. 2 on Bataan and to Australia by submarine in early May. She served in Australia, New Guinea, and then Leyte until near the war's end. Beyond being an account of her experiences in the Philippines, McKay's story is useful for understanding the problems of women in military service. The book concludes with wartime recollections of three former members of Company 'A,' 194th Tank Bn., Russell Swearingen, Walter Straka, and Henry Peck, all survivors of the Death March and subsequent imprisonment in Japan.

**470**    Monahan, Evelyn M., and Rosemary Neidel-Greenlee. *All This Hell: U.S. Nurses Imprisoned by the Japanese*. Lexington, KY: University Press of Kentucky, 2000. Pp. xi, 228. The authors mine interviews given to the Army Nurse Corps Oral History Program in the early 1980s, and a few they conducted themselves, to try to find something new to say about the army and navy nurses' experiences in the Philippines and Guam. The nurses' stories are always interesting, but the authors are especially uninformed about events in the Philippines. They make Lewis Brereton a colonel commanding Clark Field and put MacArthur at the head of something they label "Allied Forces Philippine Command." Appendices provide the nurses' names and personal information.

**471**    Norman, Elizabeth M. *We Band of Angels: The Untold Story of American Nurses Trapped on Bataan by the Japanese*. New York: Random House, 1999. Pp. xv, 327. The subtitle is exaggerated (the American nurses were among the very few army personnel *not* trapped on Bataan, and some of their stories were in print almost as soon as the first escapees made their way to Australia), but this account of the ordeal of the army nurses, based largely on interviews the author conducted with twenty nurses, is well-told and more revealing than others. Norman discusses personality conflicts, the process by which some were selected to escape and the acrimony it engendered, and tells what happened to the nurses after the war.

**472**    Redmond, Juanita. *I Served on Bataan*. Philadelphia and New York: J.B. Lippincott Co., 1943. Pp. 167. Reprinted by Garland Publishers, NY, 1984. Army nurse Redmond arrived in the Philippines in September 1940, spent a year at Stotsenburg, and then reported for duty at Sternberg General Hospital in Manila. Redmond was at "Little Baguio" on Bataan before escaping to Corregidor and then to Australia by PBY in April 1942. Redmond's was the earliest and still best-known account of the army nurses' ordeal in the Philippines, on which Paramount Pictures supposedly based its 1943 film "So Proudly We Hail."

**473**    Thompson, Dorothy Davis. *The Road Back: A Pacific POW's Liberation Story*. Lubbock, TX: Texas Tech University Press, 1996. Pp. viii, 160. A civil service nurse with the army who had lived in China and the Philippines before the war, Dorothy Davis remained at Sternberg Hospital to care for its few remaining Filipino patients after army medical personnel left for Bataan. She spent two years in Santo Tomas until being evacuated to Goa, Portuguese India, where American internees were exchanged for Japanese, and continued to New York aboard the *Gripsholm* (for which the US government billed her $575, paid by monthly deductions from her future army-officer husband's paycheck). Davis returned to the Philippines as an army nurse during the Philippine Campaign of 1944-45.

**474**    Tomblin, Barbara Brooks. *G.I. Nightingales: The Army Nurse Corps in World War II*. Lexington, KY: University Press of Kentucky, 1996. Pp. ix, 254. Includes a rather antiseptic account of the experiences of army nurses at the various posts in the Philippines when war began, on Bataan and Corregidor, and at Santo Tomas. The author contextualizes events in the Philippines by reference to Helen Nicolay's wartime hagiography, *MacArthur of Bataan* (1942).

**475**    Sterner, Doris M. *In and Out of Harm's Way: A History of the Navy Nurse Corps*. Seattle, WA: Peanut Butter Publishing, 1996. Pp. ii, 390. Twelve navy nurses were stationed in the Philippines at the Cañacao naval hospital in December 1941. One (nurse Ann Bernatitis, the first recipient of the Legion of Merit, Legionnaire) accompanied the army to Bataan and was eventually evacuated by submarine to Australia. The other eleven were left behind to be captured in Manila and detained at Santo Tomas and Los Baños until liberated in February 1945. Their stories are told here, largely through lengthy extracts from interviews.

**476**    Williams, Denny. *To the Angels*. San Francisco: Denson Press, 1985. Pp. 225. An army nurse since 1930, Williams arrived at Ft. Mills in 1936 and was later transferred to Sternberg Hospital. There, among other things, she assisted at the birth of Arthur MacArthur. She had to leave the army when she married William B. Williams, a local salesman for Texaco, in 1939, but later served as a nurse on Bataan and Corregidor and spent the war interned at Santo Tomas. Her husband, a 1925 graduate of VMI, was called to active duty on the outbreak of war. He served with the 31st Infantry and was one of the POWs killed on the *Enoura Maru*, on 9 January 1945.

Note: An account of a Philippine Army nurse's experiences on Bataan is found in entry 393.

### Civilians

**477**    Brines, Russell. *Until They Eat Stones*. Philadelphia and NY: J.B. Lippincott Co., 1944. Pp. 340. Brines' account begins with the Japanese capture of Manila, where he and other journalists remained as the US and Philippine forces withdrew to Bataan. Brines and his family were interned in Santo Tomas and in 1943 repatriated to the US.

**478**    Colley, George S. *Manila-Kuching and Return, 1941–1945.* San Francisco: Privately Published, 1951. Pp. 54. (First published in 1946.) A civilian construction contractor with Bechtel, Colley was tasked with preparing storage facilities, airfields, and other military engineering projects at Sangley Point, Cavite, and Mariveles. He provides a few details of those projects. Colley, his wife, and several other Americans attempted to escape to Australia but were captured in Borneo and imprisoned at Berhala and Kuching, Sarawak.

**479**    Gunnison, Royal Arch. *So Sorry, No Peace.* New York: The Viking Press, 1944. Pp. 272. Like Brines [entry 477], Gunnison was in Manila when the Japanese arrived. He had visited Clark Field and other areas near the front lines, but his account of the fighting reads like USAFFE news releases. He later interviewed Uno [entry 526] and offers a slightly different version of Wainwright's surrender than appears in Uno's book.

**480**    Lee, Clark. *They Call It Pacific: An Eye-Witness Story of Our War Against Japan from Bataan to the Solomons.* New York: The Viking Press, 1943. Pp. 374. A surprisingly candid (given its wartime publication) tale of America's lack of preparation in the Philippines by a journalist who had spent several years in China before arriving in Manila in mid–November 1941. Lee visited soldiers on the fronts in Baguio, Bataan, and Corregidor, and escaped to Cebu in late February 1942. He and other journalists reached Australia aboard the *Doña Nati* on 30 March 1942.

**481**    Marquardt, Frederic S. *Before Bataan and After: A Personalized History of Our Philippine Experiment.* Indianapolis and New York: The Bobbs-Merrill Co., 1943. Pp. 315. Born in the Philippines, where his parents were school teachers, but educated in the US, the author became a journalist for the *Philippines Free Press* in 1928. He returned to the US for medical treatment just before the war began. Marquardt's theme is that Filipino loyalty and sacrifice on Bataan was proof of the wisdom and altruism of America's colonial policy in the islands. When he sticks to what he personally knows, the book is fascinating, but his comments on MacArthur and Bataan read like newspaper propaganda.

**482**    Sayre, Francis Bowes. *Glad Adventure.* New York: The MacMillan Co., 1957. Pp. xii, 356. Sayre (whose name, according to contemporary Manila newspapers, was pronounced "sir") was High Commissioner to the Philippines from August 1939 to June 1942, during which his relationship with both Quezon and MacArthur steadily deteriorated. Here he is outspokenly critical only of his boss, Secretary of the Interior Harold Ickes. Sayre recalls his attempts to push forward civil defense in the months before the war, life in Malinta Tunnel after the war began, and has some interesting things to say about Quezon's relationship with MacArthur. Sayre and his party escaped Corregidor by submarine on 23 February 1942.

**483**    Willoughby, Amea, with Lenore Sorsby. *I Was on Corregidor: Experiences of an American Official's Wife in the War-torn Philippines.* New York and London: Harper & Brothers, 1943. Pp. v, 249. The author and her husband, Woodbury, arrived in Manila with High Commissioner Sayre's party in 1939. "Woody" was Sayre's executive assistant and later financial adviser. The Willoughbys were among the dozen members of Sayre's official family who went to Corregidor on 24 December 1941. They left by submarine for Australia in February 1942. Willoughby describes the terror and tedium of life in Malinta Tunnel with more candor than some of her companions might have wished. One chapter, "The Filipinos as We Knew Them," provides the classic depiction of the typical American opinion of Filipinos. (By "Filipinos," Willoughby means her servants.)

### USAFFE Unit Histories
### Philippine Army

**484** Alvior, Froilan B. *A Brief History of the 11th Division, Philippine Army*. Quezon City: Office of the Chief of Military History, GHQ AFP, 1973. Pp. 247. Recruited in the 1st Military District in Northern Luzon, the 11th Division saw action at Lingayen and on Bataan. Its American commanding general, William E. Brougher, tells his story in entry 560.

**485** Bueno, Delia. "A Brief History of the 61st Division, Philippine Army." Camp Aguinaldo: Office of the Chief of Military History, GHQ AFP. Bound typescript. The 61st Division was organized on Panay and saw service in the Visayas and on Mindanao first under Bradford G. Chynoweth [entry 420] and then Albert F. Christie. According to Ancheta [entry 300], this is the only PA division history that has not been published.

**486** Catalan, Primitivo M. *A Brief History of the 71st Infantry Division, PA*. Camp Aguinaldo, Quezon City: Office of the Chief of Military History, GHQ AFP, 1973. Pp. 168. Organized on Negros, most of the 71st Division's units served in Central Luzon and on Bataan under Clyde Selleck [entry 437] and the more able Clinton Pierce. The division's 73rd Regiment served on Mindanao.

**487** Cariño, Ranulfo B. *A Brief History of the 21st Division, Philippine Army*. Camp Aguinaldo: Office of the Chief of Military History, AFP, 1971. Pp. 210. Commanded by former Philippine Scout officer Mateo M. Capinpin, this division saw action at Lingayen and on Bataan.

**488** Catalan, Primitivo M. *A Brief History of the 81st Division, Philippine Army*. Camp Aguinaldo, Quezon City: Office of the Chief of Military History, GHQ AFP, 1973. Pp. 182. This Cebu-based division served on Mindanao under the command of Guy Fort, one of the few American PC officers who remained in Philippine service after the founding of the Commonwealth.

**489** Catalan, Primitivo M. *A Brief History of the 101st Division, Philippine Army*. Camp Aguinaldo: Office of the Chief of Military History, GHQ AFP, 1977. Pp. 204 (pp. 63-187 consist of a unit roster). The 101st Division, commanded by Joseph Vachon, fought on Mindanao.

**490** Catalan, Primitivo M., Froilan B. Alvior, and Isidro G. Espela. *A Brief His-*

*tory of the 91st Infantry Division, Philippine Army*. Camp E. Aguinaldo: Office of the Chief of Military History, 1973. Pp. 122. Recruited on the islands of Leyte and Samar, the 91st Division (less the 93rd Regiment, which served on Mindanao) under the command of former PC officer Luther Stevens, saw action during the retreat from Lingayen and on Bataan.

**491**    Catalan, Primitivo M., and Eduardo A. Calderon. *A Brief History of the 51st Division, Philippine Army*. Camp Aguinaldo: Office of the Chief of Military History, AFP, 1974. Pp. 219. The 51st Division was raised in southern Luzon and saw service there and on Bataan, initially under the command of Albert M. Jones.

**492**    *First Infantry Yearbook, Philippine Army*. Camp Murphy, Quezon City, 1939. Includes many photographs of Camp Murphy, a regimental roster, and a short article about the regiment's commander, Col. Mateo Capinpin. The yearbook also includes photographs of the 1939 trainees at Camp Murphy and of the 1939 ROTC summer camp cadets. The 1st Infantry formed part of the 1st Division [entry 496], although no divisional organization existed in peacetime. A copy of the yearbook can be found in the Vargas Collection, University of the Philippines.

**493**    *Golden Anniversary, 1941–1991, 41st Division, PA, USAFFE*. A 116-page booklet published by the 41st Division association on the occasion of the 50th anniversary of the division's mobilization (31 August 1991). Includes reprints of old newspaper accounts and photos of prewar training, a short history of the organization, and photos of the anniversary celebrations. The bulk of the work is taken up by a list of those assigned to the division from 28 August 1941 to 9 April 1942 (not necessarily those who actually reported for duty or served with the division after 8 December 1941), the result of ten years' research by Mariano F. Infante, the association's late historian [see also next entry].

**494**    Jubal, Exequiel D., and Soloman A. Asturias. *A Brief History of the 41st Division, Philippine Army*. Quezon City: Office of the Chief of Military History, AFP, 1974. Pp. 136. Commanded by former Philippine Scout officer Vicente P. Lim, the 41st Division saw action on Bataan. This history includes a roster of officers and list of medal recipients [see also previous entry and 57and 58A].

**495**    Peña, Ambrosio P. *Bataan's Own*. Manila: 2nd Regular Division Association, 1967. Pp. xii, 224. This well-written history of a "scratch" division formed on Bataan and placed under the command of Constabulary Chief G.B. Francisco (commissioned 1908) includes a good account of the PC's prewar years and a roster of officers and men.

**496**    Peña, Ambrosio P. *The Story of the 1st Regular Division*. Camp Murphy, Quezon City: Military History Branch, AFP, 1953. Pp. xi, 134. The forward of this book notes that it is to be the first in a series of "after action reports" for the 1941-42 Philippine Campaign divisions. The 1st Division had been little more than a paper organization before the war [see entry 492] and was not organized for active service until mid–December 1941. It fought on Bataan under Fidel V. Segundo (USMA August 1917) and Kearie L. Berry.

**497**    Pestaño, Rolando S. *A Brief History of the 31st Division, Philippine Army.* Camp Aguinaldo: Office of the Chief of Military History, GHQ AFP, 1976. Pp. 118. Recruited from Bataan and Central Luzon, the 31st Division served on Bataan under Clifford Bluemel, the American officer notorious for his denunciation of Filipino soldiers as good for little more than saluting and demanding three meals a day. He reportedly did not think much of many American soldiers, either.

Note: Another Philippine Army division, the 102nd, was created on Mindanao after the war's start from elements of the 61st, 81st, and 101st Divisions. A short history of this division can be found in *The Wainwright Papers*, vol. 3 [entry 300]. There is a comment in the US Army Philippine Department's War Plan Orange-3 (prepared in 1940-41) to the effect that a second tier of Philippine Army reserve divisions (the 12th Division, the 22nd, the 32nd, and so on) had begun forming, but apparently any personnel assigned to these organizations were soon dispersed among existing divisions.

### United States Army Units
### Philippine Scouts

**498**    Olson, John E., with Frank O. Anders. *Anywhere-Anytime: The History of the Fifty-Seventh Infantry, PS.* N.p. Privately Published, 1991. Pp. v, 238. Olson (USMA 1939) served with the 57th Infantry during the war. He emphasizes the unit's actions on Bataan but also sketches the regiment's prewar history, tells what happened to some of the men during the war, and describes the regiment's post-war reorganization and eventual inactivation. Includes list of officers, roll of honor, and list of casualties. This book was first serialized in the *BAHC*.

**499**    Rosen, Melvin H. *History of the Philippine Scouts Field Artillery.* N.p. Privately Published, 1995. Pp. 215. Bound typescript. The author, a retired army officer (USMA 1940) who served with the 2nd Battalion, 88th FA, produced only a few copies of this book. According to Rosen, Morton [entry 334] was "completely confused" about the "organization and employment of the Philippine Scout field artillery," and Rosen sets the record straight. The bulk of the work consists of appendices: reprints of articles found in the *Field Artillery Journal* in the 1920s; various documents in the author's possession or from the National Archives which relate to FA units; officers' promotion orders from 1941-42; personnel rosters (officers and enlisted men) for the 23rd, 24th, 86th and 88th FA Regiments; and a list of Philippine Scouts who died during the war. Much of this material is reprinted in entry 166.

Note: For other Philippine Scout-related books, see also entries 161–169.

### 192nd Tank Battalion

**500**    Poweleit, Alvin C. *Kentucky's Fighting 192nd Light G.H.Q. Tank Battalion:*

*A Saga of Kentucky's Part in the Defense of the Philippines.* Newport, KY: Privately Published, 1981. Pp. xi, 228. Formed in September 1940 of National Guard units from Wisconsin, Illinois, Ohio, and Kentucky, the 192nd Tank Battalion arrived in the Philippines and was assigned to Ft. Stotsenburg in late November 1941. Poweleit, who commanded the medical detachment, recounts the battalion's activities from its formation in the United States and his own experiences as a POW in diary form. He includes considerable material on the "Hell Ships." This book is an enlarged version of Poweleit's *USAFFE: The Loyal Americans and Faithful Filipinos. A Saga of Atrocities Perpetuated During the Fall of the Philippines, the Bataan Death March, and Japanese Imprisonment and Survival*, Privately Published, 1975 [see also entry 640].

**501**   Schutt, Donald A. "Janesville Tankers on Bataan." MS thesis, University of Wisconsin, 1966. Pp. viii, 252. Tells the story of Company A, 192nd Tank Battalion, whose members came from Janesville, Wisconsin, from the company's organization in 1920 (as Company I, Wisconsin National Guard) to its surrender on Bataan. Based on interviews and correspondence with veterans (including the Tank Group commander, General Weaver) or their families and the *Janesville Daily Gazette*, which closely followed the company's tribulations in the Philippines [see also entry 574].

Research note: The ABDC website (http://harrisonheritage.com/adbc/) links to several on-line versions of General Weaver's "Report of Operations of the Provisional Tank Group" (found reprinted in Ancheta, vol. 2 [entry 300]) and a history of the 194th Tank Battalion.

### 200th/515th Coast Artillery Regiment

**502**   Cave, Dorothy. *Beyond Courage: One Regiment Against Japan, 1941-1945*. Las Cruces, NM: Yucca Tree Press, 1992. Pp. xvi, 431. Unruly New Mexico National Guardsmen of the 200th Coast Artillery Regiment (Anti-Aircraft) get acquainted with Negrito tribesmen and clash with the regular army while guarding Clark Field after arriving in the islands in late September 1941. On 8 December, a portion of the 200th was sent to Manila. First known as "the provisional regiment of 200th," it was redesignated the 515th, on 19 December 1941. Both the 200th and 515th included Filipino soldiers (in his unpublished report, "Coast Artillery Operations, Philippine Islands, December 8, 1941, to May 6, 1942" [20 September 1943], Stephen Mellnik stated that 500 Philippine Army reservists were assigned to the 515th), but they are mentioned only in passing in this book, which is based on extensive interviews with veterans. There is also a 1996 revised paperback edition of this book (same title, same publisher) which includes some corrections but mostly serves to allow the author to express her concern that "Japanese propaganda"—aided by American academics—"is still successfully portraying Japan as the victim" of World War II.

**503**   Jolly, John Pershing. *History [of the] New Mexico National Guard, 1606-*

*1963*. New Mexico National Guard, Adjutant General's Department, 1963. Pp. 189. Bound Typescript. In 1940, the New Mexico National Guard's 111th Cavalry Regiment was converted to the 207th (later, 200th) Coast Artillery (AA) Regiment (following a court ruling that forced the state treasurer to make available the funds necessary to begin the costly conversion from cavalry to coast artillery). Describes prewar mobilization and training, the movement to the Philippines, and the actions of the 200th Regiment and its spin-off units in the Philippine Campaign. Of the hundreds of men lost during the war, "somewhat less than twenty [died] as a result of battle action, a remarkable record for units which engaged in combat with the invaders several times every day for four continuous months." Includes biographical profiles of the commanding officers of the 200th and 515th, Charles Sage and Harry Peck, both World War I veterans from Kansas.

**504**   Matson, Eva Jane. *It Tolled for New Mexico: New Mexicans Captured by the Japanese, 1941-1945*. Las Cruces, NM: Yucca Free Press, 1994. Pp. xii, 467. An interesting attempt at local history, in which the author examines how the families of soldiers sent to the Philippines coped with their absence and how the veterans have been memorialized in New Mexico. Focusing on the personnel of the 200th and 515th CA (AA), the author also provides a lengthy (pp. 133-462) analysis of New Mexican prisoners of the Japanese. Firm numbers have always been elusive in accounts of the Philippine Campaign, but this book suggests that not many American soldiers were killed fighting the Japanese: of 1,467 officers and men she lists as being in these units, twenty-one were killed in action (eight of those on Bataan). Another 662 died as POWs.

**505**   Melbourne, Dale. "The Men of Battery F: New Mexico Survivors of Bataan and the Philippine Campaign in the Second World War." MA thesis, Shippensburg University of Pennsylvania, 1999. Pp. iv, 127. Cursory account of the battery's experience, based in part on interviews with eight veterans of the company, some conducted by the author and others available on tape recordings in the Carlsbad (New Mexico) Museum's Bataan Collection.

**506**   Partin, Richard L. "Philippine Thermopylae: The New Mexico National Guard at the Battle of the Philippines, 1941–1942." MA thesis, New Mexico Highlands University, 1994. Pp. 181. Account of the 200th/515th Coast Artillery Regiments in the Bataan campaign, based largely on secondary sources and two interviews with veterans conducted by the author. It includes considerable detail on the regiments' weaponry, makes use of a local Spanish-language newspaper to gauge Hispanic feeling about the war, and states that Philippine Army troops were assigned to the 200th to bring it up to strength in late 1941.

Note: Yet another thesis dealing with this regiment exists: Moises T. Venegas, "The 200th Coast Artillery (AA)" (MA thesis, University of New Mexico, 1965), pp. iii, 86, but the only public holder of a copy, the University of New Mexico library, will not lend it. The ADBC website (http://harrisonheritage.com/adbc/) links to a roster of 200th CAC personnel.

*US Army Air Corps Units*
*19th Bomb Group*

**507**    Mitchell, John H. *"In Alis Vicimus": On Wings We Conquer*. Springfield, MO: Privately Published, 1990. Pp. 201. Pilots of the 19th Bomb Group (30th and 93rd Squadrons) flew B-17s to Clark Field in late October and early November 1941. There, the group incorporated the 14th Bomb Squadron, which had arrived at Clark with the first B-17s flown across the Pacific in mid–September, and the 28th Bomb Squadron, which had been in the Philippines since 1922 and which in late 1941 flew B-18s (its pilots had not yet qualified on B-17s when the war began). B-17s and LB-30s of the 7th BG joined the remnants of the 19th BG on Java in January 1942. Based largely on interviews with pilots of the group, the author gives brief histories of the squadrons and details the missions flown in the Philippines, Dutch East Indies, Australia, and New Guinea until October 1942. Mitchell provides probably the best published description of the airfields at Del Monte (includes photos and a brief history of the 5th Air Base Group which constructed fields on Mindanao from December 1941 to April 1942). The book also includes photos of burning hangars and aircraft taken at Clark on 8 December. One chapter, "The MacArthur Evacuation," sets the story straight about the role of Capt. Harl Pease (KIA, Rabaul, New Britain, 7 August 1942), the youthful looking B-17 pilot with whom—according to some authors—MacArthur supposedly refused to fly from Del Monte. The author states that Pease did not want to be caught on the ground and flew back to Australia without waiting for MacArthur's party to arrive. (Toland [351], seems to have been the first to print the story. It had been largely ignored by MacArthur's biographers, but Perret [100] resurrected it.) Lengthy appendices tell what happened to each B-17 (numbers 40-3086 and 40-3096 are apparently transposed) and list the planes and crews (and, if appropriate, passengers) of flights and missions.

*24th Pursuit Group*

**508**    Bartsch, William H. *Doomed at the Start: American Pursuit Pilots in the Philippines, 1941–1942*. College Station, TX: Texas A&M University Press, 1992. Pp. xxi, 503. Exhaustive history of the 24th Pursuit Group (formed on 16 September 1941 of the 3rd, 17th and 20th Pursuit Squadrons) in the Philippine Campaign. Based on interviews with virtually every surviving officer of the unit, the story begins with the arrival of air reinforcements for the Philippine Department's 4th Composite Group in November 1940. Bartsch's findings contribute significantly to understanding why the air force was caught on the ground on 8 December. Includes many unique photos supplied by veterans; lists squadron officers and tells what happened to them.

*48th Materiel Squadron*

**509**    McGlothlin, Frank Emile. *Barksdale to Bataan: History of the 48th Materiel Squadron, October 1940–April 1942*. Covington, LA: Privately Published, 1984. Pp.

v, 100. Originally formed as the 2nd Materiel Squadron at Barksdale Army Airfield, Shreveport, Louisiana, the unit was redesignated the 48th in January 1941 and arrived in the Philippines with the 27th Bomb Group on 20 November 1941. The squadron was at Ft. McKinley, but one detachment was sent to Mindoro in mid-December to service an airfield near San Jose. Includes photos, maps, and a unit roster.

## US Marine Corps Units

**510**   Berry, Grant John. "The Movement and Activities of the Fourth Marine Regiment from November 27, 1941, to the Capitulation of Corregidor, May 6, 1942." MA thesis, University of California, Graduate Division, Northern Section, 1951. Pp. 89. History of the 4th Marines on Corregidor based on secondary sources and interviews or correspondence with twenty veterans.

**511**   Condit, Kenneth W., and Edwin T. Turnbladh. *Hold High the Torch: A History of the 4th Marines*. Washington, DC: HQ, USMC, Historical Branch, G-3 Division, 1960. Pp. xii, 458. This history includes one chapter on the regiment in the Philippine Campaign. The 4th Marine Regiment arrived piecemeal in the Philippines on 30 November and 1 December 1941 and was transferred to army control on 22 December. The regiment was unusual in that eventually most of its members were not marines: marines numbered only 1,440 out of a regimental strength of 3,891. The remainder included, among others, forty-four men of the OSP, 148 soldiers from the Philippine Army, 720 from the PAAC, and sixty-four Philippine Scouts.

**512**   Dillman, Frank H., comp. *A Time in History: In Remembrance of the Old Fourth Marine Regiment*. N.p. n.p. [c1979] Pp. 282. Bound collection of documents and reprinted newspaper and journal articles telling the history of the Fourth Marines. Includes regimental commander Col. Samuel Howard's official "Report on the operations, employment, and supply of the old 4th Marines from September 1941 to the surrender of Corregidor, May 6, 1942" and reprints Reginald Owen's *Soochow the Marine* [entry 634]. Many of the documents relate to Dillman's POW experiences and postwar veterans' reunions.

**513**   Evans, William R. *Soochow and the 4th Marines*. Rogue River, Oregon: Atwood Publishing, 1987. Pp. xiv, 144. Photographs of prewar "shackmates" in Shanghai and the meaning of the word "poontang" are just of few of the oddities to be found in this anecdotal and entertaining history of the 4th Marine Regiment and its mascot, a dog named "Soochow," as they journeyed from China to Corregidor to POW camps. Evans was an army soldier captured on Bataan who obtained much of this information from marines he met in prison and later at veterans' reunions. (See entry 577 for Evans' account of his own imprisonment.)

**514**   Hough, Frank Olney, Verle E. Ludwig, and Henry I. Shaw, Jr. *Pearl Harbor to Guadalcanal*, Vol. 1 *History of U.S. Marine Corps Operations in World War II*. Washington, DC: Historical Branch, G-3 Division, Headquarters, US Marine

Corps, 1958. Pp. x, 439. Includes a fifty-page account of "Marines in the Philippines" based largely on Admiral T.C. Hart's unpublished "Narrative of Events, Asiatic Fleet"; the Wainwright reports [entry 300]; and Colonel Howard's report [entry 512]. By contrast to most army units in the Philippine Campaign, the marines lost more men killed in action and died of wounds (315) than died as POWs (239). (This book has been placed on the web at http://www.ibiblio.org/hyperwar/USMC/USMC-I.html.)

**515**   Miller, J. Michael. *From Shanghai to Corregidor: Marines in the Defense of the Philippines.* Washington, DC: History and Museums Division, Headquarters, US Marine Corps, 1997. Pp. 44. A "Marines in World War II Commemorative Series" account of participation in the Philippine Campaign, with numerous anecdotes and photographs. Most marines fought on Corregidor, but about seventy-five were captured on Bataan, most of whom made the Death March. All are believed to have survived. Includes a brief account of the marine air warning (radar) unit, based on interviews with survivors. This account of marine radar should be contrasted with entry 350.

**516**   Santelli, James S. *A Brief History of the 4th Marines.* Washington, DC: Historical Division, HQ, USMC, 1970. Pp. v, 68. An outline history of the 4th Marine Regiment, activated in 1914 and sent to China in 1927. It evacuated to Olongapo in late 1941 and took over from the army responsibility for beach defense on Corregidor in December. Captured with the fall of the island in May 1942, the regiment was reborn in 1944 by the consolidation of several Marine raider battalions. (This book has been placed on the web at http://www.mcu.usmc.mil/ftw/files/4thMar.txt.)

Research note: The website www.txdirect.net/users/jeturner/usmc4-00.htm includes information about marines in the Philippines and China and links to related websites, including entries 514 and 516, above.

---

# Japan's Philippine Campaign

**517**   Detwiler, Donald S., and Charles Burton Burdick, eds. *War in Asia and the Pacific, 1937–1949.* New York: Garland, 1980. 15 Vols. These volumes reprint forty-seven of 184 "studies" of Japanese military operations prepared by veterans of the Japanese military for US Army history agencies between 1945 and 1960. The studies varied widely in reliability and readability. The first twelve studies (including Japanese Monograph no. 1 [entries 345 and 356]) dealt with Japanese army land and air operations in the 1941-42 Philippine Campaign, but none are reprinted here. (Most of the Philippine Campaign studies were labeled by the army as "unedited translations," which meant that they "may not be accurate or understandable.") Volume 6 reprints study no. 24, "History of the Southern Army, 1941-45," which includes a few details of the Philippine Campaign. Microfilm and bound typescript copies of the entire series exist, under the titles "Japanese Monographs" and "Japanese Studies in World War II." A guide to the series and some of the monographs have been placed on the web at http://sunsite.unc.edu/pha.

**518**    Dull, Paul S. *A Battle History of the Imperial Japanese Navy, 1941–1945.* Annapolis, MD: Naval Institute Press, 1978. Pp. xvii, 402. The author devotes a few pages to naval support of the Philippine invasion in 1941 and includes a useful bibliography describing the availability of Japanese naval documents.

**519**    Hata, Ikuhiko, and Yasuho Izawa. *Japanese Naval Aces and Fighter Units in World War II.* Translated by Don Cyril Gorham. Annapolis, MD: Naval Institute Press, 1989. Pp. xvi, 442. Very detailed compilation of biographies of naval fighter aces and of unit histories, including those that participated in the December attacks on Luzon airfields (3rd Air Group, Tainan Air Group) and one that participated in the attack on Davao (*Ryujo* Fighter Squadron). Includes many photographs and appendices listing pilots, casualties, etc. According to the editors, there is a companion volume dealing with Japanese army air fighter units, recently published in English by Grub Street, London, 2001.

**520**    Hayashi, Saburo, in collaboration with Alvin D. Coox. *Kogun: The Japanese Army in the Pacific War.* Westport, CT: Greenwood Press, 1978. Pp. xiv, 249. First published in Japanese in 1951 and in English by the Marine Corps Association in 1959. Devotes a few lines to placing the Philippine Campaign in the context of the army's southern operations. According to the authors, "Fourteenth Army Headquarters paid but scant heed to intelligence received after December 25, [1941,] to the effect that the main American Army forces were moving from Manila toward Bataan and Corregidor," but they do not explain why.

**521**    Jose, Rico [Ricardo] T. "The Pacific War in the Philippines: A Preliminary Survey of Published Material in Japanese." In *Bulletin of the American Historical Collection,* vol. 17, no. 1 (January-March 1989): 102-114. (The author's first name is mistakenly given as "Federico" in the table of contents.) Lists numerous official and unofficial Japanese-language publications dealing with World War II in the Philippines, describes their genesis and contents, tells how easy or hard the books are to find, and identifies those that have been translated into English. The author also provides brief translations from some of the sources: "The section on the [Bataan] Death March in *Hito Koryaku Sakusen* [Philippine Conquest Operations] is titled 'The So-Called 'Death March.' It quotes General Wachi (Homma's Chief of Staff) as saying that the Japanese guards also marched the whole length of the route—with full pack, rifle, helmet and other equipment besides, while the prisoners didn't carry anything... . He further states that the Japanese soldiers gave the prisoners food before eating themselves."

**522**   Nobuhiko, Jimbo. *Dawn of the Philippines*. Tokyo: Privately Published, 1959. Pp. 37. This pamphlet by a Japanese officer who served in the 1941-42 Campaign includes the claim that a Japanese army order given in Manila on 9 April 1942 stipulated that American and Filipino troops captured on Bataan were to be executed. This pamphlet is difficult to find, but the relevant quote can be found in entry 584. See also entry 330.

**523**   Sakai, Saburo, with Martin Caidin and Fred Saito. *Samurai!* New York: E.P. Dutton and Company, 1957. Pp. 382. The author was a Japanese naval air ace who took part in the attack on Clark Field on the first day of the war and is credited (see his biography in entry 519) with shooting down Colin Kelly's B-17. Aviation author Daniel Ford offers a critical and informed commentary about this book at www.danford.net/samurai.htm

**524**   Shimada, Koichi. "The Opening Air Offensive Against the Philippines." In *The Japanese Navy in World War II*, 2nd ed. Edited and translated by David C. Evans; Introduction and commentary by Raymond O'Connor. Pp. 71-104. Annapolis, MD: Naval Institute Press, 1986. Pp. xxi, 568. As a staff officer with the Japanese navy's Eleventh Air Fleet in 1941, the author participated in planning the attack on the Philippines. He credits the Japanese success in easily winning air superiority to the capabilities of the Zero fighter aircraft. The author also recalled that pre-attack photo missions drew attention to "the existence of extensive fortifications" on Bataan. These photos were "immediately sent to the Fourteenth Army for more careful study." The article appeared in the book's first edition (1969) and in *Proceedings of the U.S. Naval Institute* 81 (January 1955).

**525**   Swinson, Arthur. *Four Samurai: A Quartet of Japanese Army Commanders in the Second World War*. London: Hutchinson, 1968. Pp. 266. Includes a biography of General Masaharu Homma and an account of the conquest of the Philippines. According to Swinson, despite Homma's concern that American forces might withdraw into Bataan and upset the army high command's schedule of operations, he was ordered to make the capture of Manila, and not enemy field forces, his main objective in the 1941-42 Campaign. The army high command considered Filipino-American forces to be "third class and unworthy to face [the Japanese army] in battle" and had an equally low opinion of General MacArthur. Of Morton's [entry 334] assertion that Homma expected the defeat of Fil-American troops on Bataan to be an easy task, Swinson replies that "the opposite view seems far more probable." Swinson also writes that the Japanese found in Manila "complete plans for the defense of Bataan and Corregidor [HPD WPO-3]" about which Japanese spies had known nothing. An appendix lists staff officers of the 14th Army.

**526**   Uno, Kazumaro. *Corregidor: Isle of Delusion*. Shanghai: The Mercury Press, [1942]. Pp. 114. This blatant propaganda piece was authored by a Utah-raised journalist serving with the Japanese army. Uno arrived on Corregidor just after the surrender and lectured the hapless American POWs about how they had been "deluded" by their superiors into thinking they were fighting for a just cause and would be rescued from their predicament. Includes many photographs and some interesting observations on conditions on Corregidor. Uno claims to have carried messages to some of the marines from their girlfriends in China. Morton [entry 334] accepted Uno's version of Wainwright's surrender as generally reliable, although the version Uno gives in this book differs in detail from the one Gunnison [entry 479] claims to have gotten from him. A brief account of Uno's journalistic career is given in Yuji Ichioka, "Japanese Immigrant Nationalism: The Issei and the Sino-Japanese War, 1937-41," *California History* 69, no. 3 (Fall 1990).

**527**   Yu-Jose, Lydia N., and Ricardo Trota Jose. *An Annotated Bibliography on Philippines-Japan Relations, 1935 to 1946.* Manila: De La Salle University, 1998. Pp. 100. This annotated list of books, dissertations, pamphlets, newspaper and journal articles, and published primary documents includes a few titles that deal with the prewar army and the 1941-42 Philippine Campaign.

---

# Prisoner of War Accounts

## GENERAL GUIDES

**528**   *American and Allied Personnel Recovered from Japanese Prisons: A Pictorial History Recorded by Replacement Command, AFWESPAC.* Manila: US Army Forces Western Pacific, Replacement Command, November 1945. [Pp. 51.] Numerous photographs of recovered American and allied military and civilian prisoners at the 5th and 29th Replacement Depots established eighteen miles southeast of Manila in 1945. All recovered American army colonels and generals are pictured and identified by name, as are some junior officers, enlisted men, and civilians. One page of photos depicts ex-POWs returning to Corregidor to recover items buried there in 1942.

**529**   Daws, Gavan. *Prisoners of the Japanese: POWs of World War II in the Pacific.* New York: William Morrow and Company, 1994. Pp. 462. Stunning account of the American and European prisoner of war ordeal. Although Daws conducted hundreds of interviews and read many published and unpublished sources, he concentrated on the experiences of four American prisoners, two captured on Wake, one on Java, and one in the Philippines, Forrest Knox of the 192nd Tank Bn. According to Daws, "there is no comprehensive up-to-date list of published works on POWs" and such a list is impossible to compile given that most POW memoirs are privately published. He estimates their total numbers "in the hundreds." Daws prepared an extensive topical bibliography; it was not published with the book but could be requested separately. Levin [entry 535] dismissed this book as "race-obsessed, confused, and morally obtuse," as well as biased against the British.

**530**   Falk, Stanley L. *Bataan: The March of Death*. New York: W.W. Norton & Co., 1962. Pp. 224. Based on the author's master's thesis ("The Bataan Death March," Georgetown University, 1952), this "first attempt to tell the whole story of what happened after Bataan surrendered" remains the standard account of the Death March. Falk estimated that about 9,900 Americans participated in the March, of whom between 600 and 650 died. Filipino deaths numbered anywhere from five to ten thousand. Abraham [entries 539-40] told the Belotes [interview in the Belote Papers, entry 273] that Falk's estimate of US deaths was too high. See also entry 352.

**531**   Hatch, Gardner, chief ed. *American Ex-Prisoners of War*. Vol. 1. Paducah, KY: Turner Publishing, 1988. Pp. 184. Photographs and reminiscences of members of the American Ex-POW Association. Not all were POWs of the Japanese in World War II, but many were and include former Philippine Scouts and Philippine Army soldiers. A second volume appeared in 1991.

**532**   Kerr, E. Bartlett. *Surrender and Survival: The Experience of American POWs in the Pacific, 1941–1945*. New York: William Morrow and Co., 1985. Pp. 356. The author, son of an officer who was captured in the Philippines and died as a POW, draws on published sources, unpublished diaries and memoirs, and several dozen interviews for this detailed account. Kerr estimated that some 22,000 Americans were captured in the Philippines and that about 11,400 survived the war. Condon-Rall and Cowdrey [entry 309] state that 25,580 army and navy personnel were captured in the Philippines of whom 10,650 died. Waterford [entry 538] estimates that 17,000 Americans were captured in the Philippines of whom 11,000 survived.

**533**   Knox, Donald. *Death March: Survivors of Bataan*. New York: Harcourt Brace Jovanovich, 1981. Pp. xxv, 482. Oral history based on the recollections of sixty-eight American veterans of the Philippine Campaign and subsequent prisoners of the Japanese, not all of whom experienced the Death March. Three of those interviewed served with the Philippine Army.

**534**   LaForte, Robert S., Ronald E. Marcello, and Richard L. Himmel, eds. *With Only the Will to Live: Accounts of Americans in Japanese Prison Camps, 1941–1945*. Wilmington, DE: Scholarly Resources Inc., 1994. Pp. xxxvii, 286. The University of North Texas Oral History Program collected several hundred interviews with American veterans of the war in the Pacific and of prisoners of the Japanese. This volume includes extracts from interviews with fifty-two former POWs, many of whom were captured in the Philippines. One, Capt. William G. Adair, is identified as having commanded the 1st Bn., 21st Infantry, "Philippine Division" (the editors presumably mean 21st Division, PA). The interviews are organized by topical chapters, starting with "Capture" and ending with "The Ordeal Ends." Within each chapter are subheadings such as "attitudes toward surrender" ("A bunch of us had already decided that we weren't going to surrender," remembered one corporal: "We'd seen evidence of some of the things the Japs did to prisoners. We'd seen some Filipino Scouts who had been overrun, and they had been very badly mutilated"), "American discipline" (not much in evidence, it seems), "attitudes toward non-Americans" ("I hated the Japs," and still do; "I liked the Chinese"; the English were the "filthiest people I've ever seen in my life," but the French were even worse), and so on. The other volumes of this series are *Remembering Pearl Harbor: Eyewitness Accounts by U.S. Military Men and Women* (1991), and *Building the Death Railway: The Ordeal of American POWs in Burma, 1942–1945* (1993).

**535**   Levine, Alan J. *Captivity, Flight, and Survival in World War II*. Westport, CT: Praeger, 2000. Pp. x, 258. This survey of prison camp experiences and escapes (including Nazi concentration camps) and attempts to keep from being captured, includes two chapters on Asia and the Pacific. Levin's stories of escape and evasion are mostly drawn from published primary and secondary accounts, but for the Philippines he also consulted interrogations of escaped prisoners (such as Mellnik, Dyess, Gause and Osborne), in Record Group 319, US National Archives. For some reason, Levine is of the opinion that "relatively few Americans have published narratives of their experiences" as POWs.

**536**   Miller, Audrey Jane Furman. "The Bataan Death March and Japanese Responsibility." MA thesis, San Diego State College, 1965. Pp. 115. The author exculpates the Japanese "high command" from responsibility for the Death March. Rather, the terrible ordeal reflected "individual Japanese [acts of] cruelty and sadism." "Most of the deaths resulted from disease and starvation," she claims. Based mostly on secondary sources, war crimes trial transcripts, and interviews conducted in 1965 with five American survivors of the March.

**537**   Taylor, William Marion, Jr. "Hell Ships: Voyages of Japanese Prison Ships, 1942-1945." MA thesis, Mississippi State University, 1972. Pp. v, 119. Overview of prison ship conditions, based largely on a few published POW accounts and interviews. Much of this thesis (pp. 54-104) consists of an account of the voyage of the *Oryoku Maru* and the further ordeals of its survivors.

**538**   Waterford, Van. *Prisoners of the Japanese in World War II: Statistical History, Personal Narratives and Memorials Concerning POWs in Camps and on Hellships, Civilian Internees, Asian Slave Laborers and Others Captured in the Pacific Theater*. Jefferson, NC: McFarland & Co., 1994. Pp. xi, 394. The author (whose real name is Willem F. Wanrooy) describes all aspects of the POW experience in this standard reference work. Chapter topics range from "the world of the camp prisoner" to the issuance of "the POW medal" by the US Congress in 1985. Other chapters enumerate the prison camps, civilian internment camps, and ships carrying prisoners to Japan. He identifies thirty prison camps and ten civilian internment camps in the Philippines. The camp and ship names given by Waterford are not always those used by POW authors, but where possible ship names, sailing dates, and camp names given in the following POW memoirs have been confirmed by reference to Waterford.

## Personal Accounts

**539**   Abraham, Abie. *Ghost of Bataan Speaks*. New York: Vantage Press, 1971. Pp. 244. An enlisted man with the 31st Infantry, Abraham was liberated at Bilibid and then assigned to a body recovery detail on Bataan, an account of which takes up about one-half the book.

**540**   Abraham, Abie. *Oh God Where Are You?* New York: Vantage Press, 1997. Pp. xix, 599. Enlargement of Abraham's earlier work [previous entry], with much more on prison life and the graves recovery detail. Abraham spent about nine years in the Philippines and through recreated conversations works in the names and hometowns of hundreds of soldiers and civilians he knew or learned of in the islands. This book is a moving tribute to them.

**541**   Abraham, Theodore A., Jr. *"Do You Understand, Huh?" A POW's Lament, 1941-1945*. Manhattan, KS: Sunflower University Press, 1992. Pp. 237. This fictionalized account of the wartime experiences of an American civilian captured on Wake Island and imprisoned in China and Japan includes, for reasons that go unexplained, several photographs of Las Piñas, Philippines, where American POWs built an airfield during the war.

**542**   Alabado, Corban K. *Bataan, Death March, Capas: A Tale of Japanese Cruelty and American Injustice*. San Francisco, CA: Sulu Books, 1995. Pp. ii, 120. Despite some factual errors (contrary to the author's recollection, Napoleon Valeriano was not a West Point graduate), Alabado recalls little-known aspects of the war behind the lines on Bataan, where he was a sergeant and third lieutenant in the 31st Division, PA, supply unit, followed by his experiences on the Death March and as a prisoner (much of which time he spent on a vehicle-recovery detail on Bataan). "American Injustice" refers to the 1946 Rescission Act, which the author condemns in an afterward.

**543**   Alexander, Irvin. *Surviving Bataan and Beyond*. Edited by Dominic J. Caraccilo. Mechanicsburg, PA: Stackpole Books, 1999. Pp. ix, 340. Alexander (USMA 1919) was a quartermaster officer at Ft. Stotsensburg on 8 December 1941. He served as an advisor to the 71st Division, PA, on Bataan and survived both the Death March and the *Oryoku Maru*. After spending a few months at Fukuoka, Alexander was moved to Camp Jinsen, Korea, where he was liberated at war's end. In 1949, Alexander wrote this account of his wartime experiences, beginning with the evacuation of Stotsenburg and ending with his return to the United States in October 1945. It is particularly strong on fighting on Bataan and his relationship with the Philippine Army. The editor is familiar with the standard published

Philippine Campaign literature and had the additional benefit of having access to many letters Alexander sent home from May to December 1941.

**544** Anselmi, Vickie Annette. "Colonel Robert Besson: Japanese Prisoner of War, 1941–1945." MA thesis, Northwestern State University of Louisiana, 1985. Pp. viii, 275. An adviser to the 23rd Infantry, 21st Division, PA, Besson had the unhappy experience of being one of the first American soldiers captured by the Japanese in the Philippines (on 26 December 1941). He began keeping a diary while a prisoner in 1943, backdating entries to 8 December 1941. (Among Besson's first work details as a POW was cleaning up a building to be used as an officers' brothel.) This MA thesis is an edited copy of his diary. Through the use of secondary sources and interviews with people such as Besson's widow, the editor has attempted to identify the people and places mentioned in the diary. Anselmi's attempt to obtain more information about the Japanese prison guards mentioned by Besson elicited a five-line response from the Japanese government's Department of Welfare informing her (in Japanese) that "the records of those Japanese who worked at the prison camps are not made public."

**545** Armstrong, Raymond P. *San Hyaku Go (305): Tales of a Prison Camp Horsetrader, May 6, 1942—November 1, 1945.* Eugene, OR: ACO Publishing, 1992. Pp. iii, 300. Written by Armstrong in 1946-48, the book was edited for publication by his widow after Armstrong's death in 1988. Captured on Ft. Drum and briefly a POW at Lipa, the author spent much of the war at Cabanatuan numbers 1 and 3, where his trading skills brought him a "prison-camp fortune" and kept him in fairly good health (a few pounds under normal weight) until he went to Japan on the *Matti Matti Maru (Canadian Inventor)* in July 1944. After working at several mostly unnamed camps in southern Japan, Armstrong ended the war at "camp no. 12" (Fukuoka?), a coal-mining camp where a few Americans mingled with Dutch and British POWs.

**546** Ashton, Paul, ed. *And Somebody Gives a Damn!* Santa Barbara, CA: Ashton Publications, 1990. Pp. xxi, 418. The author decided he could "improve [the] historical account" given in *Bataan Diary* [next entry] by editing the writings of others who had seen different aspects of the fighting on Bataan and Corregidor. The accounts of Dr. (Major) Willard Waterous, army nurse Josie Nesbit, and Dr. (Colonel) James Gillespie, describe medical conditions in hospitals on Bataan and other army medical facilities during the fighting and later in Bilibid prison. Waterous, an army surgeon who had served at Sternberg Hospital from 1919 to 1922 and returned to the Philippines to establish a civilian medical practice in 1923, also contributes an account of medical conditions in the Philippines before the war. The book reprints extracts from diaries and first-person accounts describing such things as the voyage of the hospital ship *Mactan* [entries 309, 326, 337, and 609] marines on Corregidor, and the experience of nurse Leona Gastinger, who escaped to Australia. It includes a large collection of maps and photographs.

**547** Ashton, Paul. *Bataan Diary.* Santa Barbara, CA: Ashton Publications, 1984.

Pp. xvi, 463. A recently recruited army doctor assigned to the Ft. McKinley hospital in June 1941, Ashton served with the 12th Medical Battalion (or Regiment), the 33rd Infantry Combat Team (of the 31st Division, PA), and finally the 51st Division hospital on Bataan. Ashton served as the prison doctor on work details in Tayabas and Bataan and was freed at Bilibid in February 1945. The last 100 pages of the book reprint records from the "Board Concerning Services Rendered American POWs in the Philippines During World War II."

**548**   Baker, Donald L. *Life—On Rice*. New York: Carlton Press, 1963. Pp. 51. Baker arrived in the Philippines in July 1940 and was assigned to a coast artillery regiment on Corregidor, a boring, "heart-breaking" place, from which "many men ... rode back to the States locked up in a section of some Army transport ship," although he found the place "quite agreeable." This short book describes mostly his imprisonment at the Yodogawa Steel Yards at Osaka from November 1942. Includes a list of POWs at the camp.

**549**   Bank, Bertram. *Back from the Living Dead*. Tuscaloosa, AL: Privately Published, n.d. Pp. 108. Major Bank was an air corps officer captured on Bataan. His account starts on the day of capture and continues to his release from Cabanatuan on 30 January 1945. Portions of his story appeared in the St. Louis *Globe-Democrat* in October 1945.

**550**   Barker, Robert A. *Philippine Diary: A Journal of Life as a Prisoner of War*. Chicago: The Robert A. Barker Foundation, 1990. Pp. xvii, 156. Barker (USMA 1938) was a 31st US Infantry officer who died aboard the *Oryoku Maru* in December 1944. This book reprints brief diary entries Barker kept from 24 May 1942 to 5 June 1944, when he was a POW at Davao. Barker gave the diary to a fellow POW who remained at Bilibid.

**551**   Bergee, Lee K. *Guest of the Emperor: The Personal Story of Ex-POW Frank O. Promnitz, U.S.M.C.* High Ridge, MO: Four Freedoms Press, 1987. Pp. 250. Promnitz had been stationed at Cavite Naval Yard where he served aboard the USS *San Felipe*, which had the job of ferrying naval personnel from Cavite to Manila and back again. Promnitz recalls every bar he visited around Cavite and some other details of prewar life. On Corregidor he was posted near the south dock. After stints at Bilibid and Cabanatuan, he was imprisoned at Hitachi, Japan, from early 1944. Author Bergee tells Promnitz's story in the first person, embedding it in a larger account of the Philippine Campaign (obviously based on considerable knowledge of the Campaign literature, although he cites no sources), which can make it difficult to know whether an event is something in which Promnitz participated or about which Bergee read. POWs, the author has Promnitz say, "will always remember the blunders and miscalculations [MacArthur] made during those early days of the war."

**552**   Berry, F. Langwith. *A Few Memories as a Prisoner of War*. N.p.n.d. Pp. 80. The author, an officer with the 86th FA (PS), tells of the Death March, the POW camp at Davao (the famous escape getting only a passing mention), surviving the

*Oryoku Maru*, and imprisonment at Fukuoka camp no. 1. Berry's four months in the islands before the outbreak of war are hardly mentioned, but the book includes several poorly reproduced photos of a prewar artillery encampment near Dagupan.

**553**   Berry, William A., with James Edwin Alexander, *Prisoner of the Rising Sun*. Norman, OK: University of Oklahoma Press, 1993. Pp. xiv, 241. With a reserve commission in navy intelligence but no training of any kind, Berry arrived in Cavite in November 1941. He was, by his own account, a glorified messenger boy. Captured on Corregidor, he was sent to Cabanatuan where he participated in a controversial escape criticized in other POW memoirs (because of the danger of retaliatory executions). He was recaptured and confined at Bilibid, where he remained until liberation.

**554**   Bilyeu, Dick. *Lost in Action: A World War II Soldier's Account of Capture on Bataan and Imprisonment by the Japanese*. Jefferson, NC: McFarland & Co., Inc., 1991. Pp. vii, 343. The author enlisted in the army in 1938 and arrived in the Philippines in April 1941. Stationed on Ft. Hughes (G Btry, 59th CA Regiment), Bilyeu was reassigned with several hundred others to be infantry soldiers on Bataan at the end of December 1941. Bilyeu was shipped to an unidentified camp in Japan in late 1944.

**555**   Bocksel, Arnold A. *Rice, Men and Barbed Wire*. Hauppauge, NY: Michael B. Glass & Associates, 1991. Pp. v, 158. Bocksel had been an engineering officer in the merchant marine before joining the army in 1941 and arriving in the Philippines in September. He served as chief engineer aboard the Corregidor-based army mine planter *Harrison*, and he explains how the harbor mine system worked. Captured when Corregidor surrendered, Bocksel was among the first group of POWs transported north, to Manchuria, in October 1942.

**556**   Bodine, Roy L. *No Place for Kindness: The Prisoner of War Diary of Roy L. Bodine*. Ft. Sam Houston, TX: Ft. Sam Houston Museum, 1983; reprint, 1995. Pp. xv, 87. Bound typescript. Bodine was a dental officer assigned to Sternberg Hospital in September 1939 (and had been an army dependent in the islands in 1924-25). The diary entries run from 19 October 1944 to 8 September 1945. Bodine survived the *Oryoku Maru* and was imprisoned at Jinsen, Korea, from April 1945 to liberation.

**557**   Boisclaire, Yvonne. *In the Shadow of the Rising Sun*. Bella Vista, CA: Clearwood Publishers, 1996. Pp. x, 186. (A 2nd edition appeared in 1997.) Robert Davis, mess sergeant for D Battery, 515th CA Regiment (AA), recalled for the author every miserable detail of his life as a POW. He sailed to Japan aboard the *Nagato Maru* in November 1942 and was imprisoned at Umeda Bunsho (near Osaka), Tanagawa, Takefu, and Tsuruga. Davis managed to keep a list of his battery members throughout the war. One, detached from the unit and serving on Corregidor, was killed in action; of the remaining seventy-two, thirty died as POWs.

**558**   Brain, Philip S., Jr. *Soldier of Bataan: Retrospective Observations of a Thoughtful Survivor*. Minneapolis, MN: Rotary Club of Minneapolis, 1990. Pp. 95. Reprints three talks Brain, a veteran of the 194th Tank Battalion, gave reflecting on his POW experiences before the Minneapolis Rotary Club in 1965, 1983, and 1986. Brain was captured on Bataan, imprisoned at Davao, and sent to Japan in September 1944.

**559**   Braly, William C. *The Hard Way Home*, Washington, DC: Infantry Journal Press, 1947. Pp. xi, 282. Colonel Braly was the Operations Officer on Harbor Defenses staff. He arrived in the Philippines in July 1939, but the book recalls only the senior-officers' POW routine in camps in the Philippines, Taiwan, and Manchuria.

**560**   Brougher, William E. *South to Bataan, North to Mukden: The Prison Diary of Brigadier General W.E. Brougher*. Edited by D. Clayton James. Athens, GA: University of Georgia Press, 1971. Pp. xxiii, 207. Lt. Col. Brougher arrived in the Philippines in 1939 to serve with the 57th Infantry. Although commissioned since 1911, it was his first assignment to the islands. He was promoted to command of the 11th PA Division, and James recounts Brougher's and the division's experiences up to the surrender of Bataan. Most of the book (pp. 40-192) reprints Brougher's prison diary entries, from 1 January 1943 to 5 September 1945, during which Brougher was in camps in Taiwan and Manchuria. The 1942 entries were lost.

**561**   Brown, Charles M., *et al.*, comps. *The Oryoku Maru Story*. Magalia, CA: Oryoku Maru Memorial, 1983. [Pp. 63] Pamphlet "compiled by four survivors of the *Oryoku Maru* in the hopes that, by its very existence, we might find other survivors" and inform the relatives of non-survivors of "the true story of the *Oryoku Maru*." Includes navy photographs of the sinking ship, maps, list of POWs aboard the ship, and copies of the summaries of the trials of Japanese soldiers charged with causing the deaths of POWs aboard the ship. Some of these documents are reprinted in Lawton [entry 608].

**562**   Brown, Charles Thomas. *Bars from Bilibid Prison: Poems*. San Antonio, TX: The Naylor Co., 1947. Pp. xx, 129. Poems written on Bataan and at Bilibid. Includes a short history of the prison.

**563**   Brown, Robert Morris "Vanderbilt," with Donald Permenter. *"I Solemnly Swear": The Story of a GI Named Brown*. New York: Vantage Press, 1957. Pp. xiii, 203. Brown was an army corpsman in charge of the Bottomside dispensary on Corregidor and well into his third year of duty in the Philippines when the war began, but he says little about prewar life in the islands. His reputation was tarnished by a too-close association with POW collaborator Sgt. John David Provoo. Brown claimed to be a member of the Vanderbilt family—a name with patriotic connotations—to save himself from the ire of other POWs and to obtain favors, since the POWs assumed the wealthy Vanderbilts would repay any loans after the war. (An officer who had lent him money actually sued him for its return after the war.) A POW at Davao and a survivor of the *Oryoku Maru*, Brown was freed at Jinsen, Korea.

**564**    Bumgarner, John R. *Parade of the Dead: A U.S. Army Physician's Memoir of Imprisonment by the Japanese, 1942–1945*. Jefferson, NC: McFarland, 1995. Pp. x, 212. A medical reserve officer, Bumgarner was called to active duty in December 1940 and arrived in the Philippines in February 1941. Assigned to Sternberg and then to Hospitals 1 and 2 on Bataan, he offers one of the more detailed recollections of peacetime army life in the islands as well as conditions on Bataan. Several chapters describe the voyage from the US, army life in Manila, and medical work at Sternberg, with some attention paid to soldier-Filipino relations. After the surrender, Bumgarner remained on duty at Hospital no. 2. After the usual detours (Cabanatuan, Bilibid), he was sent to Japan in March 1944 aboard the *Enoura Maru* (this ship is listed in Waterford [entry 538] but not this voyage) and ended the war in a camp at Bibai, Hokkaido.

**565**    Bunker, Paul D. *Bunker's War: The World War II Diary of Col. Paul D. Bunker*. Edited by Keith A. Barlow. Novato, CA: Presidio Press, 1996. Pp. ix, 309. Bunker (USMA 1903) commanded the Seaward Defense Command (batteries of the 59th, 91st, 92nd and 1st Philippine Army coast artillery regiments) on Corregidor and other fortified islands of Manila Bay. He had been assigned to the Philippines in 1915-17, again in the mid-1930s, and volunteered to return yet again in 1940. Bunker was contemptuous of Philippine Army soldiers but has harsh things to say about many of his American comrades, too. The diary entries begin on 3 January 1942 and record mostly the minutiae of life under siege. Even a senior officer could have little understanding of the "big picture." The second half of the diary records Bunker's life in a senior officers' POW camp until his death in 1943 at Karenko, Taiwan.

**566**    Carson, Andrew D. *My Time in Hell: Memoir of an American Soldier Imprisoned by the Japanese in World War II*. Jefferson, NC: McFarland, 1997. Pp. ix, 304. The author, a veteran of the 59th CA Regiment, provides an extensive account of life in Ft. Drum during the fighting and the "special treatment" meted out to the fort's survivors following the surrender. After incarceration at Bilibid and Cabanatuan camps 1 and 3, Carson was transported to Japan aboard the *Nissyo Maru* in July 1944. He spent the remainder of the war at Fukuoka camp no. 23, where he worked in a coal mine and was subjected to medical experiments by Japanese doctors.

**567**    Chunn, C[Alvin]E[llsworth], ed. *Of Rice and Men: The Story of Americans Under the Rising Sun*. Los Angeles and Tulsa, OK: Veterans' Publishing Company, 1946. Pp. 230. "Begun," writes Chunn, a major with the 45th Infantry (PS), "as a morale project in Cabanatuan Prison Camp Number 1 in 1942" offering "an outlet to the ambitions of writers and artists" in the camp. This is the resultant collection of poems, drawings, diary entries, stories and photographs. A few stories, by men who were there, depict the surrender on Bataan. Chunn intended to write a history of the Philippine Campaign and wrote down the experiences of many officers in prison camp, but this book is as far as he got.

**568**   Coleman, John S., Jr. *Bataan and Beyond: Memories of an American POW.* College Station: Texas A & M University Press, 1978. Pp. x, 210. Made commanding officer of the 27th Materiel Squadron at Nichols Field a few days before the start of the war, Coleman later saw considerable action with the Air Corps Regiment on Bataan, which he commanded the last two days of the Bataan Campaign. Coleman was shipped to Japan in November 1942 aboard the *Nagato Maru*, and most of the book tells of his experiences at the Yodogawa Steel Mill near Osaka and at Zentsuji and Roku Roshi prison camps.

**569**   Coone, Herbert W. *The Sequential Soldier.* Baltimore: Gateway, 1992. Pp. xvi, 262. Coone was surgeon for Co. A, 803rd Engineer Battalion, which was assigned to build an airfield near Camp O'Donnell before the war. Captured near Kindley Field on Corregidor in May 1942, Coone was later the POW doctor for work details at Lipa, Batangas, and Camp Murphy. (He also spent time at Bilibid and comments on hostility between US Army and Navy men there.) Coone went to Taiwan aboard the "Benjo Maru" (real name *Haru Maru*) in October 1944, and remained at Taihoku camp no. 6 for the remainder of the war. Pages 184-262 include lists of POWs at various camps and a roster of the 803rd Engineer Battalion (consisting of companies A, B, and C, the latter company originally the 809th Engineer Bn.).

**570**   Cordero, V. N. *My Experiences During the War with Japan.* N.p. n.d. (Printed by Zerreiss & Co., Nuremberg, Germany, [c1950].) Pp. 62. An animated remembrance of the author's prison experiences follows a much less revealing account of action with the Philippine Army in south Luzon and on Bataan. Puerto Rico-born Cordero commanded the 52nd Infantry ("Hijos de Bicol") during the retreat into Bataan and later took command of the 72nd Infantry Regiment. Cordero had published a lengthier Spanish-language account of his experiences as *Bataán y la Marcha de la Muerta* (Madrid: Afrodisio Aguado, 1957).

**571**   Czerwien, Anthony. *POW: Tears That Never Dry.* Monroe, NY: Library Research Associates, Inc., 1994. Pp. 107. Chicago-born Czerwien enlisted in the air corps in August 1940 and arrived in Manila with the 17th Pursuit Squadron in December 1940. A few pages describe the unit's experiences at Nichols and Iba Fields in the year before the war. Czerwien became one of the air corps' "provisional infantrymen" on Bataan. He participated in the Death March and for over two years (May 1942-September 1944) remained on a work detail at Clark Field. In October 1944 he boarded the *Haru Maru* for Camp Heito, Taiwan, and later continued to Camp Osikura, Japan.

**572**   Day, Kenneth W. *Forty-Nine Days in Hell: The Story of the Oryoko [sic] Maru.* Santa Fe, NM: Bataan Veterans' Organization, n.d. Pp. 22. Pamphlet (also published in the *Ex-POW Bulletin* in 1952-53) describing the fate of those who sailed toward Japan from Manila on the *Oryoku Maru* on 13 December 1944. Of the 1,619 who began the voyage, an estimated 300 reached Japan; half of those did not survive to war's end. Several pages of this pamphlet consists of extracts from "Peart's Journal" [entry 636].

**573**   Donovan, William N. *P.O.W. in the Pacific: Memoirs of an American Doctor in World War II.* Edited by Josephine Donovan, with Ann Devigne Donovan. Wilmington, DE: Scholarly Resources, 1998. Pp. xvii, 182. Donovan arrived in the Philippines in late 1940 and was a surgeon with the 45th Infantry (PS) on Bataan. He was one of those officers who accompanied Col. Thomas Doyle, the regiment's commanding officer, to Corregidor when Bataan fell. Other accounts accuse Doyle of deserting his regiment, but Donovan claims that MacArthur had ordered that Doyle be evacuated from the Philippines. Donovan's recollections of service on Bataan and Corregidor, as a POW at Bilibid and at the Port Area camp, aboard a hell ship (name uncertain but apparently the *Haru Maru*, which left Manila on 3 October 1944), and at Shirakawa, Taiwan, are contextualized by the editors (his daughter and wife) by reference to the standard Philippine Campaign and POW histories. A particularly interesting and unusual aspect of this book is a chapter, "The Home Front," which recounts how Donovan's wife dealt with her husband's captivity. Donovan also testified at Provoo's trial in the 1950s.

**574**   Dopkins, Dale R. *The Janesville 99: The Bataan Death March.* Janesville, WI: Privately Published, 1981. Pp. iii, 45. Tells what happened to the members of Company A, 192nd Tank Battalion, whose members were from Janesville, Wisconsin. Two were killed in the Philippine Campaign (one, the company commander, accidentally); another sixty-two died as prisoners of war [see also entries 500–501].

**575**   Dyess, William E. *The Dyess Story.* Edited, with a biographical introduction, by Charles Leavelle. New York: G.P. Putnam's Sons, 1944. Pp. 182. Classic account of the Death March by a pilot of the 21st Pursuit Squadron. Dyess, one of the ten who escaped from Davao in April 1943 [see entries 586, 590, 608, 620, and 623], was the first recovered POW who had experienced the Death March. Until then, the US had little information about what had become of the men who had surrendered on Bataan. The government sat on Dyess's explosive story until January 1944, when it was published by *The Chicago Tribune*, in a series of articles upon which this book is based. Dyess had died the month before in an airplane crash in California.

**576**   Emerson, K.C. *Guest of the Emperor.* Arlington, VA: Privately Published, 1977. Pp. 136. Bound typescript. The author arrived in the Philippines in January 1941 and was a company commander in the 12th Quartermaster Regiment (PS). His account commences with surrender on Bataan. Emerson was transferred to Japan aboard the *Nagato Maru* in November 1942 and spent much of the war at the "better than average" Zentsuji camp. In June 1945 he was sent to a small camp in the mountains, Roku Roshi, where prisoners cleared land and planted potatoes. Includes a roster of POWs transferred from Zentsuji to Roku Roshi and photographs and diagrams of the camp.

**577**   Evans, William R. *Kora!* Rogue River, OR: Atwood Publishing Co., 1986. Pp. xiv, 157. The author, one of the better ex-POW storytellers, was a member of the 200th CA Regiment who survived the Death March, Camps O'Donnell and Cabanatuan, the Las Piñas airfield work detail (includes diagrams of each camp), and a trip to Japan aboard the "Benjo Maru" (which he identifies as the *Haru Maru*) in October 1944. He ended up in a camp at Kosaka, Japan.

**578**   Fitzpatrick, Bernard T., with John A. Sweetser III. *The Hike into the Sun: Memoir of an American Soldier Captured on Bataan in 1942 and Imprisoned by the Japanese until 1945.* Jefferson, NC: McFarland & Co., Inc., 1993. Pp. xi, 243. Drafted into the army in April 1941 and assigned to the 194th Tank Battalion, the author devotes considerable space to prewar activities in the Philippines. He was struck by the contrast between the intensive training being done in the US and the "slow motion existence" in the islands. Fitzpatrick survived the Death March, O'Donnell, Cabanatuan (where he worked on a food distribution detail at Cabanatuan under Maj. Thomas Smothers, father of the "Smothers Brothers" comedians), and imprisonment at Fukuoka, Japan. He reprints some common surrender photos and offers interesting commentary concerning the conditions under which the photos were taken and some of the people in them.

**579**   Flake, Lester W. *The Remnant.* N.p. Privately Published, 1981. Pp. 150. Stories of enlistment, fighting in the Philippines, captivity, and liberation told by New Mexico veterans of the 200th/515th and 60th Coast Artillery Regiments, with the focus on the experiences of enlisted man Wallace Hall of the 200th CAC.

**580**   Fortier, Malcolm Vaughn. *The Life of a P.O.W. Under the Japanese: In Caricature as Sketched by Col. Malcolm Vaughn Fortier.* Spokane, WA: C. W. Hill Printing, 1946. Pp. 150. 241 pencil drawings (the first, dated 25 April 1942, shows a scene at Camp O'Donnell; the last, dated 20 August 1945, depicts a camp in Manchuria) by Col. "Bob" Fortier, senior advisor to the 41st Division, PA, on Bataan. Fortier had these drawings published for the benefit of fellow prisoners, and the book concludes with a list of men with whom Fortier was incarcerated. (The original drawings were given to another former POW when Fortier died in 1958 and have since disappeared.)

**581**   Gautier, James Donovan, Jr., with Robert L. Whitmore. *I Came Back from Bataan.* Greenville, SC: Emerald House Group/Blue Ridge Publishing, 1997. Pp. 215, A1–A14. Engrossing account of fighting on Bataan, the Death March, and imprisonment by an aircraft mechanic with Headquarters Squadron, 27th Bombardment Group (Light), a unit that arrived, without its aircraft, just days before the outbreak of war. Much of the book describes Gautier's POW experiences on a fifteen-man truck-driving detail at Baguio (from May 1942 to May 1944) before volunteering for transfer to Japan in July 1944, where he worked until liberation as a coal miner at Omuta (Fukuoka camp no. 17). Unusually, the author provides the names of POW collaborators. Appendices list members of his bombardment group.

**582**   Gloria, Claro C. *All the Way from Bataan to O'Donnell.* Quezon City: Privately Published, 1978. Pp. viii, 118. A teacher at De La Salle college and a prewar reserve officer, Gloria was called to active duty in September 1941 and assigned to the 2nd Regular Division on Bataan. Gloria devotes considerable attention to the relationship of American to Filipino officers and refutes postwar claims by some veterans that Americans were better fed on Bataan than Filipinos. As POWs at Camp O'Donnell, the author writes, some senior Filipino officers were harsher on the men than were the Japanese.

**583**   Goodman, Julien M. *M.D.P.O.W.* New York: Exposition Press, 1972, Pp. 218. The author was a medical doctor who served at hospital no. 1 on Bataan, but this book deals entirely with his POW experiences. Goodman missed the Death March, but remained at O'Donnell until it closed in January 1943, was transported to Taiwan aboard the *Haru Maru* in October 1944 and to Japan in January 1945. He spent the remainder of the war at Senryu camp no. 24 near Nagasaki, a small camp with mostly British and Australian prisoners.

**584**   Gordon, Richard M., with the assistance of Benjamin S. Llamzon. *Horyo: Memoirs of an American POW.* St. Paul, MN: Paragon House, 1999. Pp. xxix, 274. Gordon, an enlisted man with the 31st Infantry who arrived in the Philippines in October 1940, provides a detailed account of army life in prewar Manila, fighting on Bataan (including an evaluation of Wainwright's leadership), and prison life at O'Donnell and Cabanatuan. Gordon was among the early groups to travel to Japan, aboard the *Nagato Maru* in November 1942, where he was imprisoned at Mitsushima for the rest of the war. A major purpose of Gordon's book is to draw attention to the execrable conduct of many American POWs: doctors who sold medications, soldiers who plundered fellow prisoners, officers—especially reservists and national guard officers—without the least regard for their men. Many of these men, Gordon claims, have become today "professional prisoners of war," peddling stories of supposed heroics. Contrary to many, many, other accounts, Gordon also claims that homosexuality was not uncommon after the POWs had recovered from the effects of the early months of imprisonment. Gordon also discusses the monuments at war-related sites in the Philippines and US. Appendices include photographs of prewar and current sights in Japan and the Philippines, a list of West Point graduates who died as POWs of the Japanese, and a list of POWs at Mitsushima (Tokyo camp 2-d) in November 1942.

**585**   Grady, Frank J., and Rebecca Dickson. *Surviving the Day: An American POW in Japan.* Annapolis, MD: Naval Institute Press, 1997. Pp. xii, 274. An army radio operator, Grady had been in the islands six years as enlisted man and officer when war broke out. Assigned to the 228th Signal Operations Company at Ft. Santiago, the author was USAFFE custodian of codes and ciphers. His tasks included encoding intercepted Japanese messages for retransmission to code breakers in the United States (although he was not involved in the intercepting and decoding of enemy message traffic). Captured on Corregidor and imprisoned at Cabanatuan, Grady and several others were pointed out to the Japanese by an American officer as knowledgeable about army codes. Grady was sent to Japan for further interrogation where, curiously, the Japanese did not then press him to reveal what he knew of US cryptographic equipment and techniques.

**586**   Grashio, Samuel C., and Bernard Norling. *Return to Freedom: The War Memoirs of Col. Samuel C. Grashio, USAF (Ret.).* Tulsa, OK: MCN Press, 1982. Pp. ii, 166. A pilot with the 21st Pursuit Squadron, Sam Grashio was one of the few who kept flying until the surrender of Bataan. Grashio survived the Death March, O'Donnell, and Cabanatuan, and volunteered for a 1,000-man work detail that left for Davao in October 1942. He was one of a group of ten POWs who successfully escaped from the Davao camp in April 1943. Here, Grashio provides the recollections and historian Norling draws on other primary and secondary sources to put them in context [see also entries 575, 590, 608, 620, and 623].

**587**   Hamilton, James M. *Rainbow Over the Philippines.* Chicago: Adams Press, 1977. Pp. 53. A senior NCO with the 200th CA (AA), Hamilton was one of those sent to Manila to form the 515th CA (AA) on 8 December after the attack on Clark Field. Hamilton claims that "contrary to general belief, [the 200th CAC] had the very latest [anti-aircraft] equipment" at war's start. He remained in the Philippines throughout the war, at Cabanatuan and Ft. McKinley POW camps before being freed at Bilibid. Hamilton wrote this account in 1945 and published it in 1974. This edition includes a "1977 Update" describing a visit made to the Philippines that year by several 200th CA veterans.

**588**   Haney, Robert E. *Caged Dragons: An American P.O.W. in WW II Japan.* Ann Arbor, MI: Sabre Press, 1991. Pp. xiv, 267. A marine serving at Tientsin when the China marines left for the Philippines in late 1941, Haney moved from Olongapo to Sangley Point to Mariveles to Cavite before finally ending up on beach defense at Caballo Island. Taken to Japan in mid-1942 (no ship name provided), Haney was successively imprisoned at Wakayama, Osaka camp no. 1, and Notogawa. This is one of the more reflective records of the POW experience (including the problems of postwar adjustment to civilian life). Like many veterans, Haney believes that the major problem besetting the American and Filipino forces in 1941-42 was poor senior leadership.

**589**   Harrison, Thomas R. *Survivor: Memoir of Defeat and Captivity—Bataan, 1942.* Salt Lake City, UT: Western Epics, 1989. Pp. xii, 223. An ROTC graduate of the University of Utah, Harrison volunteered for Philippine duty in mid-1941. He served several months with the 88th FA (PS) at Stotsenburg before being assigned as an instructor with the 21st Division. He includes a good description of the types of artillery used in the campaign and devotes about one-half of the book to the fighting on Bataan. Harrison went to Japan aboard the *Nagato Maru* in November 1942 and was liberated at Roku Roshi.

**590**   Hawkins, Jack. *Never Say Die.* Philadelphia: Dorrance & Co., 1961. Pp. 196. A Fourth Marines' officer captured on Corregidor, Hawkins and two fellow marines (Lt. Mike Dobervich and Capt. Austin Shofner) at Cabanatuan volunteered for the work party sent to Davao, from where they planned to escape. Although there had been "only a handful of collaborators and informers" at Cabanatuan, too many men had "sank to the level of animals or worse." The marines alone had maintained their "discipline and group spirit," and only reluctantly at Davao did Hawkins and his comrades involve themselves with the two other parties that eventually escaped. Hawkins remained in Mindanao for several months as a guerrilla before a submarine took him to Australia. One of the ten escapees, Lt. Leo Boelens, was later killed fighting on Mindanao; in addition to Hawkins, four other of the remaining nine published accounts of the escape [see entries 575, 586, 608, 620, and 623]. Hawkins remained in the marines after the war and was later involved in the Bay of Pigs operation.

**591**   Hayes, Thomas. *Bilibid Diary: The Secret Notebooks of Commander Thomas Hayes— POW, The Philippines, 1942–45*. Edited by A.B. Feuer. New York: Archon Books, 1987. Pp. xxii, 248. Hayes, a naval medical officer since 1924, reported for duty at Cavite in August 1941 and in December became the chief medical officer of the 4th Marine Regiment. His diary begins on 2 July 1942 and continues to 17 September 1944. Hayes died aboard the *Enoura Maru* on 8 January 1945. Hayes has harsh words for many, by name, in this candid account of Bataan and imprisonment at Bilibid. The original of this diary, written on Bureau of Immigration deportation forms, has been on display in the Naval Historical Center, Washington Naval Yard. This book was reprinted by Pacific Press in 1999 under the title *FDR's Prisoner Spy: The POW Diary of Cdr. Thomas Hayes, USN*. The title refers to a brief essay about the voyage of the USS *Milwaukee* to the Azores in April 1941, that the author speculates was intended to give the Germans a target that could lead to US entry into the war. He claims that Hayes had been doing "spy" work since "around the year 1936" and was included in the voyage to establish a spy network on Azores. Fever claims that Hayes was sent to the Philippines to do the same.

**592**   Hibbs, Ralph Emerson. *Tell MacArthur to Wait*. New York: Carlton Press, 1988. Pp. 252. Reprinted by Giraffe Books, Quezon City, 1996. Hibbs, surgeon to the 2nd Bn., 31st US Infantry, recalls the easy and companionable living in Manila—especially once the officers' wives and families left in mid-1941—in the six months before the outbreak of war. The book's content is evenly divided between describing fighting on Bataan and life as a POW. Hibbs was freed from captivity at Cabanatuan in January 1945.

**593**   Hildreth, Jim. *Thank You, America, for Bringing Me Home*. Sonora, CA: Studio One, 1994. Pp. xi, 110. In this anecdote-filled memoir, the author, a cook and radioman aboard the sub-tender *Canopus*, claims to have received a navy-transmitted war message early on the morning of 8 December 1941. He carried the message to the Cavite base commander, who—as Hildreth tells the story—read it, turned out his bedside lamp, and went back to sleep. Captured on Corregidor, Hildreth went to Japan in July 1943 (no ship name provided) to Omuta camp no. 17.

**594**   Hileman, Millard E., and Paul Fridlund. *1051: An American POW's Remarkable Journey Through World War II.* Walla Walla, WA: Words Worth Press, 1992. Pp. xi, 373. A member of the 698th Ordnance Squadron who arrived at Clark Field in mid-1941, Hileman and six other soldiers decided to escape from Bataan rather than surrender. He never became a guerrilla (it seemed too much like being back in the army) but lived with friendly Filipinos until surrendering in June 1943, by which time it had become clear that his continued freedom was too much of a burden on the civilian community. Hileman confronts in unsparing detail his mental and physical collapse aboard the *Nissyo Maru* in July 1944. He spent the remainder of the war at Fukuoka camp no. 3.

**595**   Hitchcock, W. Pat. *Forty Months in Hell.* Jackson, TN: Page Publishing, 1996. Pp. 186. This 4th Marines veteran (enlisted 1939) captured on Corregidor was a POW at Cabanatuan, Bilibid, and Las Piñas before boarding the *Nissyo Maru* in July 1944 for Japan, where he was imprisoned at Oeyama (Osaka no. 3). Includes a few observations on life in China and around Subic Bay just before the war. Hitchcock has few kind words for his fellow prisoners and includes a chapter justifying the dropping of the atomic bombs.

**596**   Holloway, Carl Milner. *Happy, the POW: A Short History About a Long Ordeal.* Brandon, MA: Quail Ridge Press, 1981. Pp. 78. Brief account of fighting on Corregidor and captivity in Japan written for family and friends. US Marine Holloway had been in Shanghai for a few months before arriving in the Philippines in November 1941. He was on the Las Piñas work detail and went to Japan in early 1944.

**597**   Howell, John Benjamin. *42 Months in Hell: My Life as a Prisoner of the Japanese, World War II.* 2nd ed. Muskogee, OK: Privately Published, 1971. Pp. 47. (A first edition appeared in 1970.) The author's unit, E Battery, 59th CAC, surrendered on Fort Drum. After surviving the special treatment meted out to Drum's garrison, Howell was at Cabanatuan no. 3 before being shipped to Japan, where he was imprisoned at what he refers to as camp no. 23, on Kyushu. Despite hunger, beatings, and hard work in nearby mines from June 1944 to September 1945, no prisoner died at the camp. A recurring theme of this brief work is Howell's contempt for American officers, who lived better than the enlisted POWs and were quick to inform on men who transgressed prison rules.

**598**   Hubbard, Preston John. *Apocalypse Undone: My Survival of Japanese Imprisonment During World War II.* Nashville, TN: Vanderbilt University Press, 1990. Pp. x, 263. The author arrived in the Philippines in August 1941 and was assigned to the 330th Signal Company (later redesignated the 409th) at Nichols Field. Hubbard is unusually critical of fellow prisoners and, less unusually, of the prewar army officer corps in the Philippines. From July 1942 to July 1944, he was on the permanent party of POWs at Bilibid and was then sent to Narumi prison camp, near Nagoya, Japan.

**599**   Ingle, Don. *No Less a Hero.* N.p.: Privately Published, 1994. Pp. xiv, 298.

Dramatized, explicit, and embellished account of prewar nightlife in Manila, relationships with Filipinas, fighting on Bataan, and POW life by a veteran of the 31st Infantry. Ingle was on the harsh Nichols Field POW work detail, went to Japan to an unidentified camp aboard the *Nissyo Maru*, and later returned to Japan to testify at war crimes trial. The book includes many photos of Japanese prison guards.

**600**   Jackson, Calvin G. *Diary of Col. Calvin G. Jackson, M.D.* Ada, OH: Ohio Northern University Press, 1992. Pp. 273. Short entries, some along the lines of "slept well, lugao again for breakfast" but others very detailed, in a daily diary the author managed to keep from 20 February 1941 when he reported for active duty in Ohio to his arrival back in San Francisco on 3 October 1945. A medical officer, Jackson was assigned to the 12th Medical Regiment (PS) after arriving in the Philippines in August 1941 and later served with the 51st Division, PA, in southern Luzon and on Bataan. He was transferred to Hospital no. 2, apparently because he could not get along with Philippine Army doctors. "Gen. [Albert M.] Jones had told us many times to kick their asses," an admonition Jackson seems to have taken literally and for which he was officially reprimanded by MacArthur. He was a POW at Davao before being transported to Japan aboard the *Noto Maru* in September 1944, where he was imprisoned at Shinagawa and Ashio.

**601**   Jacobs, Eugene C. *Blood Brothers: A Medic's Sketch Book.* Edited by Sam Rohlfing. New York, NY: Carleton Press, 1985. Pp. 128. The author, in the Philippines from July 1940, was the post surgeon and hospital commander at Camp John Hay upon the outbreak of war and includes some details of prewar life at the post and a brief derisory account of the training school conducted for senior officers there in late 1941. Unable to join the forces on Bataan, Jacobs served with Col. Guillermo Nakar's 14th Infantry (a unit created in north Luzon in February 1942) in Cagayan until surrendering to the Japanese in June 1942. He survived the *Oryoku Maru* and was liberated at Mukden. Includes a partial list of the medical staff at Camp John Hay.

**602**   Jolma, Roy, as told to Nan Austin Gardner. *P.O.W. 972.* Carmel, CA: Magaling, 1995. Pp. 58. An air force enlisted man who arrived in the Philippines in mid-1940, Jolma ended up on Corregidor maintaining aircraft at Kindley Field until sent to Bataan to fight. He was imprisoned at Tarlac, Baguio, and Cabanatuan and went to Japan in July 1944 to Fukuoka camp no. 3 aboard the *Nissyo Maru.* At times, this book reads more like what the author read about the war, rather than what he personally experienced.

**603**   Jones, Betty Boellner. *The December Ship: A Story of Lt. Col. Arden B. Boellner's Capture in the Philippines, Imprisonment and Death on a World War II Japanese Hellship.* Jefferson, NC: McFarland, 1992. Pp. xvi, 120. An army reserve officer and World War I veteran (no overseas service) from New Mexico, Boellner arrived in the Philippines in November 1941 and was assigned as an adviser to a Philippine Army unit in the Visayas. This book consists of letters and photographs he sent home from October 1941 to April 1942. A prisoner at Davao, Boellner was one of those who later died aboard the *Oryoku Maru*.

**604**   Keith, Billy. *Days of Anguish, Days of Hope.* Introduction by Robert Preston Taylor. Garden City, NY: Double Day, 1972. Pp. 216. Keith tells the story of Lt. Robert Taylor, army chaplain (and later major general and USAF chief of chaplains) who arrived in the Philippines in May 1941 to become regimental chaplain of the 31st Infantry. According to Keith (whose book has a number of factual errors), the main purpose in writing the book was to understand why the Japanese treated POWs and their own men "so cruelly" and to answer "what really took place on the 'hell ships,'… about which so little has been written." Taylor survived the *Oryoku Maru* and was freed at Mukden.

**605**   Kellett, Wanda Liles. *Wings as Eagles.* New York: Vantage Press, 1954. Pp. 105. (A second edition appeared in 1976.) The author writes this book in the first person, as if she were her husband, who was captured in the Philippines. J.D. Kellett, an air corps engineer, escaped to Corregidor when Bataan fell. As a POW, he was on the Nichols Field detail and then sent to Oeyama camp, near Osaka, in early 1944. Waterford [entry 538] comments that treatment at this camp of American and British POWs "was not particularly harsh," but Kellett writes that the camp "teamed with bullies, stool pigeons, thieves and traitors," none worse than his American officers, who beat enlisted men, one even to death. At war's end, according to Kellett, the prisoners seized weapons from the guards, beat the senior English POW officer, and killed the Japanese camp commander. (Hitchcock [entry 595], confirms the hatred the POWs felt for the Japanese and the POW camp leaders, whom he said fled with the Japanese guards at the end of the war, but not these details.)

**606**   King, Otis H. *The Alamo of the Pacific: The Story of the Famed "China Marines" on Bataan and Corregidor and What They Did to the Enemy as POWs.* Fort Worth, TX: Privately Published, 1999. Pp. 237. The author claims to have been not quite fifteen years old when he enlisted in the marines in 1939. He served briefly in China before being assigned to the 1st Separate Battalion at Cavite. Includes some interesting details about marine preparations for war. King later escaped to Corregidor when Bataan fell. He was among the first POWs shipped to Japan, aboard the *Lima Maru* in September 1942 (ship name not listed in Waterford). Much of the book describes acts of sabotage carried out by the POWs at camps in the Philippines and Japan, some he participated in and some he heard about from other POWs.

**607**   Knox, Ralph M. *The Emperor's Angry Guest: A World War II Prisoner of the Japanese Speaks Out.* Middletown, CT: Southfarm Press, 1999. Pp. 271. An airplane mechanic assigned to the 28th Bomb Squadron at Clark Field from June 1941, Knox witnessed the 8 December bombing of the field. Knox was at Del Monte when MacArthur arrived. Contrary to the stories told in MacArthur's biographies that two B-17s carried MacArthur's party and a small amount of personal luggage from Mindanao to Australia, Knox claims that he and other enlisted men loaded a third B-17 with footlockers, clothing, chairs, "two particularly heavy mattresses," and "little Arthur MacArthur's toys." It is an intriguing anecdote, but as Stanley Falk asked in his review in *The Journal of Military History* 65, no. 3 (July 2001): How did all that stuff get to Mindanao from Corregidor on a crowded PT boat with no one else noticing it? Knox went to Japan aboard the *Tottori Maru* in October 1942 and was imprisoned at Kawasaki camp no. 5. He claims that during the war the Red Cross collected $40 a month from his parents to present him with care packages, none of which he received. Appendices include a roster of the 28th Bomb Squadron.

**608**    Lawton, Manny [Marion R.]. *Some Survived.* With an Introduction by John Toland. Chapel Hill, NC: Algonquin Books, 1984. Pp. xix, 295. Better-than-average memoir of prison life with a few remarks concerning prewar events by a reserve officer who arrived in the Philippines in October 1941 and served as an adviser to the 1st Battalion, 31st Infantry, 31st Division, Philippine Army. Lawton was a POW at Davao and includes accounts of the April 1943 escape by McCoy and nine others [see entries 575, 586, 590, 620, and 623], a second successful escape by two enlisted men in October 1943, and an escape by six officers (of eleven who tried) in March 1944 (none of the latter published a POW memoir). Lawton was freed at Jinsen, Korea, in August 1945. An appendix lists 1,607 prisoners who were aboard the "hell ships" *Oryoku Maru*, *Enoura Maru*, and *Brazil Maru*.

**609**    Leber, Hal. *The Silver Dollar Boys—Pacific.* Clovis, CA: Privately Published, 1991 [1992?]. Pp. 263. Oral history based on interviews with members of Fresno Chapter #1, American Ex-Prisoners of War. Includes accounts of prewar life in the Philippines, fighting on Bataan and Corregidor, the Death March, and prison camp experiences by veterans of the 59th CAC, 60th CAC, 19th Bomb Group, 27th Bomb Group, 27th Materiel Squadron, 3rd Pursuit Squadron, 24th Pursuit Squadron, 34th Pursuit Squadron, 680th Ordnance Squadron, First Separate Marine Battalion, 192nd Tank Regiment, 194th Tank Regiment, 200th Coast Artillery, 31st Infantry, 4th Marines, and assorted naval units. An appendix reprints many documents relating to the hospital ship *Mactan* [see entries 309, 326, 337, and 546].

**610**    Lee, Henry G. *"Nothing But Praise."* Culver City, CA: Murray & Gee, Inc., 1948. Pp. 93. This collection of Lee's oft-cited poems is followed by a brief biography, extracts from letters Lee sent home between June 1941 and March 1942, and extracts from his history of the Philippine Division's military police company. Lee survived the sinking of the *Oryoku Maru* only to die aboard another ship in Takao Bay, Formosa, in January 1945.

**611**    Leek, Jerome B. *Corregidor G.I.* Culver City, CA: Highland Press, 1948. Pp. 335. Leek enlisted in the 250th CA Regiment, California National Guard, in September 1940, transferred to the regular army, and arrived in the Philippines in June 1941 for duty with the 60th CAC (AA), at Ft. Mills. Leek seems to have been interested in everything going on around him, and his book is a mine of minutiae about life on Corregidor, Camp John Hay, Manila and elsewhere (including comments on the Philippine Scouts and Philippine Army). Leek was rescued from Cabanatuan in January 1945. Appendices include lists of those liberated at Cabanatuan, those who participated in the raid on the camp, and personnel roster of Hq. Battery, 60th CA (AA).

**612**   Levering, Robert W. *Horror Trek: A True Story of Bataan, the Death March and Three-and-a-Half Years in Japanese Prison Camps.* Dayton, OH: Hortsman Printing Co., 1948. Pp. xi, 233. The author was a civilian employee of the procurement section of the army engineering office in Ft. Santiago hired to negotiate military construction contracts. He retreated to Bataan with the Office of the Chief of Engineers (along with six other civilians who had arrived in the islands with him, of whom he and one other survived the war). According to Levering, it was "red tape" as usual on Bataan: "In the matter of supplies, no one could procure a much needed brush knife or a piece of cable without the high cost of delay going through the maze of official channels. Tons of the equipment which we burned on the night of surrender could have been expended against the enemy, had we been a little more realistic in meeting the demands of the time." In November 1942 he was among a group of 400 POWs chosen to work on a labor detail in the Manila Port Area, which thanks to an heroic naval POW commander and the relatively benign Japanese reserve officer in charge, was apparently one of the least severe POW experiences in the Philippines. Levering was sent to Japan aboard the *Nissyo Maru* in July 1944. An appendix reprints letters from fellow POWs. One of the more interesting is that of John H. Riley, a sailor on Corregidor who recounted his experiences as one of the boat crew that met the submarines that resupplied the island and took off passengers.

**613**   Locke, A. J. *Kobe House P.O.W. No. 13.* Privately Published, [c1999]. Pp. 184. Arthur Locke was a veteran infantryman who had already served two hitches in China and the US when he reenlisted for air corps service in the Philippines. He was at Nichols and Clark Fields from October 1939 to the start of the war. Of the Death March, Locke says that the guards were not especially severe where he was, no one was killed trying to get water, and he did not see the beheading and bayoneting that others speak of. He volunteered to go to Japan on the *Ryuku Maru* in October 1942 (a *Ryukyu Maru*, sunk near Timor in 1943, is listed in Waterford [entry 538]). It was not a "hell" ship. According to Locke, there were only fifty POWs on board; the voyage was the easiest part of his prison years. He was assigned to a camp he calls "Kobe House," one of the better POW destinations, where there were few Americans but many British and Australian POWs. Like many others, he comments that American officers did nothing for the enlisted men and that the Commonwealth soldiers helped each other but that amongst the Americans it was every man for himself, an attitude that Locke believes contributed to the death of many American POWs.

**614**   Machi, Mario. *The Emperor's Hostages.* New York: Vantage Press, 1982.

Pp. x, 90. Machi arrived in the Philippines in October 1941 and served briefly at Sternberg before being sent to care for the wounded at Stotsenburg. On Bataan he was attached to Headquarters Co., 31st Infantry. He kept a diary until the surrender and includes some extracts here. (He gave the diary to a Filipino he met along the Death March and asked that it be mailed to Machi's home in San Francisco, which the man did.) After surviving the Death March, O'Donnell, and Cabanatuan (experiences which disillusioned him less about the Japanese than about his fellow Americans), Machi was at Bilibid and scheduled for transfer to Japan in October 1944 but illness kept him behind, and he was freed when MacArthur returned. Machi intermixes his POW experiences with memories of his childhood as the son of an Italian immigrant and concludes with a plea for Americans to show more appreciation for the "loyalty and devotion of the Filipino people to Americans." A slightly longer version of this book was published as *Under the Rising Sun: Memories of a Japanese Prisoner of War* (Miranda, CA: Wolfenden, 1994), pp. 176.

**615**    Mapes, Victor L., with Scott A. Mills. *The Butchers, the Baker: The World War II Memoir of a United States Army Air Corps Soldier Captured by the Japanese in the Philippines.* Jefferson, NC: McFarland & Company, 2000. Pp. viii, 240. Mapes was an enlisted man with the 14th Bomb Squadron who survived the attack on Clark Field on 8 December. He was among 600 men of the 19th Bomb Group sent to Mindanao at the end of December. Imprisoned at Davao and Lasang, Mapes was a survivor of the *Shinyo Maru*. Appendices include a list of soldiers who surrendered at Dansalan, Mindanao, and a list of survivors of the *Shinyo Maru*.

**616**    Marek, Stephen. *Laughter in Hell.* Caldwell, Idaho: The Caxton Printers, 1954. Pp. 256. Tells the stories of POWs E. L. Guirey, a sailor with Patrol Wing 10 captured on Corregidor, and H.C. Nixon, a marine captured on Guam. They were eventually imprisoned together at Umeda Bonshu, Osaka, where POWs worked as stevedores on the nearby docks.

**617**    Martin, Adrian R. *Brothers from Bataan: POWs, 1942–1945.* Manhattan, KS: Sunflower University Press, 1992. Pp. xiv, 334. A biography—or more precisely, a string of extracts from contemporary letters written by Martin and others combined with reminiscences of veterans in chronological order—of Adrian Martin, who served with the 200th CAC, was captured on Bataan, and died in Japan in June 1945. The author is Martin's nephew. This book is one of the better sources for information about army life in the Philippines before the outbreak of war.

**618**    Masterson, Melissa. *Ride the Waves to Freedom: Calvin Graef's Story of Survival.* Hobbs, NM: Southwest Freelance, 1999. Pp. 108. An enlisted man with the 200th CAC, Graef was one of eight soldiers (out of about 1,800 POWs) to survive the sinking of the *Arisan Maru* on 24 October 1944. Graef was one of five who sailed to China in a lifeboat. (The other three were picked up by the Japanese.)

He describes that experience, as well as fighting on Bataan, the Death March, Davao, and his escape through China back to the United States.

**619**   McBride, Myrrl W. "From Bataan to Nagasaki: The Personal Narrative of an American Soldier." MA thesis, Sul Ross State Teachers College, 1948. Pp. ix, 290. A veteran of the 200th CA Regiment (AA), McBride briefly describes prewar life at Ft. Stotsenburg and fighting on Bataan. His POW experiences were unusual: He walked away from a work detail at O'Donnell and stayed with Filipino friends before sneaking back into the camp; he walked away from another road building detail in northern Luzon; recaptured, he was imprisoned for several months in Baguio, before being sent to Cabanatuan. He went to Japan aboard the *Nagato Maru* in November 1942. (He claims the seven POWs who died aboard the ship were officers killed by other prisoners when discovered to have been hoarding food and water). He was a POW at Yodagawa Steel Works at Osaka for most of the war before being transferred to Fukuoka no. 27 to work in coal mines near the war's end. He then spent several weeks sightseeing before reporting to allied military authorities. McBride learned to speak Japanese with some fluency and has much to say about Japanese and Korean civilians.

**620**   McCoy, Melvyn, and Stephen Mellnik, as told to Welbourn Kelley. *Ten Escape from Tojo.* New York and Toronto: Farrar & Rinehart, 1944. Pp. 106. First published account of the famous escape from the Davao POW camp [see also entries 575, 586, 590, 608, and 623].

**621**   McCracken, Alan. *Very Soon Now, Joe.* New York: The Hobson Book Press, 1947. Pp. 186. A naval officer who commanded a gunboat in China and arrived in the Philippines the morning Cavite was bombed, McCracken was captured on Corregidor. Later, as one of the older POWs at Davao, McCracken led a slightly less precarious life than others. He and three other naval officers manned a small motor launch that often took them away from camp. McCracken was freed at Bilibid in February 1945.

**622**   McGee, John Hugh. *Rice and Salt: A History of the Defense and Occupation of Mindanao During World War II.* San Antonio, TX: The Naylor Co., 1962. Pp. xviii, 242. McGee (USMA 1931), a prewar Scout officer who commanded Muslim soldiers at Pettit Barracks and later adviser to the 101st PA Division (experiences he describes in two lengthy chapters), was a POW at Malaybalay and Davao. McGee escaped the Japanese near Zamboanga by jumping overboard from a ship transporting POWs north in June 1944. McGee wanted to remain and fight as a guerrilla but soon left for Australia. The self-promoted American officers who commanded guerrilla forces on Mindanao, it seems, did not care to have a West Pointer around. Includes maps, POW camp drawings, and appendices that list POWs in Mindanao.

**623**   Mellnik, Stephen M. *Philippine War Diary, 1939–1945.* Rev. ed. New York: Van Nostrand Reinhold Co., 1981. Pp. 346. First edition published as *Philippine Diary, 1939-1945* in 1969. Mellnik (USMA 1932) was assigned to the 91st CA (PS), in October 1939. He was later reassigned to USAFFE staff and subsequently captured on Corregidor. About half the book covers the period before his capture. Mellnik escaped from the POW camp at Davao and made his way to Australia [see also entries 575, 586, 590, 608, and 620].

**624**   Middleton, T. Walter. *Flashbacks: Prisoner of War in the Philippines.* Forward by Ralph Roberts. Alexander, NC: Alexander Books, 2000. Pp. 191. The author was an enlisted man with B Co., 803rd Aviation Engineers, which had the task of developing an airfield at Del Carmen. The author survived the Death March and went to Korea on the *Tottori Maru.* He was experimented on at Mukden by the infamous Unit 731. Includes an unusual story about marching through the mountains of northern Luzon in mid-1942 with a small group of information-gathering Japanese soldiers.

**625**   Miller, Jesse L. *Prisoner of Hope.* Englewood, CO: Privately Published, 1989. Pp. 188. The author, an aircraft mechanic with the 20th Pursuit Squadron, spent a year in the prewar Philippines "homesick and lonesome" (he did not care for the normal soldierly pursuits and had no interest in the islands or their people), but his strong faith in God sustained him as a POW. After the war, he returned to the Philippines as a missionary and started one of the first Overseas Christian Servicemen's Centers. Includes many drawings of prison camp activities.

**626**   Moody, Samuel B., and Maury Allen. *Reprieve from Hell.* New York: Pageant Press, 1961. Pp. 213. (At least four editions exist, the last published in 1991.) An enlisted man with the 91st Bomb Squadron (27th Bomb Group), Moody was in the Philippines less than two weeks before the war started. The book begins with Moody's arrival in Japan in 1946 to testify at the war crimes trials, and then relates his experiences as a POW, from the Death March to Japan. Moody went to Japan in July 1944 and was imprisoned at Narumi. Includes information on what became of former prison guards.

**627**   Morrett, John J. *Soldier Priest.* Roswell, Georgia: Old Rugged Cross Press, 1993. Pp. 312. (There is also a 1983 edition.) Assigned to the 88th Field Artillery Regiment (PS), at Ft. Stotsenburg after arriving in the Philippines in August 1941, Morrett served as a battalion ammunition and supply officer on Bataan. Transported to Davao Penal Colony in November 1942, he was aboard the *Shinyo Maru,* and he and other survivors of its sinking were rescued by guerrillas and evacuated by submarine in October 1944. The second half of this book recounts the author's postwar life as an Episcopal missionary in China and Hawaii.

**628**   Nix, Asbury L. *Corregidor, Oasis of Hope: 50th Anniversary, Bataan-Corregidor.* Amherst, WI: Palmer Publications, 1991. Pp. xxx, 215. (Distributed by Trade Winds Publications.) Nix arrived in the Philippines in July 1939 and was a mechanic in the army quartermaster's heavy maintenance shop in the Port Area. He writes little about the prewar period but includes numerous prewar army-related photos. Captured on Corregidor, he remained with a POW work detail on the island for several years until shipped to Hanawa camp in Japan aboard the

*Noto Maru* in September 1944. This is an excellent book by a well-informed author. Appendices include rosters of personnel at the Port Area Depot, 1939-41, the POW camp on Corregidor, POWs aboard the *Noto Maru*, and at Hanawa.

**629**   Nordin, Carl S. *We Were Next to Nothing: An American POW's Account of Japanese Prison Camps and Deliverance in World War II.* Jefferson, NC: McFarland, 1996. Pp. 256. Like most of this publisher's POW narratives, Nordin's (based on a diary he kept during the war) is a mine of information, about both his prison experiences and fighting the Japanese on Mindanao. The author was part of a detachment of the 2nd Quartermaster Supply Squadron (Aviation), 5th Air Base Group, sent to Mindanao in late November 1941 to build the airfield at Del Monte before surrendering on 10 May 1942. A POW first at Malaybalay, then Davao, and Labang, Nordin shipped to Japan aboard the *Canadian Inventor* (*Matti Matti Maru*) in July 1944 and was imprisoned at Yokkaichi until liberation. Includes a roster of the supply unit's personnel and postwar photographs of prison camps on Davao.

**630**   Norquist, Ernest. *Our Paradise: A GI's War Diary.* Hancock, WI: Pearl-Win Publishing Co., 1989. Pp. 389. The author was an army medic who arrived in the Philippines in October 1941. He devotes a few pages to his pre-surrender experiences at McKinley, Corregidor, and on Bataan, but the book mostly reprints diary entries the author kept from 23 April 1942 to 7 October 1945. They are filled with the minutiae of POW life in the Philippines and Japan and include many names ("in case relatives or survivors may find them of value"). Taken to Japan on the *Noto Maru*, Norquist was imprisoned at Omori and Wakasennin.

**631**   Oatman, Earl R. *Bataan: Only the Beginning.* Riverside, CA: Privately Published, 1991. Pp. xv, 344. This enlisted man with the 34th Pursuit Squadron was at Del Carmen before the war and fought with the provisional infantry on Bataan. The unit's remaining officers, Oatman writes, spent their time awarding each other medals and left the men to fend for themselves at the time of surrender. Oatman and a colleague simply ran away during the Death March and lived with Filipino families in Zambales and Pampanga before surrendering to the Japanese in July 1943. Oatman went to Japan on the *Matti Matti Maru* and was imprisoned at a camp in the Kobe area. Oatmen comments on how much more disciplined the British and Canadian POWs were by contrast to the Americans and admits to having "mixed feelings" when learning after the war about the "Hell Ships" that had been sunk. According to Oatman, it was mostly officers who died. They had made up the rosters that sent enlisted men to Japan first, leaving themselves the last—and, as it turned out, most vulnerable—to go. Includes a roster of the 34th Pursuit.

**632**   Oliver, William P., Jr. *Diary of William P. Oliver, a Prisoner of the Japanese in the Philippine Islands.* Cedar Rapids, Iowa: The Torch Press, 1947. Pp. 71. Brief diary entries by POW Oliver (a junior officer whose unit is not identified) dating from 30 April 1942, when he was a patient at hospital no. 1 on Bataan, to

26 June 1944. As one of the Davao POWs, Oliver felt that the "foolish few" who escaped the camp had "no regard for those left behind." Oliver died aboard an unidentified ship (*Arisan Maru*) in October 1944. The diary had been buried in the Philippines, where it was recovered and sent to his family.

**633**    Olson, John E. *O'Donnell: Andersonville of the Pacific.* Privately Published, 1985. Pp. 194. (Reprinted in 1998.) Olson (USMA 1939) was an officer with the 57th Infantry (PS) and became the personnel adjutant at O'Donnell POW camp with the job of preparing the daily strength reports of American prisoners. This is a richly detailed account of conditions at O'Donnell with drawings, photos, and lists of casualty figures. Olson also describes how bodies were recovered and identified after the war.

**634**    Owen, Reginald, and Paul Lees. *Soochow the Marine.* London: Putnam and Company, 1951. Pp. vi, 218. The book begins with how the dog "Soochow" became the Fourth Marines' mascot but soon becomes the story of Lees, a marine captured on Corregidor. Lees worked at the port area until transferred to Nichols Field, where POWs enlarged the airfield at what was one of the harshest POW work details in the islands. Lees ended up at Ft. McKinley, where a few hundred sick POWs were left largely to fend for themselves while waiting to die. He was freed at Bilibid in February 1945. Soochow spent most of the war at Cabanatuan, where fear of the marines' wrath kept other POWs from eating him [see also entries 512 and 513].

**635**    Parish, Phil. *One Thirteen-Millionth.* N.p.: Privately Published, 1986. Pp. iii, 127. Because of his age (he was 32), Parish could have stayed in the US when his unit, Co. A, 192nd Tank Battalion, went to the Philippines. He was captured on Bataan and assigned to various POW work details (including Clark Field) until transferred to Japan aboard the *Noto Maru* in September 1944, where he worked in a iron ore smelter near Takaoka (Nagoya camp no. 6). When liberated, each ex-POW was given a going-away gift! He sold the set of six wooden salad bowls he received to souvenir-hunting sailors.

**636**    Peart, Cecil J. *Peart's Journal.* Washington, DC: Privately Published, [1995]. Pp. 58. Bound typescript. Photocopy of the 1946 original, then found in the US Navy Hospital Corps Archives. This is a diary kept by navy pharmacist's mate Peart, from 13 December 1944 to 6 June 1945. Peart survived the *Oryoku Maru*, imprisonment at Fukuoku, Japan, and Hoten, Manchuria.

**637**    Petak, Joseph A. *Never Plan Tomorrow.* Fullerton, CA: Aquataur, 1991. Pp. 500. The author "became a combat photographer with the Photo Section, 228th Signal Corps, after being transferred out of the 2nd Observation Unit [Squadron?] and the 4th Chemical Company." Captured on Corregidor, Petak was the photographer who took some of the standard signal corps photos included in many books on the war in the Philippines. He wrote this book in 1947 "as a psychiatric aid" and decided to publish it primarily to serve as a history of the POW camp at Mukden, Manchuria, where he arrived in November 1942 after sailing from

Manila aboard the *Tottori Maru*. Includes a roster of the "original group" at Mukden, a reprint of all four pages of the 8 May 1942 issue of the *Manila Tribune* (announcing Wainwright's surrender of all USAFFE forces), and photos taken in the Mukden area.

**638**   Playter, John. *Survivor*. Bolivar, MO: Southwest Baptist University, 2000. Pp. 158. A second lieutenant in the army reserve, Playter was called to active duty in summer 1941 and sent to the Philippines to serve with the 88th FA (PS). He provides anecdotes about life at Stotsenburg, fighting on Bataan, the Death March, experiences at O'Donnell and Cabanatuan, and, especially, imprisonment at Davao and Lasang. He made no effort to escape; those that did, he writes, "were considered heroes in the eyes of the news media. But [he and others] consider[ed] them very selfish and self-centered." Playter, one of 83 survivors (of 750 POWs) of the sinking of the *Shinyo Maru* near Zamboanga, was evacuated by submarine to Australia in September 1944. Includes several photographs of the Davao penal colony taken in 1955.

**639**   Porwoll, Kenneth, as told to Mary O'Brien Tyrrell. *But Not Alone*. St. Paul, MN: Memoirs, Inc., 1997. Pp. 90. Porwoll, a veteran of Company A, 194th Tank Battalion, had a few copies of these somewhat sanitized POW stories published for his family members. Shipped to Japan in October 1943 (aboard the *Coral Maru*?), he spent the remainder of the war at Niigata camp no. 5. Includes maps, drawings depicting life as a POW, photographs of Porwoll and his family, and an extract from an official 1945 report on conditions at Camp O'Donnell.

**640**   Poweleit, Alvin C., and James C. Claypool. *Kentucky's Patriot Doctor: The Life and Times of Alvin C. Poweleit*. Ft. Mitchell, KY: T.I. Hayes Publishing, 1996. Pp. 119. Autobiography of Dr. Poweleit, with the few pages dealing with his experiences in the Philippines largely reprinted from *USAFFE* [entry 500]. Includes some additional details about his failure to receive the medals he was recommended for by tank commander Brig. Gen. James Weaver. The problem was that Weaver (whom Poweleit admired) and Wainwright (whom he did not) did not get along, and Wainwright turned down Weaver's medals requests.

**641**   Provencher, Bobbie Ann Loback. *Frenchy's War*. n.p. n.d. [c1999] [Pp. 118] Bound typescript. This is a brief narrative of the life and military career of the author's father, Raymond Joseph "Frenchy" Provencher, focussing on his experiences as a POW at Cabanatuan and Clark Field. An enlisted marine captured on Corregidor, Provencher was taken to Japan aboard the *Noto Maru* and imprisoned at Nagoya Camp no. 6, Takaoka. Much of the book consists of photographs Provencher took while serving with the 60th CAC on Corregidor in 1935-37 and with the 4th Marines in China in 1940-41.

**642**   Quinn, Michael A. *Love Letters to Mike: Forty Months as a Japanese Prisoner of War, April 9, 1942 to September 17, 1945*. New York: Vantage Press, 1977. Pp. 331. Col. Quinn, a one-time Philippine Scout officer (1918-19), was the chief motor transport officer on Bataan. These letters to "Mike" (his wife) and his children were written in diary form while a POW at O'Donnell and Tarlac, and in Taiwan and Manchuria. They deal mostly with camp routine, but occasionally he comments on personalities and events on Bataan. Quinn was not an admirer of MacArthur's staff: "What in the name of God [he writes] MacArthur was thinking of in taking the riffraff with him to Australia and leaving the best on the Philippine Islands to rot on Bataan, is beyond me."

**643**    Renfro, Robert L. *A Total Eclipse.* n.p.n.d. [Ft. Worth, TX: Privately Published, 1992] Pp. [ix,] 130. Renfro's love of airplanes led him to enlist in the air corps in 1939 and ship for the Philippines in 1940. His 28th Bomb Squadron was ordered to Australia at the end of December 1941, but Renfro did not make it: He ended up serving as an infantryman near Davao. The first third of the book describes the author's experiences until surrendering on 10 May 1942. Renfro says virtually nothing about imprisonment on Mindanao, but six months later, he and 300 other volunteers were sent to Bilibid and then Japan in October 1942 aboard the *Toro Maru* (*Tottori Maru?*). The rest of the book reprints brief entries from a diary "all the POWs were told to keep" by the Japanese commander of Renfro's camp, Kawasaki no. 5.

**644**    Reynolds, Bob [Robert Victor]. *Of Rice and Men.* Philadelphia: Dorrance & Company, 1947. Pp. 182. A sergeant with the 34th Pursuit Squadron at Del Carmen, Reynolds fills the first third of his memoirs with anecdotes about fighting Japanese infiltrators in southern Bataan and methods of supplementing the unit's meager food rations. He survived the Death March only to be driven promptly back on a work detail to Bataan and then Calumpit (thus avoiding O'Donnell and the worst days at Cabanatuan). As such, he had relative freedom to visit nearby Filipino families. He sailed to Japan aboard the *Canadian Inventor* (*Matti Matti Maru*) in July 1944 and was imprisoned at Funatsu. The author devotes a considerable portion of the text to relating his experiences with Filipino and Japanese civilians. When their small ex-POW contingent left Funatsu at the end of the war, the entire village came to the train station to see them off!

**645**    Ruby, James. *James Ruby, Family Memories, His POW Diary, The Story of His Philippine Captivity.* N.p. n.d. [1994]. Pp. xxxvii, 111. Newly enlisted UCLA graduate Ruby arrived in the Philippines in July 1941 for duty at the Ft. McKinley hospital. The diary includes entries as a POW, the first dated 25 December 1942 and the last 1 October 1944. Prewar materials include a few photographs of McKinley and local villages. Ruby died on the *Oryoku Maru.* (The ship name is not given in the book, but he is listed on the recreated ship roster [see "research note"].) The attitudes he expresses toward the Japanese are atypical. He was a messenger at Camp O'Donnell and had, he reported, "the opportunity to see the Japanese at first hand more than most." His conclusion? "I can't help but respect them for their fairness and decency in their dealings with us."

**646**    Rutledge, Tillman J. *My Japanese POW Diary Story.* New York: Vantage Press, 1997. Pp. x, 130. Rutledge managed to keep a brief diary throughout the fighting on Bataan and during imprisonment. This book reprints the short diary entries fleshed out by the author's recollections of the events. An active member of the ADBC, the author mentions many names, where possible tells what happened to the men after the war, cautions against believing veterans' tall tales, and vents his rage on ignorant—and safe at home—"do-gooders and cry babies" who criticize President Harry Truman for authorizing the dropping of the atomic bombs on Japan, an act that saved the lives of thousands of prisoners. He was a POW at Lipa, Batangas, and Las Piñas, before going to Japan aboard the *Nissyo Maru* in July 1944, where he was at Tanagawa and Fukuoka no. 11. Rutledge, who arrived in the Philippines in April 1941, offers one of the few published accounts of prewar basic training with the 31st Infantry at Ft. McKinley's "B" Range.

**647**   Schloat, Don T. *Freedom! Bataan—POW—Pvt.* Valley Center, CA: Privately Published, 1995. Pp. iv, 352. (Earlier published in a shorter version as *Tales of Bataan*). Part factual, part fictionalized, experiences of a teenage recruit who arrived in the islands in August 1941 and spent most of his time at the McKinley hospital "making gonorrhea slides from infected soldiers." His formal military training consisted of learning to march, salute, and wear a gas mask. Schloat claims he was not issued any field service equipment until 8 December 1941, and had to be shown how to use it by a Filipino orderly. On Bataan, Schloat served at "Little Baguio" and as a POW volunteered for the work detail at Puerto Princesa. He survived the massacre of POWs there because he had earlier escaped and when recaptured was sent to Bilibid. Schloat is one of the less inhibited POW authors. He also includes some excerpts from the diary of James Ruby [see entry 645].

**648**   Scott, R. Jackson. *90 Days of Rice*. Pioneer, CA: California Traveler, Inc., 1975. Pp. 217. The author served with the marine anti-aircraft unit at the Cavite Naval Yard. He describes aerial attacks early in the war, service at Mariveles, and small unit action at Longoskawayan Point. Convinced by their experiences in China that the Japanese would kill POWs, he and other marines swam to Corregidor when Bataan fell. They then escaped to Cavite and wandered around southern Luzon before being captured and sent to various prison camps. (Netzorg [entry 19] quotes another reviewer as commenting that "'aspects about the story [rendered it] incredible.'") Scott went to Japan aboard an unnamed ship and devotes much of the book to describing his experiences at a mining camp located about twenty miles southwest of Nagasaki. He questions the decision to drop an atomic bomb on Nagasaki, even if doing so saved POW lives.

**649**   Shabart, Elmer. *Memoirs of a Barbed Wire Surgeon*. Oakland, CA: Regent Press, 1997. Pp. 180. Sent much against his will to the Philippines in August 1941, medical officer Shabart was assigned to the 12th Medical Regiment (PS). After capture, Shabart was among the earliest group of POWs sent north, to Mukden, in early October 1942, where he had remarkable success in saving the lives of wounded and sick prisoners. Most of this book addresses the difficult circumstances of providing medical care in Manchuria.

**650**    Sheya, Mel[vin]. *Pacific Pandemonium*. N.p. Privately Published, 1950. Pp. 96. This is mostly an account of beach defense on Corregidor by a "China Marine." Of his service in China, Sheya comments that at first he "couldn't quite get used to the sight of seeing Marines and the pert Chinese girls walking nonchalantly down the streets," but he soon "fell in line with the rest of the crowd." After capture, Sheya was transported to Mukden in November 1942 and in May 1944 to Toyama, Japan.

**651**    Sides, Hampton. *Ghost Soldiers: The Forgotten Epic Story of World War II's Most Dramatic Mission*. New York: Doubleday, 2001. Pp. 342. Sides' much-acclaimed account of the 1945 rescue of 513 POWs at Cabanatuan by American soldiers of the 6th Ranger Battalion and Filipino guerrillas is interspersed with recollections by American veterans of the Bataan Death March, the massacre of POWs at Palawan, prison camp life, and the ordeal of the *Oryoku Maru*. Sides estimates American deaths on the Death March at 750, and suggests that the March was occasioned by the Japanese desire to move prisoners from Bataan as rapidly as possible in order to launch an attack on Coregidor.

**652**    Smith, Stanley W., edited by Duane A. Smith. *Prisoner of the Emperor: An American POW in World War II*. Niwot, CO: University Press of Colorado, 1991. Pp. xii, 138. A naval dental officer assigned to the Asiatic Fleet in August 1940 (USS *Blackhawk*), the author was stationed at Cañacao at war's start. He was assigned to a field hospital established at Holy Ghost College and then to St. Scholastica, where he was working when captured by the Japanese. We "anxiously awaited orders to leave" Manila, he recalled, but none came. Transported to Japan in March 1944, Smith claimed to be one of the "first Americans ... to enter Tokyo on their own after the cessation of hostilities."

**653**    Stamp, Loren E. *Journey Through Hell: Memoir of a World War II American Navy Medic Captured in the Philippines and Imprisoned by the Japanese*. Jefferson, NC: McFarland & Co., Inc., 1993. Pp. xv, 135. In the navy since 1935, the author reenlisted in 1939 for China duty and ended up at Cañacao. In July 1940, he was reassigned to the USS *Canopus* and served as medical corpsman for several submarine crews. During the fighting he was assigned to the 4th Marines at Mariveles and on Corregidor. Stamp remained on the Corregidor work detail to 1943 and survived the *Oryoku Maru*. Freed at Hoten, Manchuria, Stamp returned home by air via Calcutta, Cairo, Casablanca, and Bermuda. Includes list of naval medical personnel in China and the Philippines at start of war and what happened to them.

**654**    Stewart, Sydney. *Give Us This Day*. New York: W.W. Norton, 1957. Pp. 254. (Many editions.) The author (his unit could not be determined, but he is said to have served in the medical corps) was a prisoner at Davao and a survivor of the *Oryoku Maru*. According to Netzorg [entry 19] reviewers praised the literary qualities of this book, which was published first in France in 1950. An obituary of Stewart from the *New York Times* (5 April 1998) that explains the background to his writing this book is located at http://www.sirius.com/~neilm/Stewart,Sydney.html.

**655** Taylor, Vince. *Cabanatuan: Japanese Death Camp.* 2nd ed. Waco, TX: Texian Press, 1987. Pp. 208. A 1st edition appeared in 1985. Recounts the story of John Allen McCarty, an enlisted soldier who arrived in the Philippines with the 200th Coast Artillery (AA) Regiment. A survivor of the Death March, Taylor was freed from Cabanatuan in January 1945. Appendices list those who freed them, and those who were freed.

**656** Tenney, Lester I. *My Hitch in Hell: The Bataan Death March.* Washington, DC: Brassey's, 1995. Pp. xviii, 220. The author enlisted in B Company, 192d Tank Battalion, Illinois National Guard, on 12 October 1940. The unit was federalized in late November 1940, and after a period of training at Fort Knox, Kentucky, and Camp Polk, Louisiana, sailed for the Philippines aboard the *Hugh L. Scott* (formerly the SS *President Pierce*). It arrived on 20 November 1941 and took up position near the airstrip at Clark Field. Captured on Bataan, Tenney participated in the Death March, escaped from Camp O'Donnell and served briefly with a guerrilla unit before recapture. He was later on work details on Bataan, at Cabanatuan, sailed aboard the *Toro Maru* (*Tottori Maru?*), and spent the remainder of the war at Fukuoka camp no. 17, described by the author as having "the most brutal and inhumane commander and guards of any camp in all of Japan." He pulls no punches in describing the brutal treatment meted out to Filipino civilians and POWs by the Japanese, and sometimes by fellow prisoners.

**657** Thomas, Ed. *As I Remember: The Death March of Bataan.* Sonoita, AZ: Privately Published, 1990. Pp. iv, 256. Sgt. Thomas' small outfit of signal corps men and Filipino workers erected the radio intercept antenna that was to connect to the prewar Ft. McKinley tunnel complex. Later commissioned, Thomas (who had been in the Philippines since March 1940) directed the laying of the submarine cable from Corregidor to Bataan. Imprisoned at Cabanatuan after surviving the Death March, Thomas writes that by late 1944 POWs realized that it would be dangerous to travel aboard ship to Japan and made every effort to avoid being sent there. He was one of 513 left behind at Cabanatuan to be rescued in January 1945. This book is a mine of detail about prison life, and the author's evaluation of fellow prisoners is considerably more positive than many others.

**658** Towery, Ken, with an introduction by William F. Buckley. *The Chow Dipper.* Austin, TX: Eakin Press, 1994. Pp. xii, 423. Autobiography of long-time journalist Towery, who served as Senator John Tower's chief of staff and was deputy director of the US Information Agency. The first quarter of the book deals with the author's World War II experiences. As an 18-year old enlistee, Towery was assigned to Battery C, 60th CAC, in March or April 1941. He provides a particularly vivid account of life with an anti-aircraft artillery unit on Morrison Hill (where he met MacArthur once). Towery was among the first to sail north, aboard the *Tottori Maru*, in October 1942 and was imprisoned at Hoten camp no. 1.

**659**    Vance, John R. *Doomed Garrison: The Philippines (A POW Story)*. Ashland, OR: Cascade House, 1974. Pp. 248. Vance (USMA November 1918) was a senior army finance officer in the Philippines and as such knew most of the leading American and Filipinos officers and government officials. The book is filled with fascinating detail concerning island personalities, the financial problems relating to the mobilization of the Philippine Army in August 1941, and life in Malinta Tunnel. Captured on Corregidor, Vance was imprisoned with other senior officers at Tarlac until eventually sent to Manchuria. Includes several maps (one of Manila shows army property in the city).

**660**    Verity, George L. *From Bataan to Victory*. New York: Carleton Press, 1992. Pp. 274. The many spelling and factual errors in this book grate, but the author's recollections of his prison experiences at Tanagawa (November 1942–January 1943), Zentsuji (to June 1945), and Roko Rushi (to September 1945) are revealing. Verity, a non-flying officer assigned to the 93rd Squadron, 19th Bomb Group, was at Clark Field at war's start and later commanded base maintenance troops at Cabcaben Field. Includes drawings made at the POW camps.

**661**    Vining, Virgil V. *Guest of an Emperor*. 2nd ed. N.p. n.p., 1994. Pp. 351. A navy petty officer, Vining spent several years in the Philippines and China with the Asiatic Fleet before the war, serving aboard a destroyer and a minesweeper. Captured on Corregidor, he provides an extensive account of the Nichols Field detail. Vining was on the first working party assigned there in July 1942 and remained until October 1943. Sent to Japan aboard the *Nissyo Maru* in July 1944, he was imprisoned at Narumi, near Nagoya, where he worked on a locomotive-building factory. Like other navy ex-POWs, Vining was able to fly back to the US from Japan, rather than be processed through Manila like most army ex-POWs.

**662**    Waldron, Ben D., and Emily Burneson. *Corregidor: From Paradise to Hell*. Freeman, SD: Privately Published, 1988. Pp. xiii, 234. Chatty account of prewar and prisoner of war life by an enlisted man with the 60th Coast Artillery Regiment (assigned to Battery Chicago) who had been in the Philippines since October 1940. Imprisoned at Cabanatuan and Bilibid, Waldron was transported to Japan in July 1944 to Funatsu camp. Waldron includes a story of soldiers at Battery Chicago fighting off a Japanese assault on Morrison Hill just before Corregidor's surrender, but no such battle took place. For a comparison of Waldron's account with the official battery report, see "The So-Called Battle of Morrison Hill," posted at the Corregidor Historical Society website (http://corregidor.org/ct&n_index.html).

**663**    Wallace, John W. *POW-83*. Chatham, NY: The Gray Rider Publishing Co., 1999. Pp. 264. Tells the story of Cpl. John Mackowski, Co. A, 803rd Aviation Engineers, assigned to build an airfield at O'Donnell. The author includes much detail on prewar training in the US and life at O'Donnell. Mackowski was sent to Corregidor in February 1942 to help keep Kindley Field flyable. As a POW, he was at

Davao and Lasang and was one of those who escaped when the *Shinyo Maru* was sunk. Includes a list of the ship's 83 survivors.

**664**   Weinstein, Alfred A. *Barbed-Wire Surgeon*. New York: The MacMillan Co., 1948. Pp. x, 310. Arriving in the islands in July 1941, the war's outbreak found the author at the Ft. McKinley hospital. He then worked at several hospitals set up in schools in Manila before going to Bataan and undergoing the usual POW experiences at O'Donnell, Cabanatuan and in Japan. He became involved with the daughter of Jewish refugees in Manila and returned to marry Hanna Kaunitz at war's end and mentions a number of American and Filipino civilians he knew in the city. Netzorg [entry 19] states that this is "one of the few books of the period that veterans both seek and actually read."

**665**   Weiss, Edward W. *Under the Rising Sun*. N.p.: Privately Published, 1992. Pp. vi, 238. The author's experiences as a soldier and POW were atypical. Arriving in the Philippines in May 1940, Weiss was a radio operator at Ft. Santiago and Camp John Hay until October 1941, when he and several other radiomen were assigned to the *Don Estaban*, a ship chartered by the army to carry supplies to Australia and New Guinea, and, once the war began, to take personnel off Corregidor to the southern islands and bring supplies back. (Weiss shares anecdotes about some of the passengers, including Quezon and Osmeña.) The ship was attacked by the Japanese and abandoned near Mindoro. Weiss made his way to Panay, Cebu and eventually southern Negros, where he hid with other Americans until attempting to sail to Australia in June 1942. Captured en route, Weiss was one of fourteen Americans imprisoned at the Tan Toey POW camp on Ambon Island. Nine of the fourteen survived, as did 121 of 528 Australian POWs. A longer second edition of this book appeared under the same title in 1995. It included additional photographs and more information on what became of the author and others mentioned in the book.

**666**   Whitcomb, Edgar D. *Escape from Corregidor*. Chicago: Henry Regnery Co., 1958. Pp. 274. A B-17 navigator with the 19th Bombardment Group, Whitcomb arrived in the Philippines in October 1941, escaped to Corregidor when Bataan fell, then made his way to the mainland where he was captured. He eventually managed to pass himself off as a civilian and was repatriated aboard the *Gripsholm* in December 1943.

**667**   Wills, Donald H., with Reyburn W. Myers, *The Sea Was My Last Chance: Memoir of an American Captured on Bataan in 1942 Who Escaped in 1944 and Led the Liberation of Western Mindanao*. Jefferson, NC: McFarland & Co., Inc., 1992. Pp. xvii, 169. The author served with the 26th Cavalry on Bataan. He was hospitalized at the time of surrender and thus escaped the Death March. Wills escaped captivity by jumping off a ship taking POWs from Davao in June 1944 (shortly after McGee [entry 622] had done so). Most of the book describes his service with guerrillas on Mindanao.

**668**   Wright, John M., Jr. *Captured on Corregidor: Diary of an American P.O.W.*

*in World War II.* Jefferson, NC: McFarland, 1988. Pp. viii, 181. A straightforward detailed narrative of the author's experiences, based on entries in a diary he was able to keep, beginning with the day of surrender on Corregidor. A coast artillery officer (USMA 1940) with the 91st CAC, Wright spent nearly a year on Corregidor ("not a bad place to be," according to Wright, who weighed more when he left the island as a POW than he had when he arrived in November 1940) as part of a 191-man POW workcrew. After returning to Bilibid and Cabanatuan, Wright was chosen for the ill-fated *Oryoku Maru* detail. He was at Fukuoka camp no. 1 from January to April 1945 and ended the war at Jinsen, Korea.

Research note: The ADBC website (http://harrisonheritage.com/adbc/) has a partial list of Hell Ship sailing dates, lists the POWs aboard the *Arisan Maru,* and links to a list of *Oryoku Maru* POWs (or go direct to http://www.geocities.com/oryokumaru/search.html). The American Ex-Prisoners of War organization maintains a website (http://www.ax-pow.com) with considerable POW-related information and links to related websites.

---

# Military Medals and Insignia

**669**   Baja, Emanuel A. *The Medal for Valor, The Distinguished Conduct Star, The Distinguished Service Star.* Manila: Juan Farjardo Press, 1933. Pp. 178. The outspoken Major Baja is not content to list the recipients of these awards (to 31 December 1932) but takes to task his superiors for apparently giving one to virtually anyone—in the PC's senior ranks, at least—who wanted one.

**670**   Basso, Aldo P. *Coins, Medals and Tokens of the Philippines.* Menlo Park, CA: Chenby Publishers, 1968. Pp. v, 136. A "military decorations and medals" section covers the Spanish, Revolutionary, American, Japanese, and Republic periods, with photographs or line drawings of most of the awards.

**671**   Basso, Aldo P. *Coins, Medals and Tokens of the Philippines, 1728–1974.* 2nd ed. Quezon City: Privately Published, 1975. Pp. 184. Basso deleted the section on military medals and decorations from this edition, intending, he wrote, to publish a separate work on the topic. He never completed this task, but Reynolds [entry 679] states that much of his work "is derived from Basso's partially completed manuscript." The second edition includes a large listing of pre and postwar military and constabulary tokens used in post/base exchanges.

**672**   Emerson, William K. *Encyclopedia of United States Army Insignia and Uniforms.* Norman and London: University of Oklahoma Press, 1996. Pp. xvi, 674.

Includes photographs and descriptions of collar insignia and other uniform badges distinct to the Philippine Scouts and Philippine Constabulary.

**673**    Hood, Jennings, and Charles J. Young. *American Orders & Societies and Their Decorations*. Philadelphia: Bailey, Banks & Biddle Co., 1917. Pp. 107. Reprinted by the London Stamp Exchange, 1991. Includes membership criteria and illustrations of the decorations of the Military Order of the Carabao and the Military Order of Moro Campaigns. The latter was open to any soldier who participated in any expedition against the Moros from 15 July 1903 to 31 December 1904. The book also includes membership information but no medal illustration for the National Society of the Army of the Philippines [see entries 122 and 177].

**674**    Laslo, Alexander J. *The Interallied Victory Medals of World War I*. 2nd rev. ed. Albuquerque, New Mexico: Dorado, 1992. Pp. 130. This edition of the leading reference work on World War I victory medals includes a chapter on the PC victory medal and the very rare Philippine National Guard medal. Laslo could only speculate on the origin of the PNG medal, but subsequent research has confirmed that the medal was offered by the PNG association to its members in late 1934 or early 1935.

**675**    Meixsel, Richard B. "Officers and Medals of the Philippine Constabulary." In *The Journal of the Orders and Medals Research Society* [London] 34, no. 3 (Autumn 1995): 157, 171–76. Details of PC and prewar Philippine Army medals concentrating on the medals worn by Brig. Gen. Clarence Bowers, the last American Chief of Constabulary, and Col. Robert Duckworth-Ford, a British-born officer who was superintendent of the PC Academy in Baguio until his retirement in 1932. (Unpublished research by Duckworth-Ford's grandson has revealed that the colonel made up most of the biographical information he provided to the PC—and to his own family—including his place of birth, year of birth, and even his name.) Based on correspondence with those families and illustrated with photos of the officers and of the Philippine Army medal awarded to Dwight Eisenhower. Reprinted in *BAHC* 24, no. 1 (January–March 1996): 74–81, minus portions of the photographs described in the text.

**676**    Peterson, James W. "Awards of the Philippine Constabulary." In *The Medal Collector* 16, no. 12 (December 1965): 2–4. Brief account that includes photos of PC World War I Victory Medal, long-service medal, and Medal for Valor. *The Medal Collector* is also known as the *Journal of the Orders and Medals Society of America*.

**677**    Peterson, James W. "The Philippine Constabulary Campaign Medals." In *The Medal Collector* 19, no. 8 (August 1968): 26–29. Unillustrated description of the prewar Visayan, Luzon, and Mindanao-Sulu campaign medals.

**678**    Reynolds, Robert H. "The Philippine Distinguished Service Star." In *The Medal Collector* 48, no. 2 (March 1997): 28–33. Photographs of five different styles of the medal, from pre–Commonwealth to Republic periods.

**679**   Reynolds, Robert H. *Philippine Medals.* Glassboro, NJ: Orders and Medals Society of America, 1998. Pp. ii, 96. This slim book consists of black and white photos and brief descriptions of most (but not all) military medals of the Spanish, American, and Republic periods. Includes medals awarded by the Spanish government to its soldiers for service in the Philippines but not medals awarded by the US government to its soldiers for service in the Philippines. For those, see entry 681.

**680**   *Soldier Heroes: A Handbook of the Winners of the Major Medals Awarded by the Philippine Constabulary and the Armed Forces Since 1902.* Manila: National Media Production Center, 1981. Pp. viii, 242. Color photos of currently awarded medals and badges are followed by a list of winners of the Medal for Valor (recipients for 1911, 1913, 1914, and 1927 have been excluded for unstated reasons). Also listed are the post-1944 winners of the Distinguished Conduct Star, Gold Cross, Distinguished Aviation Cross, and Military Merit Medal.

**681**   Strandberg, John E., and Roger James Bender. *The Call of Duty: Military Awards and Decorations of the United States of America.* San Jose, CA: R. James Bender Publishing, 1994. Pp. 383. This is one of the more comprehensive catalogs of US military medals. Some of the text must be read with caution, but the book includes numerous color photos of the Philippine Congressional Medal and the Navy-Marine Corps and Army Philippine Campaign (Insurrection) Medals. Eligibility for the latter medals extended to 1906 for some sailors and marines and to 1917 for some soldiers. About 126,000 soldiers served in the Philippine-American War but only about 44,000 Philippine Campaign Medals were issued.

A list of the first 6,179 recipients of the Congressional medal, an award authorized for about 17,000 soldiers who had agreed to remain on duty in the Philippines after their enlistment contracts had expired in late 1898, has been published as *Philippine Congressional Medal Issue Records* (Ft. Myer, VA: Planchet Press, 1994), compiled and edited by Thomas D. Thiessen, Douglas C. Scott, and Albert F. Gleim. Records for an additional 5,000 or so recipients have been lost. JoAnn Williams and Robert H. Reynolds have compiled a companion *Philippine Campaign Service Medal Issue Records* (Privately Published, 1997). Actual medal recipients never approach the number of authorized recipients because all of the above medals were authorized and distributed several years after the war had ended, and most veterans (or the families of deceased veterans) either did not know about the medals or did not care to apply for them. Recipients tended to be men who had remained on active duty or were members of regimental associations or veterans groups.

**682**   Wheatley, Todd. "The Military Order of the Carabao." In *Journal of the Orders and Medals Society of America* 46, no. 7 (July 1995): 8-22. Includes a brief history of the order (originally known as The Order of the Carabao of the Philippines), biographical sketches of some of its leading members, and photographs of its membership medals. The article is reprinted in entry 135.

# Appendix 1

# A Note on Prewar Military Newspapers and Journals

Newspapers and newsletters were common features of US and Philippine military units and posts. Semi-official in nature, the papers kept soldiers informed of unit activities and serve scholars today as sources of local color. Camp Stotsenburg published *Stotsenburg Growls* in the 1920s, one issue of which has been reprinted in entries 290 and 293. A lengthy search of archival collections failed to discover additional issues. The 30th Infantry, with which George Marshall served on Mindoro in 1902-1903, distributed *Bamboo Breezes*, used by Forrest Pogue in preparation of Marshall's official biography [entry 207]. The Naval Historical Center in Washington, DC, holds copies of the Cavite navy yard weekly, also titled *Bamboo Breezes*. It began publication about 1926. *Military Digest* was published weekly at Fort McKinley starting about 1910 (a single copy seen in private collection only). The 45th Infantry (PS) Officers' Association sponsored a regimental quarterly, *The Whizz Bang*. Copies from 1921-22 have been donated to the Philippine Scouts Heritage Society at Ft. Sam Houston, Texas, and portions reprinted in *The Philippine Scouts* [entry 166]. "Manila's Own," the 31st US Infantry, sponsored *Here and There with the Thirty-First* starting in 1919. Several volumes from the early 1920s can be found in the NY Public Library and at the army museum at Ft. Sill, Oklahoma, where the regiment was once posted after World War II. *The Fifty-Seventh Infantry Review* was a monthly publication begun in early 1922 by officers of that regiment. A few issues are included in the Eugene Ganley papers at USAMHI. Travelers to the Philippines aboard the USAT *Grant* in the 1930s published *The Whisperin' Wave*, assorted copies of which are found in manuscript collections at USAMHI. More difficult to find is *Republic-ation*, an early 1930s newsletter of the USAT *Republic*. The USS *Houston*, flagship of the Asiatic Fleet in 1941, had a ship's paper, the *Blue Bonnet*, copies of which are included in the Cruiser *Houston* Memorial Collection in the library of the University of Houston. *Typhoon* was a bi-monthly of the Asiatic Fleet's Destroyer Squadron.

Philippine military (or military-related) publications include *The Volunteer*, published beginning in 1931 by the National Volunteers. No complete run appears to exist but assorted issues can be found in several US and Philippine archives. *The Corps* was the journal of the PMA. The Philippine Constabulary's monthly, *Khaki and Red*, began publication in 1921 but did not appear on a regular basis until "revived," according to a story in the *Philippines Herald* (10 November 1925), in late 1925. The New York Public Library appears to hold the only remaining publicly available run of this important journal, beginning with the January 1926 issue. From June-July 1940, the Philippine Army Reserve Officers' Legion supported the profusely illustrated monthly *Citizen Army*. The US Library of Congress holds the only known collection (which ends with the October 1941 issue) of this journal.

Philippine Army post newspapers also existed. *The Camp Dau Journal* chronicled events at that important Philippine Army camp (located on the Stotsenburg reservation). The only issues which appear to remain are a few dated mid–1939, found in the Johnson Hagood Papers, South Carolina Historical Society, Charleston. The Philippine Army's School for Reserve Commissions (SRC) at Camp Ord, Tarlac, is known to have published *The Rifle*, but no copies appear to have survived. The *Camp Murphy Chronicle* was supposedly the only army fortnightly in the Philippines, but, again, no copies appear to exist.

Prewar US Army journals evidenced periodic enthusiasm for the Philippine garrison, and articles about both American and Philippine Scout units can be found in the appropriate arm or branch journal. These include the *Infantry Journal* (the April 1927 issue consisted entirely of articles about the Philippines), *Coast Artillery Journal*, *Field Artillery Journal*, *Journal of the Military Service Institution of the United States*, and *Military Engineer*. Other useful publications include the army's "hometown newspaper," the *Army and Navy Journal* and the short-lived pre-World War I *Army and Navy Journal of the Philippines* (briefly continued under the title *Army and Navy Weekly*). The *Air Service News Letter*, published from 1919 and retitled *Air Corps News Letter* in 1926, saw limited distribution but is available on microfilm, through 1935. It provides a detailed look at air corps-related life and activity in the prewar Philippines up to mid-1941. US Army journals also carried occasional articles about the activities of the Philippine Army and Philippine Constabulary. In addition, all of the English-language Manila newspapers (most of which can be found on microfilm at the Library of Congress) devoted extensive coverage to the army and navy in the Philippine Islands.

# Appendix 2

# A Note on United States Army Official Histories

The institutional history series, *United States Army in World War II*, often referred to as the "Green Series" or "Green Books" (because the original volumes had green covers) is now complete and comprises seventy-eight volumes. While many make mention of the Philippines, the volumes included in this bibliography [entries 312, 327, 331, 334, 335, 348, 350, and 355] are those which give more than passing reference to prewar events in the islands and to the Philippine Campaign of 1941-42. Publication dates are those of original publication. Many of the books have been reprinted frequently and can be found in both hard and soft-cover. The army has also published guides to the series (the first appeared in 1955), in which each volume's content is summarized. The most recent is Robert D. Adamczyk and Morris J. MacGregor, eds., *United States Army in World War II: Reader's Guide* (Washington, DC: US Army Center of Military History, 1992), pp. ix, 174. (It is on the web at www.ibiblio.org/hyperwar/USA/USA-Guide/index.html.) In 1997, a commercial firm, The National Historical Society, reprinted the series, with the maps once found in the individual volumes now contained in two separate atlases.

# Appendix 3

# A Note on Dissertations and Theses

Most doctoral dissertations and masters theses dealing with Philippine military history topics are presented in either Philippine or United States universities. Copies of virtually all doctoral dissertations completed in the United States are held by University Microfilms International (UMI) of Ann Arbor, Michigan, which offers them for sell in a variety of formats. UMI also publishes several dissertation guides, most of which appear annually. The first edition of UMI's *Comprehensive Dissertation Index* was published in 1973 and listed dissertations completed in the United States and other countries from 1861 to 1972. A second edition encompassed 1973 to 1982, and the series now appears annually. The *Index* lists not only United States dissertations, but also those submitted to Canadian, Australian, and many European and Asian universities. Currently, the only Philippine school found in the *Index* is the Los Baños campus of the University of the Philippines. UMI also publishes separately *American Doctoral Dissertations*. Finally, UMI offers *Dissertation Abstracts International*, which lists North American and European dissertations and summarizes the contents and findings of their authors. For the most part, UMI can provide copies only of US and Canadian dissertations.

There is no comprehensive listing of masters theses completed at universities in the United States. UMI publishes an annual *Masters Abstracts International* but less than one hundred degree-granting institutions contribute to the listing and not every department within those institutions participates. An older series is *Master's Thesis Directories*, which first appeared in 1952. Its title and format have changed over the years, but it too lists only a fraction of the masters theses completed in the United States each year.

American, Canadian, and British-authored dissertations dealing with military-related topics are periodically listed in *The Journal of Military History*, published quarterly for the Society of Military History by the George C. Marshall Foundation at the Virginia Military Institute. These listings (thirty to date [July 2002]) supplement *Doctoral Dissertations in Military Affairs: A Bibliography*, published by the library of Kansas State University, Manhattan, Kansas, in 1972.

# Abbreviations

| | |
|---|---|
| AA | Antiaircraft |
| AB | Air Base |
| ADBC | American Defenders of Bataan and Corregidor |
| AEF | American Expeditionary Forces (World War I) |
| AFB | Air Force Base |
| AFP | Armed Forces of the Philippines |
| BAHC | *Bulletin of the American Historical Collection* |
| BG | Bomb/Bombardment Group |
| BIA | Bureau of Insular Affairs |
| CAC | Coast Artillery Corps |
| DBC | Defenders of Bataan and Corregidor |
| FA | Field Artillery |
| FEAF | Far East Air Force |
| HPD | Headquarters Philippine Department |
| MTB | Motor Torpedo Boat |
| OSP | Off Shore Patrol |
| PA | Philippine Army |
| PAAC | Philippine Army Air Corps |
| PAF | Philippine Air Force |
| PC | Philippine Constabulary |
| PMA | Philippine Military Academy |
| PNG | Philippine National Guard |
| PNL | Philippine National Library |
| POW | Prisoner of War |
| PS | Philippine Scout(s) |
| PT | Patrol Torpedo boat |
| US | United States |
| USA | United States Army |
| USAF | United States Air Force |
| USAAC | United States Army Air Corps |
| USAAF | United States Army Air Force |
| USAFFE | United States Army Forces Far East |
| USAMHI | United States Army Military History Institute, Carlisle, Pennsylvania |
| USAT | United States Army Transport |

| | |
|---|---|
| USFIP | United States Forces in the Philippines |
| USMA | United States Military Academy |
| USMC | United States Marine Corps |
| USN | United States Navy |
| USNA | United States Naval Academy |
| USNH | United States Naval Hospital |
| WPO | War Plan Orange |

# Author/Name Index

*References are to entry numbers*